9738
?

D1186911

CANE: Camberwell Assessment of Need for the Elderly

CANE: Camberwell Assessment of Need for the Elderly

A needs assessment for older mental health service users

Edited by
Martin Orrell
Geraldine Hancock

Published by Gaskell
London

© The Royal College of Psychiatrists 2004

Gaskell is an imprint of the Royal College of Psychiatrists,
17 Belgrave Square, London SW1X 8PG

Gaskell is a registered trademark of the Royal College of Psychiatrists.

All rights reserved. Except where indicated below, no part of this book may be reprinted or reproduced or utilised in any form or by any electronic, mechanical, or other means, now known or hereafter invented, including photocopying and recording, or in any information storage or retrieval system, without permission in writing from the publishers.

Photocopying and translation
The material that appears in Appendices 1–3 may be photocopied by individual researchers or clinicans for their own use without seeking permission from the publishers.

Please contact the publishers if you wish to translate the CANE (or any other material in this book) into another language.

British Library Cataloguing-in-Publication Data
A catalogue record for this book is available from the British Library.

ISBN 1-904671-06-3

Distributed in North America by Balogh International, Inc.

The views presented in this book do not necessarily reflect those of the Royal College of Psychiatrists, and the publishers are not responsible for any error of omission or fact.

The Royal College of Psychiatrists is a registered charity (no. 228636).

Printed in the UK by Cromwell Press Ltd, Trowbridge, Wiltshire.

Contents

Acknowledgements

The authors would like to express their thanks to John Basson, Pamela Taylor, Martin Butwell, Tim Green, James Noak, Lisa Davies, Morven Leese, and the staff and service users who made the development of this assessment possible.

Contributors

Dr María Teresa Amboage   Consultant Psychiatrist, Division of Psychiatry, Complejo Hospitalario Universitario Juan Canalejo, A Coruña, E-15006, Spain

Dr Olakunle Ashaye   Consultant Psychiatrist and Honorary Senior Lecturer, Mental Health Services for Older People, Lister Hospital, Coreys Mill Lane, Stevenage, Herts SG1 4AB, UK

Dr Mohat Bhat   Consultant in the Psychiatry of Old Age, South Essex Partnership (NHS) Trust, Basildon Hospital, Basildon, Essex SS16 5NL, UK

Professor Heike Dech   Professor of Social Medicine and Consultant for Old Age Psychiatry, Department of Social Psychiatry, Hanover Medical School, Carl-Neuberg-Str., 30625 Hanover, Germany

Dr Elizabeth Field   Clinical Psychologist, Mental Health Services for Older People, 6 Radnor Park Avenue, Folkestone, Kent CT19 5HN, UK

Isabel Fraguela   Psychologist, Specialist in Gerontology, A Coruña, Spain

Dr María Jesús García   Consultant Psychiatrist, Division of Psychiatry, Complejo Hospitalario Arquitecto Marcide-Prof. Novoa Santes, Ferrel, E-15405, Spain

Dr Suki Greaves   Specialist Registrar in Old Age Psychiatry, St Thomas's Hospital, London SE1 7EH, UK

Sir John Grimley Evans   Professor Emeritus of Clinical Geratology, Nuffield Department of Clinical Medicine, University of Oxford, UK

Bob Hammond   Health Manager, Petersfield Centre, Petersfield Avenue, Harold Hill, Romford, Essex RM3 9PB

Dr Geraldine Hancock   Clinical Research Fellow, Department of Mental Health Sciences, University College London, Wolfson Building, 48 Riding House Street, London W1N 8AA, UK

Juanita Hoe   Clinical Research Nurse, Department of Psychiatry and Behavioural Sciences, University College London, Wolfson Building, 48 Riding House Street, London W1N 8AA, UK

Dr Steve Iliffe   Reader in Primary Health Care, Department of Primary Care and Population Studies, University College London, Royal Free Campus, Pond Street, London NW3 2QG, UK

Professor Cornelius Katona   Dean, Institute of Health Sciences, University of Kent, Canterbury, Kent, UK

Jan Lambert — Clinical Governance Facilitator, Mental Health Services for Older People, Evington Centre, Leicester General Hospital, Gwendolen Road, Leicester LE5 4QF, UK

Dr Gill Livingston — Reader in Old Age Psychiatry, Department of Psychiatry & Behavioural Sciences, University College London, Wolfson Building, 48 Riding House Street, London W1N 8AA, UK

Dr Raimundo Mateos — Professor of Psychiatry and Coordinator of the Psychogeriatric Unit of the Complejo Hospitalario Universitario de Santiago (CHUS), Departamento de Psiquiatría, Facultad de Medicina, Santiago de Compostela, E-15782, Spain

Professor Wielant Machleidt — Professor of Social Psychiatry and Head of Department of Social Psychiatry, Department of Social Psychiatry, Hanover Medical School, Carl-Neuberg-Str., 30625 Hanover, Germany

Dr Mark D. Martin — Learning Disabilities Service, 192 Hob Moor Road, Small Heath, Birmingham B10 9JH, UK

Professor Martin Orrell — Professor of Ageing and Mental Health, Department of Mental Health Sciences, University College London, Wolfson Building, 48 Riding House Street, London W1N 8AA, UK

Dr Richard Prettyman — Senior Lecturer and Honorary Consultant, Mental Health Services for Older People, Bennion Centre, Glenfield Hospital, Groby Road, Leicester LE3 9DZ, UK

Dr Tom Reynolds — Consultant Psychiatrist, Clare Mental Health Service for Older People, Cappahard Lodge, Tulla Road, Ennis, Co. Clare, Ireland

Dr Barbora Richardson — Consultant in Old Age Psychiatry, Department of Psychiatry, Princess Alexandra Hospital, Hamstel Road, Harlow, Essex, UK

Dr Peter Simmons — Consultant in Old Age Psychiatry, Hertfordshire Partnership NHS Trust, Queen Elizabeth II Hospital, Welwyn Garden City, Hertfordshire AL7 4GH, UK

Professor Graham Thornicroft — Head of Health Services Research Department, Section of Community Psychiatry (PRISM), PO Box 29 , Health Services Research Department, Institute of Psychiatry, Kings College London, De Crespigny Park, London SE5 8AF, UK

Dr Mike Walker — Consultant in Old Age Psychiatry, Hertfordshire Partnership NHS Trust, Lambourn Grove, Hixberry Lane (off Hill End Lane), St Albans, Hertfordshire AL4 0TZ, UK

Martin Walter — London South Bank University, Faculty of Health and Social Care, 103 Borough Road, Southwark, London SE1 0AA, UK

Dr Kate Walters — General Practitioner and MRC Fellow in Health Services Research, Department of Primary Care and Population Studies, University College London, Royal Free Campus, Pond Street, London, NW3 2QG, UK

Professor Bob Woods — Professor of Clinical Psychology of Older People, DSDC, University of Wales Bangor, Neuadd Ardudwy, Normal Site, Holyhead Road, Bangor LL57 2PX, UK

Dr Matías Ybarzábal — Consultant Psychiatrist, Division of Psychiatry, Hospital General de Lanzarote (Las Palmas), E-3500, Spain

List of abbreviations

CAN	Camberwell Assessment of Need
CANDID	Camberwell Assessment of Need for Adults with Developmental and Intellectual Disabilities
CANE	Camberwell Assessment of Need for the Elderly
CANFOR	Camberwell Assessment of Need – Forensic Version (including CANFOR–S, CANFOR–C and CANFOR–R)
CANFOR–C	Camberwell Assessment of Need – Forensic Version (Clinical)
CANFOR–R	Camberwell Assessment of Need – Forensic Version (Research)
CANE–S	Camberwell Assessment of Need for the Elderly – Short Version
SMI	severe mental illness
ANOVA	Analysis of variation
CADI	Carers' Assessment of Difficulties Index
CAMI	Carers' Assessment of Managing Index
CANOA	Camberwell Assessment of Need for Older Adults
CANDID	Counselling and Diagnosis in Dementia
CAPE–BRS	Clifton Assessment Procedures for the Elderly – Behaviour Rating Scale
CarenapD	Care Needs Assessment Pack for Dementia
CGA	Comprehensive Geriatric Assessment
CMHT	community mental health team
CPA	Care Programme Approach
CSRI	Client Service Receipt Inventory
GDAS	Goldberg Depression and Anxiety Scales
GDS	Geriatric Depression Scale
GDS	Global Determination Scale
GHQ	General Health Questionnaire
GP	General Practitioner
IADL	Instrumental Activities of Daily Living
MDT	multidisciplinary team
MEAP	Multiphasic Environmental Assessment Procedure
MMSE	Mini-Mental Health Examination
NHS	National Health Service
NSF–OP	National Service Framework for Older People
PANT	Practitioner Assessment of Network Typology
PCT	primary care trust
SAP	single-assessment process

Foreword

Need is an elusive concept and in the vocabulary of politicians inevitably a slippery one. Thirty years ago, in Jonathan Bradshaw's well-known typology, four kinds of need were recognised: *expressed* need, equivalent to demand; *normative* need, based on expert opinion; *comparative* need, based on the assumption that similar people must have similar needs; and the *felt* need that people were conscious of, but had not got round to expressing as a demand. Later, it was realised that such definitions, applied in real life, could lead to people being defined as in need of something that would actually do them no good if they received it. Capacity to benefit thereby entered the scheme of things, bringing with it the inherent tension within the British National Health Service over whether treatments are provided to benefit the recipient or the Chancellor of the Exchequer. In essence, who should decide what constitutes benefit? Is health a desirable thing because it allows us to attain our personal goals or because it enables us better to serve the State? The former underpins the rationale of private medicine and is what most taxpayers think they pay their money for. Historically, however, the origins of the British Welfare State owed much to the poor health of recruits to the army for the Boer War. Use of the Health Services to maximise the utility of the population for political ends is the philosophy behind the quality-adjusted life-years that modern Health Ministers seek to buy with our money. Individual and cultural values are respected by being ignored. Quality of life is defined by reference to that charmless entity, the European Standard Consumer.

Need can be an irritant to politicians when identified in its unmet form. At one of the many low points of British politics in recent decades, the government decreed that no one should be defined as in need of a service that was not being provided. Such instant abolition of the challenge of unmet need proved too Orwellian for the tastes of the time, and was quietly dropped. It did, however, touch on the crucial issue of the relationship between needs assessment and services provision. The screening model has been better worked out and is illuminating in its systems approach. Screening instruments are designed to match the cases they define as positive to the diagnostic and treatment processes positivity leads into. Screening programmes should not be launched until those processes are in place, and are sufficient in quality and volume to meet the screening yield and the aims of the programme. But screening is typically a single- though far from simple-minded process focusing on one condition; needs assessment is necessarily a more widely based exercise, with concerns and implications that may transcend traditional service delivery divisions, in particular between health and social care. But if the concept of need is to be useful it has to be defined in terms of a specific and practicable intervention to which it will respond; needs assessment is not just a detailed acknowledgement of the imperfections of life.

There can be few more complex patterns of needs than those of ill, disabled or disadvantaged older people, and particularly older people with mental health problems. Mental and physical ill-health and social deprivation feed on each other in complex ways that defy conventional causative analysis. Well-intentioned but ill-thought-out interventions may produce paradoxical effects. Adverse events due to drugs, or increased burdens on neighbours or relatives, are as familiar as they are embarrassing to doctors and social workers. But even the basic process of transforming disability into dependent ability may increase rather than diminish an older person's unhappiness. The 'problem' as perceived by professionals may not correspond with the problem as lived by an older person, or her informal carer. Good sense, as well as respect for human dignity, requires that providers and recipients of care work as partners in defining problems and prescribing interventions.

It is against this immensely complex and challenging background that the Camberwell Assessment of Need for the Elderly (CANE) was developed. It has been conscientiously evaluated for reliability and validity, and is comprehensive in its range and perspectives. Specifically, needs are viewed from the vantage points of the older person, the informal carers and the providers. CANE can provide a systematic review of an older person's life-situation at any point of direct or indirect contact with services. It can contribute, if the times demand, to the Single Assessment Illusion of the National Service Framework for Older People, but its logical place lies more deeply in subsystems of care prescription and delivery, where the requirements of specialist expertise and broad competence inevitably conflict. A social worker must recognise the existence of an old lady's hallucinations but would be unwise to try to treat them with non-directive counselling. A doctor who does not understand the reason why the hallucinations centre on a long-dead daughter-in-law may not meet the old lady's need for relief from guilt as well as from Lewy body dementia. Yet such entwinements form the warp and woof of life-as-experienced, and their intricacies grow with the accumulating years. Services must be both analytical and integrated in their response; CANE is therefore an instrument for researchers and evaluators as well as for practitioners.

With such a major project, it is inevitable that the literature describing CANE's development and deployment has been scattered and in some aspects incomplete. This book provides a single source from which professionals and others interested will be able to explore the structure and utility of the instrument. Many readers will be struck by the ready introduction into other countries and settings of a form of assessment developed within the particulars of the British system of health and social services. For its creators, this must be a particularly gratifying endorsement of CANE's rationale and practicality.

This book is not a final report. Older people of successive generations differ in their values, needs and resources. Services evolve also, in response not just to the requirements of their users and the growth of knowledge and technology, but also to pressures from politics, finance and the aspirations of staff. Instruments such as CANE must also have the capacity and mechanisms to evolve. Here, then, must be a beginning, not an end.

John Grimley Evans
Green College
Oxford

Introduction

Geraldine Hancock and Martin Orrell

Effective and good-quality health and social care must be able to accurately and comprehensively identify and address the needs of the individual user of the service. The Camberwell Assessment of Need for the Elderly (CANE) has been specifically designed to measure the multiple needs of individuals over the age of 65 and define which of these needs are not being met. In the UK there has been widespread interest in the CANE, particularly in health settings, and now over 100 centres throughout the UK are familiar with the instrument. The CANE has been widely used in Europe including Norway, Sweden, Finland, Holland, Belgium, Austria, Ireland, Germany, Portugal and Spain, and has also been used in Turkey, India, New Zealand, Australia, Canada, the USA, Brazil and Hong Kong. Translations are available in Norwegian, Swedish, German, Spanish, Portuguese, Dutch, Turkish and Hindi. An electronic version is now available for use with laptop or handheld computers.

We have produced this book to provide comprehensive information about the CANE in a single publication, as a direct response to the growing demand within the UK and internationally. The scope of the book is intended to illustrate the versatility of the CANE in clinical practice, service evaluation and research in a range of settings. In the first part of this introduction, we discuss the background history to the assessment of need and look at the particular issues with regard to assessing needs in older people. In the second part, we introduce the chapters in the book within the three main sections. The first section looks at the original development of the CANE, and its further development and evaluation in the UK and other countries. The second section looks at the applications of the CANE in clinical practice, service evaluation and research in a range of settings. The third section comprises the manual, a copy of the CANE and the CANE–S (short version), and a training pack.

Defining need

In health care, the concept of an individual need has been defined using various terminologies, and a consensus on the definition of need is not readily apparent (Phelan *et al*, 1995). However, the disparity within the literature concerning the definition of need might be due to the differing backgrounds and frameworks of the various disciplines that use the term.

⁣ A common way of defining a need has been to consider how an individual's abilities compare with a standard population of peers. A need would then exist when the individual did not have what others of the same age and circumstances did have (Brewin *et al*, 1987). For example, it could be generally expected that a 20-year-old should be able to walk comfortably and if they could not walk comfortably for whatever reason, this would be considered a need for mobility. Other definitions of need exclude the impact of previous disabilities, such that the mobility need would no longer exist if the person had never been able to walk comfortably. Another definition automatically decrease the average expectation as the individual ages.'Gordon *et al* (1997) used such a reference point when they suggested that a need exists when a person requires 'personal attention' involving more people or more time than they had previously. Yet other definitions identify a need when a deficit in resources results in a decrease in the person's quality of life. Indeed, Xenitidis *et al* (2000) argued that a need is a quality of life measure in itself. Associating need with quality of life has the advantage of giving the individual the ability to decide when a need is present. Quality of life, however, has itself proven to be difficult to define and measure objectively (O'Brien *et al*, 2000) since by its very nature it is subjective and personal.

A commonly used definition of need has been based on interventions or treatments that were available to potentially help or alleviate the problem. This definition has the advantage of being readily translated into a need for a particular intervention that might meet the need (Slade *et al*, 1999). A definition of need that incorporated the idea of intervention has the advantage of being able to separate needs into those that are presently met and those that are not met. A met need would be defined as a situation in which the individual has difficulties in a particular area but these difficulties are being adequately provided for. An unmet need would then exist when they are not receiving the appropriate level of assessment or care. Separating needs in this way had clinical implications in that once unmet needs were identified, they led directly to appropriate interventions that should meet those needs. Meeting unmet needs was also important because the number of unmet needs was related to reduced health, poor quality of life and ongoing health-related expenses (Slade *et al*, 1999; UK700 Group, 1999).

Why assess need?

Assessment of an individual's health care needs used to be based on measures of disability and symptomatology, such that if a person had a certain disease that caused a certain level of disability, they were assumed to need a certain level of services (Neville *et al*, 1999). This system of resource allocation has been questioned, resulting in an increased emphasis on the importance of individually meaningful criteria for assessing and allocating limited health care resources (Slade & Thornicroft, 1995).

Much research has shown that basing resource allocation and individual care plans on diagnosis or measures of disability does not necessarily result in appropriate interventions for many individuals (Slade & Thornicroft, 1995). Instead, research has shown that the relationships between treatment and outcome (especially in the realms of mental health) are more complicated than simply adding up the severity of symptoms and that the process is intricately linked to each individual's needs. Thus, outcome for mental health services should be guided by an individual's evaluation of their unmet needs (Boardman *et al*, 1999). This type of model is based on vulnerability and risk, not legal status or diagnosis, so that in modern health care, emphasis should be on a whole system approach to match services with need (Department of Health, 1999). There has also been pressure for services to become patient-centred rather than service-centred and this has led to an increased emphasis on individuals' needs (Chester & Bender, 1999; Woods, 2001).

This emphasis on needs-based service allocation has also been prompted by a trend towards evidence-based costing of care. As the research had shown that individual need is closely related to effective health outcome, health care commissioners wanted to see that the services they were purchasing were based on the assessment of individual needs (Slade & Thornicroft, 1995). This shift towards looking for cost-effective evidence for health care services has been particularly important in the domains of mental health, where outcome data has always been more complicated (Ramsay *et al*, 1995; Philp, 1997).

New government policies have reflected this change in emphasis (e.g. NHS and Community Care Act 1990; National Service Framework for Older People, 2001). For example, the care programme approach (House of Commons, 1990) policy was designed to enhance the delivery of health and social care services to people with mental health problems, based on the assessment of each individual's needs. This individual needs assessment was to be completed by a keyworker, who would then facilitate the smooth delivery of services to meet the individual's needs across various health care services and settings such as in-patient, out-patient, acute hospital wards and the community (Department of Health,

1995*a*). The Carers (Recognition and Services) Act 1995 also specified that carers should have their individual needs assessed, regardless of setting, and that appropriate interventions should be available to meet their needs. The National Service Framework (Department of Health, 2001) also stresses that services should be provided based on individual need alone rather than other factors such as ability to pay, level of disability, ability to communicate or type of setting (Department of Health, 2001).

Principles of needs assessment

Assessment of needs should be comprehensive so that it goes beyond the presenting problem, and should involve whichever disciplines and agencies appear appropriate in the circumstances. It should be tailored to the individual's current and projected needs, take into account the patient's and carer's views, and be reviewed regularly. Assessments based on these multidisciplinary principles should assist services to incorporate each individual's needs into a structured, individualised care plan that is person-centred. If care plans are based on such an assessment, they should lead to the production of effective interventions that go some way towards meeting each individual's specific needs (Hughes *et al*, 2001). Additionally, this individual assessment of need can then be used to evaluate the interventions outlined in the care plan and determine whether they have been successful in meeting the person's needs.

• In the past, older people's needs (especially those that were unmet) only became apparent when the person could no longer cope and reached crisis point (Philp *et al*, 1995). If they were fortunate, monitors might have been in place, and the crisis might have been predicted and subsequently averted. If not in a crisis, presentation would normally lead to a period of assessment, usually coordinated by a multidisciplinary team (Bedford *et al*, 1996). The members of the team then drew together their various assessments, proposed management strategies and devised a suitable plan to meet the individual's needs. This multidisciplinary method of assessment and treatment has been generally accepted and found to be satisfactory in most circumstances, particularly in the delivery of mental health services (Bedford *et al*, 1996). Difficulties arose, however, when individuals did not receive this multidisciplinary assessment or when the team were unable to monitor the outcome of the individual once the crisis had passed (House of Commons, 1995; Bebbington *et al*, 1997). In particular, individual needs changed over time and although some needs were easily met, other needs could remain neglected (Brewin *et al*, 1988; Philp *et al*, 1995; Bedford *et al*, 1996).

One of the main reasons for a multidisciplinary approach to assessment and treatment of older people's problems is because mental health problems are common and often encompass various domains pertinent to the overall well-being of the individual (Hughes *et al*, 2001). These domains combine physical, social and psychological needs. In addition to the often complex nature of their difficulties, people often lack the skills and resources to enable them to benefit from available ways of meeting their needs (Chester & Bender, 1999). People with mental illness often struggle with additional problems, such as communication difficulties or public stigmatisation about mental health problems (Wing *et al*, 1992). There have also been assumptions about poor outcome and social restrictions that make it difficult for individuals with mental health problems to have their needs assessed and met effectively (Chester & Bender, 1999). Multidisciplinary teams have tried to overcome many of these factors when assessing individual needs, for example by incorporating multiple informants into their assessments to gather valid information about the person's difficulties (Slade *et al*, 1998).

The needs of older people

The increasing size of the older population of the world, and particularly that of the 'oldest old' (those over 85 years), has led to a growing recognition of the potential demands that this will make on health and social care resources worldwide. Though much debate and analysis has concentrated on the possible impacts of such demands, there has also been a growing awareness of the wider issues involved in such radically changing population demographics. Against this background, health services and social services, governments and international organisations have been eager to measure the needs of older people to help delineate the impact such population changes will have on the use of resources. Cassel (1994) highlighted the particular importance of assessing the health care needs of older people in the context of health care rationing. Moreover, the Medical Research Council's topic review on the health of elderly people in the UK (Medical Research Council, 1994) recommended that research should be focused on changing areas in health care in the community, particularly through needs-based assessment approaches.)

The frequent coexistence of disability, physical and mental illness and social problems means that older people often have complex needs, some of which may be long-term. This means that proper evaluation will be difficult without standardised methods aimed at comprehensive and systematic assessment. Maslow (1954) postulated that certain needs are 'universal' in humans generally. However, different subsections of the population will have additional more specific types of need. Thus, older people with dementia might have specific and unique needs related to their cognitive impairment, but their range of general needs would be the same as everyone else's (Murphy, 1992).

Within the realms of the mental health care of older people, widespread changes have contributed to a move away from traditional models of health care provision, with a marked decrease in the number of NHS-run continuing care wards and a rapid increase in privately funded residential and nursing care facilities (Bowling *et al*, 1991). The number of older people sustained in the community remains significantly greater than in previous decades, mainly due to the increased range and quantity of support services available in the community (Impallomeni & Starr, 1995; Chester & Bender, 1999). This move from institutional care to community care has had many advantages, such as reducing costs, encouraging ongoing involvement in the community and an emphasis on the preservation of abilities (Philp *et al*, 1995). However, it has also meant that individuals entering elderly nursing or residential care facilities are generally frailer than they would have been in the past (Wattis *et al*, 1992).

Old age has special characteristics that may affect an individual's mental health, such as the psychological effects of retirement, deteriorating physical health, loss and grief over previous capacity, loss of friends or family (Wing & Roth, 1996) and later, end-of-life issues. The prevalence of dementia also increases markedly with increased age (Chester & Bender, 1999), rising to one in four of the over 80s. Given these factors, many elderly people will require assistance from mental health services at some point, and often this will be their first contact with mental health services.

Development and evaluation of the CANE

The CANE is one of a series of needs assessment measures derived from the original Camberwell Assessment of Need (CAN; Phelan *et al*, 1995), which also includes the CAN Forensic version (CANFOR) and the CAN for Developmental and Intellectual Disabilities (CANDID). The development and psychometric properties of the CANE have been summarised in Chapter 1 by Reynolds *et al*, although this has been described more fully in Reynolds *et al* (2000). However, for an instrument to be clearly identified as having robust validity and reliability, it should be tested in other settings, under different conditions and by other research groups. Chapter 3 by Mateos *et al* and Chapter 4 by Dech and Machleidt show that the CANE can be readily used in other countries and translated into other languages, and that the validity and reliability is consistently good. This consolidates the position of the CANE as an effective and accurate measure of need. Walters and Iliffe (Chapter 2) evaluated the CANE in primary care and noted that it was a feasible tool for research, but probably too long for routine clinical use in general practice. They are currently involved in a major study, developing a short focused version for primary care.

Applications of the CANE

• The CANE can be a very useful instrument to use in clinical practice (particularly in mental health or social care settings), in care planning and in multidisciplinary team work, as it generates lists both of unmet needs and of worthwhile interventions, and allows for consideration of users' and carers' views. However, it has a wide variety of other uses, many of which have been illustrated by chapters in this book. Mateos *et al* show how it has been used as part of an epidemiological survey to map the needs of the community elderly population in northern Spain. Field *et al* (Chapter 5) conducted a survey in supported housing in the UK, and found that older people with poor social networks have higher numbers of unmet needs. A number of chapters demonstrate that the CANE can be readily used to map the needs in specific populations or services. Both Martin *et al* (Chapter 6) and Dech and Machleidt found that it was a very effective method for detailing the complex needs of people living in long-term care settings, including nursing homes. Hoe *et al* (Chapter 8) also used the CANE to look at the needs of long-term attenders of mental health day hospitals and found that many people had all their needs met. The CANE can also be used to profile the needs of new referrals to a service. Ashaye *et al* (Chapter 9) investigated the needs of new attenders at two day hospitals over a 1-year period and Bhat *et al* (Chapter 7) looked at the needs of older in-patients in general hospitals who had been referred for a psychiatric liaison assessment. Lastly, the CANE can be used for service evaluation. Ashaye *et al* looked at the effectiveness of mental health day hospitals by comparing the average number of unmet needs at admission and 3 months later, and defining which interventions had been met at follow-up. Hammond *et al* evaluated service provision for younger-onset dementia across four London boroughs by using the CANE as part of a survey of all such patients known to the various services. The results of the survey are summarised, and the high number of unmet needs in defined areas are used to clearly identify specific gaps in the service provision.

The CANE in practice

The CANE is a comprehensive measure designed to assess the needs of older people. It supports the clinical assessment process, and the underlying principles of the scale means that it models good clinical practice and the ratings are based on expert assessment. This means that clinical and professional expertise is needed to complete the CANE, and complex issues can be dealt with in the usual way by discussion and consultation with the multidisciplinary team. As a general rule, staff completing the CANE should have professional training and experience working with older people. Staff without professional training could still be involved in the CANE assessment, but should be adequately supervised and supported by an appropriate professional.

The CANE can be easily used, without extensive training, by a wide variety of professionals including doctors, nurses, clinical psychologists, occupational therapists and social workers, and the reliability remains good when used by different disciplines. Further information about 1-day training courses on the use of the CANE is available from the editors on request. However, the book is designed to provide all the information needed (which includes a detailed manual and training materials) for local teams to organise their own training seminars. As the CANE is completed via a semi-structured interview, this gives the person administering it flexibility in the phrasing and ordering of the questions. This approach is generally more acceptable to carers and patients, since the clinical interview does not need to follow a rigid format and can be varied according to the context and the individual. In addition, the ability to compare patient, carer and staff ratings can be very valuable. It highlights discrepancies in views that might suggest that additional information needs to be collected, indicating that a more detailed explanation should be given to be the patient or carer. It also helps in assessing potential problems in compliance and acceptability of treatment options. A number of studies have been carried out, using the CANE to compare the patient, carer and staff views on the needs of older people in primary care (Chapter 2 by Walters & Iliffe) and also in mental health services (Hancock *et al*, 2003).

The current version of the CANE (Version IV) has been recently modified to take into account the requirements of the 'single-assessment process' (SAP; Department of Health, 2001). It now addresses the range of sub-domains of the process, though not all are specifically listed (e.g. both falls and ability to use local transport come under the mobility section). Older people are fully involved in the needs assessment process and there is a special section noting their own views of their needs and their satisfaction with the amount of help received. Support is available for sites using the CANE in clinical practice in preparation for the full implementation of the SAP.

Using the CANE in a community mental health team (CMHT)

An older people's CMHT in West London decided to pilot the CANE for a 12-week period, and to use it as an initial holistic screening assessment for all new referrals, with a view to adopting the CANE as a routine assessment if the pilot was judged to be a success. We wrote a new operational policy to describe our system for assessing new referrals. We also initiated a single point of entry to mental health services with a new open access system that in addition to accepting referrals from health and social services, for the first time allowed referrals from carers, older people and non-statutory services.

The process of selecting a common assessment tool was through a multi-disciplinary steering group within the CMHT. The steering group was set up to consider selecting a core assessment tool for use by the entire CMHT within the context of the SAP. It was felt that the CANE was holistic and, importantly, was very much focused on the older person's view and the carer's view, as well as assessing the view of any staff involved in that person's care. The CANE had been suggested for use as an overview and as a comprehensive tool, but it was felt that with the addition of a short anxiety/depression scale and the Mini-Mental State Examination (MMSE; Folstein *et al*, 1975), it would function effectively as a screening tool for the specialist service. A further advantage was that it appeared relatively simple to use, with an easy scoring system and a clear layout. The CANE linked neatly into the care programme approach (CPA) process since it was a holistic and comprehensive assessment of need that could be completed prior to each CPA meeting to identify the areas that could be addressed in the older person's care plan. Apart from its potential as an assessment tool that could be used by all disciplines within the team, it had the additional function of providing data about the effectiveness of the service. This information could easily be extrapolated, since the scoring system clearly indicated the number of unmet needs at the point of assessment by our team and the number of unmet needs when the person had been discharged. The CANE could also be used as an interim measure of needs during allocation within the team.

There was a great deal of anxiety generated within the team by the use of a new tool, as well as the other changes, and much anxiety was initially directed towards self-referrals that the team thought would be overwhelming. We have not yet completed the pilot, but we have had a mid-way review. Our fears of being engulfed with work as a result of numerous self-referrals were not realised, and the concerns that the CANE would require an inordinate amount of time to complete have abated. We have found that, on average, carrying out a fairly complex assessment with the patient and carer takes between 60 and 75 minutes. We have also decided that we will set up training for all CMHT members. Support for the CANE as our tool of choice was not overwhelming and a number of psychiatrists seemed reluctant to use it, arguing that it was a biosocial model that deviated too much from the medical focus. Others within the team were enthusiastic. The overall views will become clearer once we have formally evaluated the experiences of both the CMHT and the older people who were involved in the process.

Acknowledgement

Kerry Mowat-Goswell for providing information and feedback about experiences in piloting the CANE for use within the Single Assessment Process and their local CMHT in London.

1 Development of the Camberwell Assessment of Need for the Elderly (CANE)

Tom Reynolds, Geraldine Hancock, Bob Woods, Graham Thornicroft and Martin Orrell

Assessing needs

Assessing the needs of older people with mental health problems has attracted various approaches. Epidemiologically based approaches have been used to look at population needs in older people (Victor, 1991; Cooper, 1993). However, individual approaches have largely concentrated on those with dementia, a group with obvious multiple and enduring needs, whose care, in health and social terms, has probably been more systematically studied than other groups of older people with psychiatric disorders (Aronson *et al*, 1992; Wattis *et al*, 1992; McWalter *et al*, 1998). Older people may also have different perceptions of their needs from those of clinicians (McEwan, 1992). Until recently, there have been no instruments specifically designed to measure met and unmet needs for the range of interventions available from mental health and social care services for older people (Hamid *et al*, 1995).

Needs assessment instruments developed in the UK were designed to measure the needs of adults under 65 with serious mental health problems. Examples include the MRC Needs for Care Assessment (Brewin *et al*, 1987), a modified version, the Cardinal Needs Scale (Marshall *et al*, 1995), the Bangor Assessment of Need Profile (Carter *et al*, 1996) and the Camberwell Assessment of Need (Phelan *et al*, 1995).

The Medical Research Council Needs for Care Assessment (Brewin *et al*, 1987) was designed to measure needs in people with long-term mental illnesses. A need was deemed to be present if a patient's level of functioning fell below, or threatened to fall below, some minimum specified level and a potentially effective remedy existed. While a number of studies suggest it has good reliability if used by trained investigators (Brewin & Wing, 1993), some problems were highlighted when it was used in hostels for the homeless (Hogg & Marshall, 1992) and for long-term in-patients (Pryce *et al*, 1993). Hogg & Marshall (1992) concluded that their data was difficult to interpret due to the failure to take account of patients' and carers' views in appropriate detail and therefore went on to develop a modified version, the Cardinal Needs Schedule (Marshall *et al*, 1995).

The Bangor Assessment of Need Profile (Carter *et al*, 1996) covers 32 items of need and allows patients and their keyworkers to give their opinion. It was specifically intended to assess the needs of those with long-term mental illness and the evaluation of its reliability involved a study on participants who had been long-stay in-patients, according to the criteria that they had been in-patients for over 1 year and had a diagnosis of a major mental illness other than senile dementia (O'Driscoll & Leff, 1993). The authors concluded that it was mainly designed to be used as a research instrument.

The Camberwell Assessment of Need (Phelan *et al*, 1995) was developed to measure the needs of people in the general adult population with severe mental illness. It measures whether a need exists in 22 domains and whether or not it is met. If help is being given, it also allows recording of the level of help being given by different agencies, from friends and relatives to statutory services. It has been shown to have good reliability and validity. Studies comparing the assessments made by staff and patients showed that both groups tended to rate similar numbers of needs but different ones, agreeing moderately on met needs but less often on unmet needs (Slade *et al*, 1996; 1998).

Needs assessment instruments for older people

New social and mental health policies have noted the influence of unmet needs on individual outcome and this has led to the need for a structured, standardised needs assessment tool (Martin *et al*, 1999). This has been highlighted in the UK by the introduction of the Single Assessment Process (Department of Health, 2001), which has emphasised the importance of standardised needs assessments across health and social care in the context of a person-centred approach. Attention turned to finding new, adequate and appropriate ways of assessing the various facets of individual health and social care needs. What was needed was a comprehensive needs assessment instrument to quantify met and unmet needs in older individuals, which had good psychometric properties, was easy to use and could measure a change in needs. This instrument should be suitable for use as an outcome measure and include the various perspectives of the health professional, carer, staff and the individual (Gordon *et al*, 1997). These differing perspectives were required because the definition of a need was somewhat subjective. A small number of person-centred tools have been designed and piloted for their utility in assessing the multi-faceted nature of needs in older people (see Reynolds & Orrell, 2001).

Wattis *et al* (1992) proposed a model for estimating the needs of people with dementia living in continuing care, by assessing their level of dependency using the Clifton Assessment Procedure for older people (Gilleard & Pattie, 1979) or the Crighton Royal Behaviour Scale (Robinson, 1961). This approach could be useful in determining the appropriateness of various continuing care settings. However, the level of dependency did not necessarily equate with level of need generally, in either a qualitative or quantitative sense, or even define what the needs were. For example, a person with mild dementia, rated as low-dependency and apparently appropriately housed in a residential home, might still have a large number of unmet or partially met needs because of poor quality of care or poor understanding of those needs. On the other hand, a person with profound dementia and with very high dependency might have few, if any, unmet needs as all aspects of daily living are receiving obvious help or intervention. Similarly Rodriguez-Ferrera & Vassilas (1998) have pointed out that it is the quality of the environment, not where it is, that matters for older people with schizophrenia.

The Care Needs Assessment Pack for Dementia (CarenapD) (McWalter *et al*, 1998) was designed for multidisciplinary team use to rate met and unmet needs of people with dementia, and their carers in the community and related settings such as day hospitals. Although it did not differentiate between information sources (e.g. interviews with the person with dementia, the carer or others involved and information from case notes), it allowed for discrepancies or differences of opinion to be recorded at the rater's discretion. Recordings were made on seven sub-scales of need (health and mobility, self-care and toileting, social interaction, thinking and memory, behaviour and mental state, house-care, and community living). The section specific to the carer allowed assessments of need over six domains: health, daily difficulties, support, breaks from caring, feelings, and information. Preliminary research suggested it has acceptable validity in a number of domains and reasonable reliability (McWalter *et al*, 1998).

The development and evaluation of the CANE

*The Camberwell Assessment of Need for older people was the first instrument designed for measuring the broad range of needs of older people, particularly those with mental health problems. It was intended for use in all settings, ranging from community out-patients to day hospitals, psychiatric assessment wards, and continuing care in hospital, nursing and residential homes. The CANE was based on the structural model of the Camberwell Assessment of Need (CAN) and had similar criteria set out for its development (Phelan *et al*, 1995), including adopting the same definition of need, as a problem or difficulty requiring intervention or assessment. The advantages of this definition were that it was clinically defined and useful, particularly for care planning by identifying needs as met or unmet. This meant that clinical/professional expertise and knowledge was necessary in order to complete the assessment and in clinical practice complex issues could be dealt with in the usual way by discussion and consultation within a multidisciplinary team. The full report of the development of the CANE and the evaluation of its reliability and validity have been reported in more detail elsewhere (Reynolds *et al*, 2000).

Development of the draft version of the CANE

The initial adaptation of the CAN was carried out by Melanie Abas, Martin Orrell and colleagues. The overall format of the CAN was preserved and a number of the topics covered were identical, although the format of questions was necessarily adapted to be more suitable to the target population. The process of adaptation took place in the context of various focus groups (Kitzinger, 1996) made up of older service users and professionals working in mental health services for older people. This resulted in a draft version called the Camberwell Assessment of Need for Older Adults (CANOA), which covered 27 different areas. The CANOA was piloted on an inner-city sample of 70 black elderly people with various mental health problems.

As part of a Delphi process (Jones & Hunter, 1996) to achieve a consensus on the style and content, a questionnaire was sent to service users, carers and professionals involved in all aspects of care of older people (psychiatrists, psychologists, geriatricians, nurses, social workers, representatives of voluntary groups and occupational therapists), asking them to rate the various topics on a 5-point scale of importance and requesting suggestions on any other areas. Following the feedback from these and subsequent focus groups (again with service users, carers and various professionals), a second draft version was prepared. This was the subject of the Consensus Conference held in London and attended by delegates who represented all the relevant professional and voluntary groups involved in care of older people. These included representatives from Age Concern and the Alzheimer's Disease Society, mental health service managers, psychiatrists, psychologists, geriatricians, general practitioners, social workers, nurses and occupational therapists.

Workshops were used to work on specific topics in the draft version, scrutinising the layout and wording in detail to make sure that it covered all of the most important areas as well as possible. Each workshop group had a core of specialists in the topics they were to cover (e.g. geriatricians and GPs covering physical health issues). Each group fed back to the whole conference after each session. The results of these sessions were collated and the feedback was used to prepare a penultimate draft version of CANE that was circulated to the conference delegates for final opinions. This draft was piloted with 10 day hospital patients, their key staff members and their carers. The final draft was prepared following these interviews, which included 24 items for patients' needs and two for carers' needs (Box 1.1). This was essentially the same document as that resulting from the conference, except for some minor changes in wording to clarify some areas and make it more 'user-friendly'. It measured both met and unmet needs, incorporated staff, patients' and carers' views of needs and

Box 1.1 Areas of need covered in the CANE

1	Accommodation	14	Psychological distress
2	Looking after the home	15	Information
3	Food	16	Deliberate self-harm
4	Self-care	17	Inadvertent self-harm
5	Caring for someone else	18	Abuse/neglect
6	Daytime activities	19	Behaviour
7	Memory	20	Alcohol
8	Eyesight/hearing/communication	21	Company
9	Mobility/falls	22	Intimate relationships
10	Continence	23	Money/budgeting
11	Physical health	24	Benefits
12	Drugs	A	Carer's need for information
13	Psychotic symptoms	B	Carer's psychological distress

had a section on the needs of carers. It also measured level of help received from informal carers as well as from statutory services. In the latest version of the CANE, a further column was added to document the ratings of the assessor (e.g. clinician or researcher) conducting the assessment

Validity and reliability

The main study to evaluate the psychometric properties (including validity and reliability) of the CANE was carried out in London and Essex in collaboration with five other centres; three in the UK (North Wales, Liverpool and Southport), one in Sweden (Jonkoping), and one in the USA (Lebanon, Pennsylvania). CANE appeared to have good face validity. In addition, the extensive development process involved rigorous scrutiny by a large number of experts, clinicians, carers and service users in the UK and other countries (see also Chapter 3 by Mateos *et al* and Chapter 4 by Dech & Machleidt). The overall consensus was that CANE covered the main areas of need for the older population. The choice of words and word length was suitable for most readers. The survey of patients ($n=35$), carers ($n=30$) and professionals ($n=55$) (psychiatrists, community psychiatric nurses, occupational therapists, social workers, geriatricians, GPs, psychologists and representatives of voluntary organisations) found that all items were rated as at least moderately important (3 on a 5-point scale), and no additional areas of need were suggested by more than two respondents from one group. The overall consensus from the surveys, focus groups and the conference was that there was a definite requirement for a needs assessment instrument for older people with mental health problems and that the CANE should fulfil that requirement.

Table 1.1 Mean number of needs identified

	Met needs	Unmet needs	Total needs
Patient ($n = 83$)	5.00	1.47	6.47
Staff ($n = 94$)	5.78	2.76	8.53
Carer ($n = 57$)	6.54	2.75	9.3

Table 1.2 Correlations between CANE and established scales

CANE item	CAPE–BRS item	Correlation
Eyesight/hearing/communication	CAPE (eyesight/hearing)	$r = 0.6$
Self-care	CAPE (bathing/dressing)	$r = 0.73$
	CAPE (appearance)	$r = 0.67$
Memory	CAPE (confused)	$r = 0.82$
Mobility	CAPE (walking)	$r = 0.74$
Continence	CAPE (incontinence)	$r = 0.85$
CANE summary score and CAPE–BRS		$r = 0.8$
CANE carers' total score and GHQ		$r = 0.58$
CANE item Carers' psychological distress and GHQ		$r = 0.6$

The total numbers of met and unmet needs for individuals assessed from the sites outlined above using the final version of the CANE are shown in Table 1.1. To investigate criterion and concurrent validity four other scales were compared with the CANE: The Clifton Assessment Procedures for the Elderly – Behaviour Rating Scale (CAPE–BRS) to rate dependency and behavioural function; Short Form 36 as a quality of life measurement; Barthel Index as a measure of functional status; General Health Questionnaire (GHQ) to measure carer stress. Table 1.2 shows that the CANE correlates with appropriate items on the CAPE–BRS and GHQ. The CANE had appropriate criterion validity with a correlation of 0.66 with the Behaviour Rating Scale from the Clifton Assessment Procedures for the Elderly (Gilleard & Pattie, 1979). Further analyses also showed that the CANE had good construct validity (Reynolds *et al*, 2000).

Data were collected on 55 'cases' for the interrater and test–retest reliability studies. Of these 41 service users, 53 staff members and 22 carers were interviewed initially with two co-raters present (interrater). Forty service users, 53 staff and 17 carers were re-interviewed one week later (test–retest). Correlations between summary scores were very high with values of $r=0.99$ for interrater scores (patients, staff and carers) and 0.8 for test–retest scores (patients) and 0.96 for that of staff and carers. Kappa values were very high for interrater reliability with all but one (0.6) at 0.75 or above, indicating excellent agreement. Kappa values for test–retest reliability were also very high for most items, indicating very good reliability.

This evaluation process found that the CANE provides a comprehensive assessment of needs for older people. By highlighting needs that are unmet it also could be used to identify interventions and resources required either for the individual or for a particular group of people. The development work on the CANE showed that it has very good psychometric properties and the instrument can be completed in 30 minutes or less. It can be used by a wide range of professionals and is easily learned without extensive training. It was also shown to be usable with a wide range of populations and settings. The results of the development and evaluation process indicated that the CANE could have a wide range of uses in clinical practice, service evaluation and research.

2 The CANE in primary care settings: its feasibility and utility as a research and clinical tool

Kate Walters and Steve Iliffe

Introduction: assessing the needs of older people in primary care

There is a well-established view, partly rooted in reliable evidence and partly fuelled by anecdote, that illness and disability in older people are under-detected in primary care settings (Williamson *et al*, 1964; Iliffe *et al*, 1991a,b; Brown *et al*, 1997), despite a long tradition of service innovation and experiment designed to optimise case finding and management for health problems in later life. This perception may persist in part because of the dominance of medical models of health, rather than models of disability, even though it was becoming clear by the early 1970s that the predominant problem among older people in the community was seen to be functional loss, not undiagnosed medical problems (Taylor & Buckley, 1987). The majority of medical problems identified by screening of older populations were either already known to the general practitioner or were not considered of major importance by the individuals concerned (Williams, 1975; Tulloch & Moore, 1979). Consultation habits appeared to have changed after the establishment of the NHS, with less evidence of under-consultation by older patients (Williams, 1974), and some signs that those who did not seek medical care were relatively well (Ebrahim *et al*, 1984).

The development of an interest in primary care for older people was less significant, and much less rapid, than the growth of geriatric medicine, but it began in the 1950s and gathered some momentum, focusing on finding a role for primary care staff – general practitioners and health visitors in particular – to complement that of specialist geriatric medicine. Were general practitioners simply to direct their older patients towards geriatricians, or was there some other task to perform, like preventing them from needing specialist care at all? Were health visitors to concentrate on the health of infants and pre-school children, or did they have a broader remit for health promotion across all age groups? Could the complex interrelationships between physical health, psychological state and social situation be understood and attended to in ways that enhanced the well-being and functional ability of the older patient?

Experimentation with population screening and assessment by different methods such as postal questionnaires, specialist nurses, case-finding computer software and dedicated clinics, and the search for 'at risk' groups, were reflected in the debates that occurred both in the Royal College of General Practice (Taylor & Buckley, 1987) and in the Health Visitors Association (British Geriatrics Society & Health Visitors' Association, 1986). Although the reporting of the approaches to primary care for older people was dominated by general practitioners, much of the actual work on the ground was pioneered by health visitors, and the underlying ideas came as much from community nursing as from medicine (Butler, 1987; Macleod & Mein, 1987). The debates that occurred are of direct relevance to those working on and with the CANE, for they identified some of the key themes that later shaped the CANE's design. Brief, non-intrusive strategies for predicting functional problems during routine consultations were needed, always qualified by the need to avoid iatrogenic risks of treating unimportant abnormalities, and of medicalising old age (Freer, 1987). The preoccupation of doctors with disease to the detriment of its social consequences, the failure to take into account the adaptive powers of older people and the tendency to underestimate the burden borne by carers were all identified as major obstacles to progress in developing more effective primary care for older people. Medical and social problems overlapped in ways that were often puzzling to clinicians; screening led to an increase in referrals to other agencies but without clear evidence of benefit in many instances, and with variations in referral rates determined as much by the referrer as by the patient's problems (Williams, 1987). Finally, at-risk groups proved harder to identify than anticipated, as more pathological events occurred outside the expected at-risk groups than in them. Models of community development and community networking (Kewley, 1984; Drennan, 1987) became attractive because they began from a social understanding of the impact of disease, and the recognition that disability is the gap between individual capability and environmental demand.

The first attempt to create a national programme of health assessment for older people in the UK, the 'over-75 health check', as prescribed by the 1990 contract for general practitioners, failed to have an impact on the burden of illness and disability in an ageing population and led to a widespread disillusionment with needs assessment for older people in general practice (Iliffe *et al*, 1999). This poorly conceived and delivered policy has impeded the development of primary care for older people for a decade, leaving innovation to occur in the USA and Europe, where the underdevelopment of primary care led to the emergence of substitute systems of comprehensive geriatric assessment and management that appeared to reduce disability. Comprehensive Geriatric Assessment (CGA) can prevent admission to hospital or placement in nursing/residential care, improve functional status and in some cases improve survival of older people (Stuck *et al*, 1993, 1995, 2002), even in those who are relatively well-functioning at baseline (Bula *et al*, 1999). Similarly, out-patient and pre-discharge in-hospital CGA has been shown to prevent functional and health-related quality of life decline in community-dwelling older people (Nikolaus *et al*, 1999; Reuben *et al*, 1999).

Although translation of methods and outcomes from other health service systems is hazardous, the tangible benefits of comprehensive geriatric assessment have stimulated new interest in assessment approaches in the UK. We are now facing a second attempt to introduce a standardised form of needs assessment for older people, driven in part by the increasing pressure to both contain the costs and still adequately meet the needs of an ageing population. The National Service Framework for Older People (NSF–OP) in the UK has revived the concept of multidisciplinary needs assessment in primary care settings (Department of Health, 2001). The second standard 'person-centred care' of the NSF–OP states that a single assessment process should be implemented to ensure a more standardised assessment process is used across all areas and agencies, standards are raised and older people's needs are assessed 'in the round'. Primary care is likely to be a key place where this single assessment process will be both triggered (particularly by general practitioners) and delivered (mainly by nurses and social care).

The idea of a single assessment process is complicated by the heterogeneity of the older population, ranging from robust nonagenarians to frail septuagenarians. There has been a recent trend for the continuing care of some of the most frail and dependent older people to be transferred from the secondary care hospital sector to private nursing and residential homes in the community (Audit Commission, 1997). The responsibility for providing care for these people, with often complex health and social care needs, now falls primarily with their general practitioners (GPs) and Primary Care Trusts (PCTs). This raises questions about how the needs of this sub-population can best be identified and met.

There is now little debate that there is a role for needs assessment of older people in primary care in the UK, but the exact form this should take remains unclear. There has been no systematic structured assessment in widespread use for the 75-and-over checks in the minority of practices that carry them out, and there is a wide variation between practices that carry out these checks and the methods they use (Brown & Groom, 1995). There was clearly a gap in information on valid, reliable multidisciplinary needs assessment instruments in primary care settings. In this context the potential for using the CANE in primary care appears considerable, both as an instrument for research purposes and as a multidisciplinary needs assessment tool for clinical use. The CANE has two important advantages: it addresses dimensions of disability 'in the round', from financial circumstances to mental state; and it triangulates the perspectives of patient, carer and professionals, allowing a discussion about what constitutes a problem to be built into the assessment of need from the outset. This makes it attractive for primary care use, and contrasts it with the traditional medical orientation of needs assessments in health care settings.

The CANE as a research tool in primary care: a feasibility study

In 1997–1998, we conducted a feasibility study to test the use of the CANE as a research tool in a primary care setting. The objectives were to test the feasibility of using the CANE in primary care and to compare the needs identified by the patient, carer, lead health professional (general practitioner or practice/district nurse) and by the researcher following these three assessments. In addition, where an unmet need was identified during an assessment, an additional brief semi-structured interview was conducted to explore help-seeking behaviour and why the need had not been met. This study will be described briefly and the implications for using the CANE as a research tool in primary care considered. Further details on methodology and results are reported elsewhere (Walters *et al*, 2000, 2001).

A systematic random sample of 1:20 of all registered patients aged 75 years and over was selected from four practices in north-west London, representing inner-city/suburban and large/small practices. Patients with advanced dementia who had no informal carer to represent their views and with terminal illness were excluded. The researcher was trained in a single one-hour session in the use of the CANE by a clinician experienced in its use. The use of the CANE was then piloted and a brief follow-up session clarified coding. For each subject agreeing to participate, a structured needs assessment using the CANE was performed in a face-to-face interview. In addition, their informal carers (a relative, friend or neighbour who assisted them in their daily living on one or more occasion per week) and lead health professional (the health professional who was identified by both the patient or carer and their general practitioner as knowing them best) were identified and interviewed. A 'met' need was recorded where the subject identified a problem but felt that there was sufficient support from either informal sources or services to meet the need. An 'unmet' need was recorded when the subject identified a problem but felt there was either no support or insufficient support from informal sources or services. The Clifton Assessment Procedures for the Elderly Behaviour Rating Scale (CAPE–BRS) was used as an additional measure of functional status (Pattie & Gilleard, 1979). Feasibility data were collected for the use of the CANE in primary care, including data on arranging/travelling to the interviews, place and length of interviews and the presence of others at the interview.

The needs (met and unmet) identified using the CANE by the patients and carers were compared to those identified by the health professionals, and kappa tests were performed to analyse the level of agreement between the patient and health professionals' assessments. This was not repeated for carers, owing to small numbers and risks of spurious results from multiple testing. The total number of needs identified by the CANE schedule was correlated against the total score on the CAPE–BRS. A thematic analysis was performed on the qualitative data on barriers to meeting unmet needs involving conceptualising and reducing data, describing categories and enabling interpretations to evolve from the data from the specific case to more general concepts (Strauss & Corbin, 1998).

Findings

In total, 55/84 (66%) of patients, 15/17 (88%) of carers and 55/55 (100%) of health professionals completed interviews. There were no significant differences using chi-squared tests between participants and non-participants in age, gender or location. Reasons given for non-participation were varied and ranged from 'too well' to 'too ill'. In the interviews with health professionals, 40 were with general practitioners (GPs), 14 with practice nurses and one with a district nurse. No hospital-based staff were identified as 'lead health professional'. A carer view alone was taken for 3/55 patients as the patients were unable to complete an interview (two had advanced dementia and one was aphasic).

The mean age of patients was 82 years (range 75–93 years), 72% were female and 6% spoke English as a second language. Overall, 50% were homeowners, 58% had no income other than the state pension, 44% lived in inner-city areas, 44% lived alone, 11% lived in sheltered accommodation and 3% in residential care. Data on the feasibility of using the CANE in primary care, including arranging and timing of interviews/CANE assessments, is detailed in Table 2.1. The mean time taken for the CANE assessments was 22 minutes with patients, 17 minutes for carers and 11 minutes for health professionals, but with a wide variation – up to 55 minutes for patients with multiple needs. The CANE was simple to use with minimal training as a structured, pre-coded interview schedule with in-built prompts. Some variables ('psychotic symptoms', 'behaviour', 'abuse' and 'alcohol') in the CANE schedule did not identify any unmet needs.

The mean number of needs identified was 6.6/24 (s.d.=4.4) per patient, of which 4.2 (s.d.=3.0) were met needs and 2.4 (s.d.=2.9) were unmet needs. A comparison of the overall frequencies of needs identified by patients, their carers, health professionals and the overall assessment by the researcher following all three interviews is illustrated in Figure 2.1. Some examples of individual social, physical and psychological unmet needs identified by patients and health professionals are illustrated in Figure 2.2. The original data has been presented elsewhere (Walters *et al*, 2000).

Many patients identified met needs in the areas of 'physical health', 'looking after the home', 'food' and 'mobility'. The patients' three most frequently identified unmet needs were with 'eyesight/hearing/communication', 'psychological distress' and 'continence', followed closely by 'company', 'information on condition and treatment' and 'memory'. Conversely, health professionals' three most

Table 2.1 Feasibility data for using CANE in primary care

	Patient interviews	Carer interviews	Staff interviews
No. of contacts made to arrange interview			
Mean no. (range)	2.1 (1–6)	1.5 (1–4)	1.2 (1–2)
Distance travelled to interview from base			
Mean distance in miles (range)	7.0 (0.5–20)	4.4 (0–10)	4.2 (0–18)
Time for CANE assessment			
Mean time in minutes (range)	22.0 (9–55)	17.3 (10–30)	10.7 (4–20)
Place of interview			
(a) Patient's home	51	13	0
(b) carers' home (if not (a))	0	2	0
(c) GP surgery	1	0	55
Other people present at interview			
(a) none	43	14	55
(b) carer	2	0	0
(c) non-carer relative	6	1	0
(d) non-carer friend	1	0	0

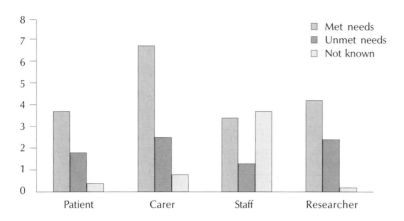

Figure 2.1 Mean needs identified using the CANE by subject

frequently identified unmet needs were 'daytime activities', 'accommodation' and 'mobility/falls'. More than a third of patients (35%) and two-thirds (67%) of health professionals reported that they did not know if the patient had a need regarding benefits, demonstrating poor knowledge of this area.

Kappa tests were performed to analyse the level of agreement between patients and health professionals (Altman, 1991). Most variables (18/24) demonstrated poor or fair agreement (kappa coefficient $\kappa \leq 0.4$). There was moderate agreement with 'self-care', 'company' and 'caring for someone else' ($\kappa = 0.4$–0.6), good agreement with 'physical health', 'food' and 'mobility' ($\kappa = 0.6$–0.8) and no variables with very good agreement ($\kappa \geq 0.8$).

Most carers identified met needs in 'looking after the home' (14/15), 'food' (15/15) and 'physical health' (12/15). High levels of unmet need were identified for 'mobility' (8/15) and 'eyesight/hearing' (7/15) 'self-care' (7/15) and 'daytime activities' (7/15). About half of the carers identified needs in 'continence' and 'memory', but in contrast to the patients' assessments, many of these were identified as met rather than unmet needs (5/8 and 5/7 respectively). Six out of 15 of the carers felt 'psychologically distressed'; in four of these, this need was unmet.

Figure 2.3 shows a scatter plot of the CANE total needs score versus the CAPE score. The scores were not normally distributed, therefore a Spearman's correlation was performed. The Spearman's rho correlation coefficient was 0.785 (significant $P \leq 0.01$, 2-tailed), thus the CANE schedule total number of needs positively correlates with the CAPE–BRS.

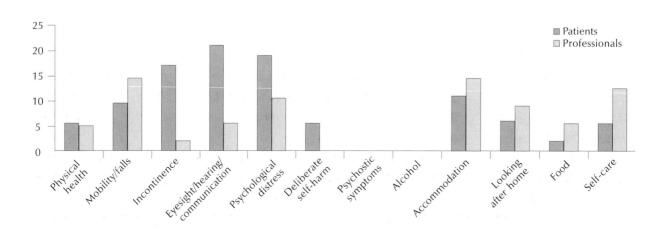

Figure 2.2 Examples of social, physical and unmet needs identified by the CANE

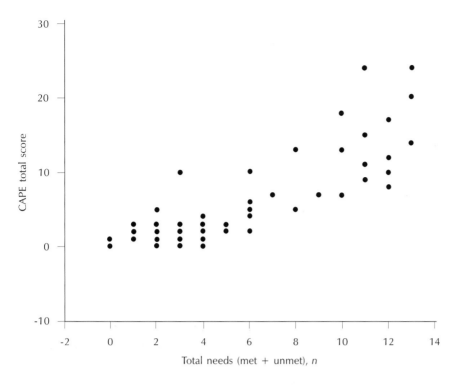

Figure 2.3 Scatter plot of total needs identified by the CANE *v.* the CAPE scale

Barriers to seeking help

One or more unmet need was identified by 31/52 (60%) of patients and 11/15 (73%) of carers. A total of 104 unmet needs were identified by the 31 patients and 11 carers and explored in semi-structured interviews. Help had been sought in only 25/104 (24%) of the unmet needs identified and in 19/104 (18%) help had been offered for the problem. We identified a range of themes from patients' explanations of why their need had not been met, which differed between those who had and had not previously sought help for the problem. These are summarised in Figure 2.4. This illustrates how, for the majority of patients who had not sought help, the overlapping themes of resignation, social withdrawal, low expectations, age attribution and problem minimisation were dominant. For those who had actively sought help, the themes were more orientated around services with issues such as costs, rationing or eligibility for services, failure of service provision or lack of information about services. Further detail and examples are reported elsewhere (Walters *et al*, 2001).

Implications

We should be careful of over-interpreting the results of the feasibility study with its small sample size. However, it does raise some interesting points. There was poor agreement between patients and health professionals about patients' needs, with a few exceptions (e.g. 'physical health', 'mobility' and 'food'). This may be because of different conceptions of the meaning of 'need', or incomplete professional knowledge on the patients' circumstances.

A wide range of needs, both met and unmet, were identified by this study in a community setting and the CANE correlated well with the CAPE–BRS in this setting and with previous work in other settings (Reynolds *et al*, 2000), giving some support to the validity of using the CANE in primary care.

Many of the needs were unmet – and most patients with unmet needs appeared reluctant to seek help due to a combination of resignation, social withdrawal and low expectations. To an extent, there was also a corresponding tendency to minimise their problems and attribute them to the normal

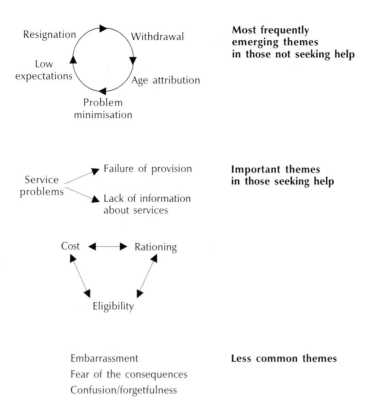

Figure 2.4 Qualitative analysis: barriers to meeting needs

ageing process. Pro-active needs assessment may help increase motivation for change and counter some of these views.

The advantage of using the CANE schedule in research in any setting is that it has the capacity both to identify met and unmet needs, and to directly compare the assessments of patient, carer and health professional. This study illustrates how a three-way assessment can yield new information and enable the researcher to compare what health professionals already know with what can be identified by interviewing patients and carers themselves. It was obviously more time-consuming to make three assessments for each person, and the relative advantages of doing this in clinical practice are less obvious. The feasibility study demonstrated that the CANE schedule is feasible to use for research in a primary care setting as a relatively quick multidisciplinary needs assessment tool that can yield important new information.

The CANE was originally developed for use in old age psychiatry and some variables (e.g. psychotic symptoms, behaviour problems) elicited very low levels of met or unmet needs when used in primary care, probably owing to a low prevalence of these problems in people living at home. Modification of the CANE and further evaluation (feasibility, validity, reliability) are recommended before any extension of its use in its present form in the assessment of people living at home. A brief instrument may have clinical applications for busy primary care practitioners, who may be able to integrate its use into opportunistic screening during their routine work. A brief primary care version of the CANE has been developed with extensive user involvement and this is being field-tested in clinical settings for feasibility of use, validity and reliability, funded by the National Health Service (London Region) Primary Care Development Programme.

The conclusion that we drew from this study is that the CANE schedule is feasible to use as a research tool in primary care and can yield new information about the unmet needs of older people. Using the CANE, it is possible to identify in people living at home the areas where there are relatively high levels of perceived unmet need that the health professionals do not already know about, such as incontinence, impaired eyesight/hearing, memory problems and information on their condition/treatment. A shorter, more focused primary care version of the CANE may have clinical applications for the routine assessment of needs in older people in the community and this is currently being tested.

The CANE as a clinical tool in primary care

The potential for using the CANE as a clinical tool in primary care was subsequently tested in two separate field studies in the same inner-London borough. In the first, the CANE was introduced into a single inner-city general practice, where it was used alongside a practice-designed 75-and-over check protocol. In the second it was introduced to a newly formed health and social care team undertaking home assessments of older people deemed vulnerable by their general practitioners. These two field tests put the CANE into the hands of experienced nurses who were not interested in the CANE's research potential, but only in its utility in everyday practice, and we were able to observe their use of the instrument.

The field test in a single practice was prompted by the practice's involvement in a project on community-oriented primary care, which explored patients' perspectives on present and future health needs (McCabe *et al*, 2000). The CANE appeared attractive because its structure requires the user to elicit and document the views of the older person, of those nearest to them, and of the professional. A head-to-head comparison of the practice's own 75-and-over checklist and the CANE revealed as much about the deficiencies and gaps of the in-house design as it did about the breadth of the CANE, but the feedback from the practice nurse who used both instruments was revealing. Her first action after learning how to administer and score the CANE, and using it with a small number of her patients, was to re-arrange the order of the domains to place difficult or embarrassing questions like those about alcohol consumption and psychotic symptoms last. This was justified by the need to collect the maximum amount of information about the other domains before the older person could withdraw from the exchange, and to minimise the potential to cause offence and jeopardise a long-term relationship. The second revelation was that very little information was collected that reflected a carer perspective. Sometimes this occurred because the older people lived alone, and friends and neighbours were simply not interviewed, and on other occasions the views of a spouse or relative were not elicited to avoid the emergence of conflicts which the professional suspected (from past knowledge) were a feature of the relationship. These insights about conflictual relationships were not documented, but were discussed by the practice nurse outside the CANE interview, and influenced decision-making. The third experience was that the depth of the CANE was not utilised, so that a completed schedule might consist of some domains partially filled in, but without detail of unmet need, and others left blank, even if they were not potentially embarrassing. The practice nurse, in using the CANE, came to the interview with her prior knowledge of the patient, which prompted her to use the instrument selectively. At the end of the study period, the practice decided to continue with their own 75-and-over checklist, modified to close the gaps identified by using the CANE, but not to continue using the CANE itself.

The second field test, carried out after the results of the first were known, involved introducing the CANE to a multidisciplinary team of three district nurses and three workers from a voluntary organisation concerned with social care for older people (Drennan *et al*, 2003). Their remit was to fashion and implement an integrated assessment and management process for individuals deemed 'vulnerable' by their general practitioner, and they were taught how to use the CANE as part of this process. After a lengthy debate within the team about the benefits and disadvantages of structured assessments (the nurses' preference) compared with patient-led dialogues about need (the perspective from the voluntary organisation), the CANE's domain order was changed, for similar reasons to those expressed in the practice field test. Enquiry about the team's use of the CANE revealed a tendency to complete it after the interview with the older person rather than during it, changing its role from a decision-support tool prompting comprehensive needs assessment to a form of documentation of needs and problems. Analysis of data obtained using the CANE is only now beginning, but an immediately obvious finding is that the team was able to raise very significant sums in benefits for many older people, while recording little or no unmet financial needs using the CANE.

The CANE in primary care: future directions

We conclude that the CANE as it stands appears to be feasible to use as a research tool in primary care settings, and valuable as an instrument for identifying unmet need. However, it has not been specifically validated in these settings, and while it is unlikely to perform differently to out-patient and day hospital old age psychiatry settings (where the original validation studies were undertaken), it should ideally be further validated in primary care and with community-dwelling populations.

The experience of its use in clinical settings in the community has been more mixed, which makes us think that modification of the CANE might be needed to make it suitable for routine primary care use. A shorter, more focused primary care-orientated version of the CANE might be useful when assessment time is often severely restricted, as it can be in general practice, and in practice and district nursing. Such a change is potentially problematic, for a reduction in scale to fit in with the limited contact time between professionals and older people risks loss of both the unique triangulation of perspectives that makes the CANE so attractive as an instrument, and the depth that leads to recognition of hidden or unmet needs. Since some domains of need are less well recognised than others a shorter instrument would need to focus on them, at the expense of being comprehensive, without losing the other important characteristics of the instrument. To this end, a brief instrument is being developed and field-tested in a study funded by the NHS executive, and if it proves useful is likely to be available from 2005.

3 The Spanish CANE: validation study and utility in epidemiological surveys

Raimundo Mateos, Matías Ybarzábal, María Jesús García, María Teresa Amboage and Isabel Fraguela

Summary

The evaluation of patients' needs comprises an important new field in planning for services and care. Older people have special characteristics that necessitate the use of specialised instruments. Within the framework of a project of epidemiological research, and given the lack of such instruments for measuring the needs of older people, the utility, validity and reliability of the Camberwell Assessment of Needs for the Elderly (CANE) were assessed. Through a process of translation and adaptation of the original English version, a Spanish version of the CANE was used in interviewing a group of 70 psychogeriatric patients and their carers (family members). The interviews were conducted by teams of two researchers, who then repeated the interviews after a period of between 7 and 15 days, in order to study interrater and test–retest reliability of the questionnaire. In addition, the Spanish version of the CANE was completed by 365 elderly persons and 66 carers during the field work of the Community Epidemiological Survey of Psychogeriatric Needs of the Catchment Area of Santiago de Compostela. In both samples, to evaluate the concurrent validity, the CANE was correlated with other instruments that measured level of dependency and carer burden. The questionnaire demonstrated excellent face validity, was easy to apply, had good concurrent validity and high test–retest and interrater reliability ($\kappa=0.65–1$ and $0.60–1$, respectively). In the clinical sample, the mean duration of the interviews was 25 minutes for participants and carers; in the epidemiological sample, it was 20 and 16 minutes, respectively. Both populations sampled and presented here suggest that the Spanish version of the CANE is a valid and reliable instrument. The CANE proved to be a useful tool when evaluating the needs of older people across both clinical and research settings. The CANE showed particular strengths in its ability to be translated easily into another language and across cultural boundaries.

Introduction

The evolution of the concept of need from medical diagnosis to a new paradigm of clinical evaluation (Brewin *et al*, 1987; Wing, 1990; Stevens & Gabbay, 1991; Thornicroft, *et al*, 1992; Pampalon *et al*, 1996) has been discussed in detail in other sections of this book. Epidemiological research has demonstrated in the past few decades, something that general practitioners have known for some time – that diagnosis and treatment needs are not interchangeable concepts (Copper, 1997; Regier *et al*, 1998; Andrews & Handerson, 1999). Also, with illnesses that are profoundly incapacitating, which is frequently the case among users of psychogeriatric services, the figure of the carer has become increasingly important as a fundamental element in defining a patient's needs (Herrman *et al*, 1994;

Light *et al*, 1994; Nolan *et al*, 1994; Philp *et al*, 1995). Given this knowledge base, it is surprising that there has been a clear lack of standardised instruments that can evaluate the needs of older people with mental disorders (Hamid *et al*, 1995).

For this reason, and taking a step in the same direction as previous epidemiological surveys carried out in the same community (Mateos & Rodríguez, 1989; Mateos *et al*, 2000), we decided to include a measure of the needs of people with psychiatric disorders and those of their informal/ principal carers. To accomplish this we considered the selection of an instrument which had the following characteristics:

(a)   standardised measurement of a comprehensive range of needs in older people;
(b)   adequate validity and reliability;
(c)   ease of learning and administering (intelligible, length of about 30 minutes);
(d)   applicability for research as well as for daily clinical use.

The CANE seemed to possess those characteristics, judging from the information made available to us by its authors and collaborators during the development and validation process (Reynolds *et al*, 2000). The CANE also had the advantage of including three separate points of view (Sartorius, 1999): that of the patient, that of the informal carer and that of the professional carer. In addition, the instrument was based on a forerunner of recognised validity, the Camberwell Assessment of Need (CAN) (Phelan *et al*, 1995), which had been designed for adult psychiatric patients and was already validated in Spain (Jiménez *et al*, 1995). This chapter summarises the validation study of the Spanish version of the CANE (Ybarzábal *et al*, 2002) and contributes new data about its functioning within the framework of an epidemiological field survey.

Method

For the creation of the Spanish version, an initial translation of the CANE was written and submitted to various professionals (psychiatrists, psychologists and social workers), who evaluated the accuracy of the original version and made slight modifications, maximising its understanding for people of low educational levels. Next, it was submitted to a discussion group made up of patients' family members, who reported that the translation was understandable and contained an adequate range of questions. None of the groups (neither professionals nor carers) mentioned other relevant items that should have been included, despite the specific request made in that regard. This final version underwent a back-translation by professional translators who had no knowledge of the original instrument and that result was reviewed by English psychiatrists (including the authors of the CANE), who considered it completely adequate. In addition, two of the authors (R.M. & M.G.) developed a Galician language version, which was very convenient when administered in our area given the high percentage of the population, particularly among older people, that use Galician as their native language.

Samples

For the validation study, 70 patients and their corresponding carers (where available) were interviewed. Some of them were under the care of the Psychogeriatric Unit of the Santiago de Compostela Catchment Area (Mateos *et al*, 1994) (the majority lived in their homes, and some lived in local senior citizens' residences); the remainder were patients who attended the Day Center of the Red Cross of A Coruña. Psychogeriatric patients who were currently in psychiatric hospitals were not included in the sample. In addition to the CANE, the Blessed Dementia Scale (Blessed *et al*, 1968) and the Spanish version of the Goldberg Depression and Anxiety Scales (GDAS) (Goldberg *et al*, 1988; Lobo *et al*, 1994) were completed in order to measure cognitive function/dependence and caregiver burden, respectively.

The second sample was collected during the Community Epidemiological Survey of the Psychogeriatric Needs of the Santiago de Compostela Catchment Area. The main objective of this survey was to measure the relationship between psychiatric morbidity and the needs of older people who lived in their homes as well as the needs of their informal carers. It was designed in two phases, and in the first a dependency and psychiatric morbidity screening was carried out with a sample of the Catchment Area of Santiago de Compostela (454 021 inhabitants, 71 402 of whom were older than 65). In the second phase, the subjects defined as possible 'cases' and a sample of the 'non-cases' were interviewed in their homes using a wider protocol, which assessed:

information from older persons:

- self-reported illnesses, self-perception of health, requests for assistance and use of medication
- functional capacity for basic and instrumental daily-life activities using the Katz Index (Dowd & Davidhizar, 1999), the Barthel Index (Wade & Collin, 1988) the IADL scale of Lawton & Brody (1969)
- level of depression and cognitive impairment using the Geriatric Depression Scale (Montorio & Izal, 1996) and the Mini-Mental State (Folstein et al, 1975)
- individual met and unmet needs using the Spanish version of the CANE;

information from informal carers:

- level of social support
- opinion about the possible cognitive decline of older people using the Informant Questionnaire on Cognitive Decline in older people (Jorm & Jacomb, 1989)
- difficulties and coping strategies using the Carers' Assessment of Difficulty Index (CADI; Nolan & Grant, 1992) and Carers' Assessment of Managing Index (CAMI; Nolan et al, 1995)
- level of distress using the GHQ–28 (Lobo et al, 1986)
- views of the participant's met and unmet needs using the Spanish version of the CANE.

In total, the CANE was completed by more than 365 elderly persons (the excess corresponds to some participants who were not included in the epidemiological survey) and 66 carers (62 were relatives and 4 were professionals). The similarity between the socio-demographic characteristics of this sample (Table 3.1), representation of the community (stratified by gender, age and environment), and the characteristics of the clinical sample, composed of incidental cases, is very interesting and confers greater external validity on the validation study of the CANE.

The interviewers had a wide range of experience in sociological and epidemiological research. Among the strategies intended to assure the reliability of the survey, we will mention two. Throughout the interviews, the interviewers assessed the apparent sincerity of the interviewees using a five-point Likert scale which produced an average score of 4.8 (s.d.=0.6) in the first phase and 4.7 (s.d.=0.9) in the second, both scores being close to maximum sincerity (5 points). To reduce possible inconsistencies between the answers obtained from participants and carers in the second phase, interviewers were asked to provide their ratings of the needs of the interviewees, scoring the third column of the CANE along with their own 'comments'.

The statistical analyses were carried out using statistical program SSPS, versions 8.0 and 10.0 for Windows.

Results

Table 3.1 summarises the socio-demographic and clinical characteristics of both the validation and the community samples. The range of diagnoses included a wide range of psychiatric illnesses: dementia, dysthymia (the two largest groups), major depression, delusional disorder, residual schizophrenic disorder and anxiety disorder, among others.

Table 3.1 Socio-demographic and clinical characteristics of the validation sample and community sample

	Validation sample		Community sample	
	Patients (*n* = 70)	Carers (*n* = 50)	Older persons (*n* = 365)	Carers (*n* = 62)[4]
Age, years				
Mean (s.d.)	76.3 (7.9)	54.6 (16.6)	76.2 (6.7)	52.0 (12.7)
Range	65–94	36–82	67–99	23–81
No carer (%)	29		82	
Gender (%)				
Male	37	20	31	6
Female	63	80	69	94
Marital status				
Single	5	15	14	11
Married	53	74	42	81
Widowed	42	11	43	6
Separated/divorced	0	0	1	2
Relationship of the carer (%)				
Spouse		30		
Daughter		63		
Daughter-in-law		7		
Wife				10
Son/daughter				52
Daughter-in-law				19
Niece				10
Granddaughter				5
Sister				3
Other				2
Diagnosis (%)				
Dementia	23			
Depression	37			
Psychosis[1]	16			
Other[2]	20			
No diagnosis[3]	4			
Domicile (%)				
Home	79			
Nursing home	21			
Status at interview (%)				
Out-patients	93			
Day hospital	7			
Geographical area (%)				
Urban	na	na	16	16
Rural	na	na	84	84

1. Psychosis includes diagnoses of schizophrenia and delusional disorder.

2. Other includes adjustment disorder, hypocondriasis, somatisation, conversion, phobia personality and alcohol misuse.

3. Absence of diagnosis includes two patients with normal bereavement and one person who was referred to the psychogeriatric unit and for whom psychiatric pathology was ruled out.

4. The four professional carers are not included.

Validity

Face validity

Beyond the obvious social and cultural differences between two countries of the EU, it seems appropriate to emphasise here similarities between the basic principles upon which the systems of social service and health assistance of Spain and England are based, such as the citizen's right to free and universal health care and social services, or the common aspiration towards interdisciplinary work. That constitutes an *a priori* incentive for any attempt at interchanging instruments meant to measure needs generally related to those health care and social services. The Spanish version of the CANE, which stems from the conceptual and operative development of the English version, described in detail in other sections of this book, was submitted for review by professionals and patients' carers, who considered its content easily understandable and relevant.

Ecological validity

The interviewers who participated in the validation as well as those of the community survey pointed out that the CANE was easy to learn and to administer. In the clinical sample, the average time required was 25 minutes per person interviewed, with little difference between subjects and carers. In the community sample, the average length for subjects and carers was 20 minutes (s.d.=10) and 16 minutes (s.d.=5), respectively.

Evidence for the feasibility of the questions is the small number of missing ratings from the epidemiological survey, despite being a semi-structured assessment that is more prone to this type of limitation. Of the 66 carers, only two left two items unanswered and another two carers each left one item unanswered. Five of the six omissions were from items of the CANE that related to the carers themselves. Of all participants (n=365), eight (2.2 %) did not answer any of the items; five of these people had dementia, one person was affected by aphasia following a cerebrovascular accident, another was seriously physically ill and the last was a person with Down's syndrome. All eight of these participants had carers who completed the interview. The average total scoring of the CANE (the sum of the first items of each section) was similar whether assessed by the subject or by the interviewer: 4.1 (s.d.=3.7) and 4.7 (s.d.=4.5), respectively. The subgroup of patients who had a carer obtained higher ratings; the averages of the scoring given by the subject, carer and interviewer for participants in this subgroup were: 9.5 (s.d.=4.4), 11.5 (s.d.=5.2) and 11.4 (s.d.=5.1), respectively.

Content validity

All persons interviewed using the CANE reported that the instrument covered the principal needs usually found in elderly people of this area. Neither in the validation study nor in the survey were needs detected that could not fit into the classification scheme of the CANE. It was noted, however, that the comments of the interviewers concerning the items that received positive scores were particularly informative.

Construct validity

Replicating the validation process of the English version, a correlation matrix was included to assess whether a positive or negative correlation existed between items about which it was expected that such a correlation would exist (convergent validity) and whether or not there was a lack of correlation between measurements about which, according to the theoretical construct, such a relationship would not be expected (divergent validity). As an example of divergent validity, one might cite the lack of correlation between items such as carers' or patients' need for information and all other items.

There was a high correlation between the scores given by the carers for the items related to 'memory' and 'self-care' ($r=0.63$; $P<0.001$), 'company' and 'daytime activities' ($r=0.75$; $P<0.001$), and 'self-care' and 'looking after the home' ($r=0.85$; $P<0.001$). The correlations are considerably lower for the answers of the patients (0.40, 0.53 and 0.60, respectively), owing to the greater level of variation in ratings obtained from patients with cognitive decline and sometimes their lack of insight into their memory or functional problems. All in all, the correlation coefficients reasonably support the construct validity of the CANE.

In the epidemiological sample, the correlation between the three pairs of items mentioned above continued to be positive but to a lesser degree, as might be expected in a predominantly healthy and more heterogeneous population. Those correlations, for the assessments given by the subject, the interviewer and the carer, respectively, were as follows; between 'memory' and 'self-care': $r=0.20$ ($P<0.001$), $r=0.33$ ($P<0.001$) and $r=0.24$ ($P<0.001$); between 'company' and 'daytime activities': $r=0.34$ ($P<0.001$), $r=0.50$ ($P<0.001$) and $r=0.57$ ($P<0.01$); and between 'self-care' and 'looking after the home': $r=0.56$ ($P<0.001$), $r=0.61$ ($P<0.001$) and $r=0.40$ ($P<0.001$). In this sample it was nevertheless possible to find the expected statistically significant correlation between other pairs of items, particularly those related to needs for memory for example and referred to in the same order, between 'memory' and 'money': $r=0.25$ ($P<0.001$), $r=0.46$ ($P<0.001$) and $r=0.50$ ($P<0.001$); between 'memory' and 'inadvertent self-harm': $r=0.28$ ($P<0.001$), $r=0.35$ ($P<0.001$), $r=0.22$ ($P<0.07$); between 'memory' and 'carer's psychological distress': $r=0.34$ ($P<0.05$), $r=0.24$ ($P<0.07$), $r=0.38$ ($P<0.001$); between 'memory' and 'looking after the home': $r=0.29$ ($P<0.001$), $r=0.35$ ($P<0.001$), $r=0.07$ (NS).

Criterion validity

Given that a 'gold standard' for assessing the needs of older people does not currently exist, Blessed's Dementia Scale was chosen to be completed with the CANE because it assesses three similar aspects: (a) changes in performance of everyday activities linked to cognitive function, (b) changes in self-care habits and (c) changes in personality, interests and drive. The equivalent items showed a correlation in the carers of greater than 0.96 (which is not strange since some are formulated in almost exactly the same way). Even though the two scales measure things which are too complex to even cautiously consider the convenience of comparing the total sum of the scorings, the correlation between the total scores is also excellent ($r=0.81$; $P<0.001$).

The GDAS, which contains two sub-scales with adequate specificity and sensitivity to detect symptoms of anxiety and depression in the general population, was used to assess the degree of psychological distress or burden of the carer. This scale also achieved a strong correlation with the CANE item carer's psychological distress ($r=0.76$; $P<0.001$). In the community sample, a certain correlation could also be expected between the degree of dependence (Barthel Index) and total score on the CANE. The correlations for the assessments of the subject, interviewer and carer were all very high: –0.7, –0.8 and –0.8, and were all statistically significant ($P<0.001$).

Reliability

The interviews were carried out by two teams of two persons each, interviewer and observer who alternated roles in order to avoid any systematic bias; both persons rated answers separately to allow for assessment of interrater reliability. The subjects were re-interviewed within 7 to 15 days in order to carry out the assessment of test–retest reliability. The results (Table 3.2) show good agreement, with κ between 0.60 and 1 for interrater reliability, and between 0.65 and 1 for test–retest reliability.

Discussion

The shortage of standardised needs assessment instruments for use with older people, and the total lack of such instruments in Spain, makes it difficult to allow comparisons of the CANE with other instruments used to assess the needs of elderly people with psychiatric disorders. Our study focused on making the first step towards further research and development of the CANE and other assessments in the future. These results support the notion that the Spanish version of the CANE is an easily learned and administered scale which provides insight into the needs perceived by the patient, the carer and the professional responsible for care of the person. The CANE also has good psychometric qualities with very satisfactory validity and reliability.

We must nevertheless point out possible limitations of the instrument. Its application can present some difficulties for certain groups of patients, such as those who show signs of significant cognitive decline, and for whom lower concurrent validity of their answers, and in particular a low correlation with the assessment made by their carers, was observed. It is certain, however, that the opportunity that the CANE offers for the carers to express their own points of view about the patient compensates for that limitation, and the problem becomes rather one of making an overall assessment of needs by

Table 3.2 Interrater and test–retest reliability of CANE: κ scores for the validation study

CANE item	Patients		Carers	
	Interrater	Test–retest	Interrater	Test–retest
1 Accomodation	1	1	0.95	0.80
2 Looking after the home	0.60	0.81	0.64	0.94
3 Food	0.63	0.90	0.72	0.87
4 Self-care	0.79	–	0.84	1
5 Caring for someone else	–	1	–	1
6 Daytime activities	0.66	0.75	0.78	0.80
7 Memory	0.72	0.88	0.76	1
8 Eyesight/hearing/communication	0.69	0.78	0.68	0.92
9 Mobility/falls	0.83	0.89	0.61	0.93
10 Continence	0.73	0.65	0.77	0.93
11 Physical health	0.71	0.86	0.67	0.7
12 Drugs	–	–	0.7	0.78
13 Psychotic symptoms	0.78	0.69	0.72	0.78
14 Psychological distress	–	0.89	–	0.70
15 Information	–	0.93	1	1
16 Deliberate self-harm	1	0.65	1	
17 Inadvertent self-harm	–	0.65	0.72	0.86
18 Abuse/neglect	1	0.79	1	
19 Behaviour	1	1	–	–
20 Alcohol	1	1	1	
21 Company	0.61	0.78	0.65	0.93
22 Intimate relationships	–	1	–	0.78
23 Money/budgeting	0.66	0.86	0.74	0.65
24 Benefits	–	1	–	–
A Carer's information	0.93	1	–	0.66
B Carer's psychological distress	–	0.88	0.75	0.85

gathering information from all informants. Where some cognitive decline is present, the patient's ratings will probably be less reliable, especially in the framework of epidemiological surveys. In addition, carers and patients do not always share the same perspective. The relevance of this aspect deserves a more detailed analysis in our survey, and in future uses of the CANE in epidemiological field surveys. In addition, the clinical interviewers reported that the instrument would be even more objective if a manual providing a more detailed list of situations that exemplify the scoring categories of the individual items was available, based on experience in its use within different participant groups and social contexts.

Acknowledgements

The team that created the original version of the CANE, in particular to Tom Reynolds, Martin Orrell and Graham Thornicroft, for their confidence and efforts in supervising the back-translation.

Matías Ybarzábal's experience in the utilization of the CANE took place at the Institute of Psychiatry (London), where he was greatly aided by Brian Cooper, who also collaborated in the revision of the back-translation of the CANE.

The Galician Association of Families of Alzheimer Victims (AFAGA) for their enthusiasm during the group discussions and the completion of questionnaires.

This study forms a part of an epidemiological research project funded by the Direccíon Xeral de Universidades/Xunta de Galicia: grant XUGA 20802A97. During the first part of the project M. Ybarzábal received a pre-graduate grant from the University of Santiago de Compostela.

A preliminary communication on this study received an award as best poster at the IX Reunion of the Spanish Gerontopsychiatric and Psychogeriatric Society (SEGP), 9–10 October 1999, Pamplona. This poster was also presented at the following international congresses: VII Congress of the International Federation of Psychiatric Epidemiology, 6–9 March 1999, Taipei, Taiwan; Symposium of the World Psychiatric Association, Section of Epidemiology and Public Health, 1–4 August 1999, Turku, Finland; IX Congress of the International Psychogeriatric Association (IPA), 15–20 August 1999, Vancouver, Canada. An expanded version of this study, coinciding partly with the content of this paper, was presented at the III Congreso Virtual de Psiquiatría, 1–28 February 2002 (website *http:// www.interpsiquis.com*) and later published in the *Revista de Psicogeriatría*, 2002, **2**, 38–44.

Obtaining the Spanish CANE

The Spanish and Galician version of the CANE can be obtained from Professor R. Mateos, Departamento de Psiquiatría, Faculted de Medicina, Universidad de Santiago de Compostela, E-15782, Spain. E-mail: mrmateos@usc.es

4 Relevance and applicability of the CANE in the German health care system

Heike Dech and Wielant Machleidt

The German health care system and needs of elderly people

Initially, we wish to discuss features of the German health care system to emphasise the relevance of assessment instruments for organising health and support services for elderly people. In contrast to tax-based national health state systems (United Kingdom, Sweden, Norway, Spain) or private health care systems (USA), the German health care system is social insurance-based (compulsory), which up to now provides compensation for individual medical and nursing services (Wild & Gibis, 2003). In this 'Bismarck' model health care system, private practice physicians, church- or municipality-affiliated hospitals, university hospitals financed by the federal state, and non-profit and for-profit insurers are incorporated. With the health care system focused primarily on in-patients and the acutely ill, there is currently still a large gap between in-patient and out-patient services (Hirsch *et al*, 1999; Hurrelmann, 1999).

It has become evident that patients' requirements of this health care system are changing. One of the core reasons for such changes is the rapid shift in the population structure, mainly as a result of the drop in the birth rate and the rise in average life expectancy. This means that an increasing number of people grow progressively older, and simultaneously the number of gainfully occupied people decreases in comparison to the percentage of pensioners (Deutscher Bundestag, 2002). Obviously, an ageing population has effects on the system of social security, especially on the health care insurance systems and on the pension funds. However, it is especially the health care system which is threatened by the demographic change, faced with new and different tasks and challenged with the need to develop new diagnostic and therapeutic options (BMFSFJ, 2001).

As older people require more frequent, more varied and longer-term medical treatment than younger people, the demand on medical services is growing. In addition, the health problems, and thus the spectrum of diseases, have been changing. In the statistics of morbidity and mortality, a shift towards chronic and degenerative diseases, as well as towards multi-morbidity and the growing incidence of cognitive impairment and dementia, can be observed (Jorm *et al*, 1987; Cooper & Bickel, 1989; Hurrelmann, 1999).

With regard to the multi-morbidity typical of old age, different sorts and 'phases' of illness and impairments appear side by side in different grades of intensity; besides this, a certain level of self-sufficiency generally remains or can be extended (Van den Akker *et al*, 1998). Not infrequently, physical problems are comorbid with psychiatric problems such as depressive disorders and/or dementia in the context of social and functional problems (e.g., isolation, malnutrition, loss of independence, inability to take care of oneself). From this simultaneous presence of multiple health disturbances in different degrees and stages derives the necessity of an equal emphasis on measures in all areas: health promotion, disease prevention, curative medicine, rehabilitation and nursing. In a future patient-centred service landscape, these areas should not be taken into account separately, but as elements of comprehensive health planning (Nikolaus & Specht-Leible, 1992; Nikolaus *et al*, 1999).

The changes in demography and in the spectrum of health needs will have far-reaching consequences for the health care system, the service structure of which should become more focused on concepts for the longer-term care of multi-morbidity patients. Among the characteristics of geriatric illnesses are their longer-term presence, their different forms of functional impairments and the difficulty of differentiating between them when they often cause and sustain each other. This results in not only a massive financial burden, but also the necessity to offer different forms of social support (Light *et al*, 1994; Cooper, 1997). Urgent new requirements of the system of medical care are emerging, concerning both the scope and profile of health and social services for older people (e.g. drug treatment, disease management, nursing, hospital bed capacities), as well as the financial consequences. Elderly people carry a higher risk of morbidity and, owing to the progressively higher number of widowed persons among them and the fact that their partners are often not in a position to cope with their care, an increased risk of requiring external support (Huckle, 1994; Dech, 2001).

The questions the health care system is currently faced with are not only of a medical nature, but concern the quality of life and the independence of elderly people. In order to take these matters into account, a profound structural change in the German health system has been in progress for the past few years, not least because of cost-cutting efforts resulting in reduced numbers of in-patient beds in favour of more out-patient services (Hirsch *et al*, 1999). This necessitates more complex and simultaneously more flexible medical services in the out-patient sector, a better interconnection of the different service components and smoother transitions from in-patient to day clinics or out-patient care (Dech, 2001). Until recently, as a result of the compensation system for single medical services, the German health care system in particular showed a lack of integrated treatment programmes or support services in the out-patient sector. The introduction of a *Pflegeversicherung* (compulsory care insurance) in Germany and the consecutive rise of out-patient care service companies and nursing services are a first result of these changes.

What emerges in the course of developing these more differentiated treatment and care facilities is that the individual services are still insufficiently adjusted to patients' needs, and frequently a lack of systematic service allocation can be observed. However, while these services are emerging, they may still lack fine-tuning regarding patients' needs, and quite often do not have a systematic approach towards planning of aid and services. At the time information was gathered for this paper, networks of out-patient treatment and care facilities were often still not cooperating systematically and coverage of an entire catchment area could not be guaranteed in all cases. Community service structures also still occasionally reflected the local interests and traditions of organisations in charge of services rather than the real needs of older people people and their relatives (BMFSFJ, 2001).

In order to meet the needs of elderly patients, who often simultaneously suffer from psychiatric disorders, physical disorders, functional impairments and social problems, systematic assessment of needs with a standardised instrument will have to be introduced to the German health services (Nikolaus, 2001; Wild & Gibis, 2003). Within this instrument, it should be possible to include functional aspects in the treatment of elderly patients, as maintaining one's independence is a major goal in the planning of care. Examination and assessment of patients by means of recording single, isolated medical aspects is an insufficient method for elderly persons. However, a standardised recording of disorders and impairments, which usually consists of a wide range of conventional scales in a 'test battery', is complicated and time-consuming. What is required is an instrument reflecting the treatment and care needs of elderly patients with psychiatric disturbances. Therefore, multidimensional geriatric assessment is a diagnostic process for systematic recording of the medical, functional, and psychosocial problems, and resources of older patients as a basis for setting up a comprehensive plan for treatment and care (Stuck, 1997). Such multidimensional psychogeriatric assessment should make it possible to draw up an initial statement for the coordinated planning of care, to set goals for treatment and rehabilitation, and to describe the course and progress; it should also contribute to more precise planning of adequate treatment and support measures. Multidimensional psychogeriatric assessment therefore records not only biomedical or psychological data, but also social and functional information as well as existing resources. This is because especially in treating elderly patients, the somatic, psychological and social factors cannot be regarded separately, and as a whole they are decisive for continuing independence, determining the need for care, and achieving maximum quality of life. Moreover, an early assessment can contribute to the prevention of further disability.

Such health planning could be made possible by the introduction of a general assessment scale for older people. The CANE is conceptualised as a general, broadly based assessment scale for elderly patients with psychiatric problems and is explicitly not restricted to single disease entities such as dementia (Reynolds *et al*, 2000). Thus, systematic application of the CANE (Reynolds *et al*, 2000) at the points of intersection between services appears feasible. This scale is also of high interest in regard to the Europe-wide harmonisation of health care systems, and potential European cooperation in the development of service models.

Translation of the scale, piloting and consensus workshops

German version

Similar to the multi-stage preparations for the development of CANE in Britain (Reynolds *et al*, 2000), a multi-stage process was conceptualised for generating and discussing a German version of the CANE. First, the CANE was translated in accordance with generally used international procedures for the translation of psychometric scales (cf. Dech *et al*, 2003). As the assessment scale was for multidisciplinary use in the geriatric sector, the translation was done health professionals from all relevant backgrounds. The translators concerned were members of professional groups considered to be the ones using the scale later on: psychiatrists, general practitioners, psychologists, social workers, and nurses. The average professional experience in that group was 4.2 years (range 1.5–13 years). The group decided not to include non-professionals in the translation procedure and the consensus workshops, as professional knowledge was considered to be required for work with the scale. However, a professional translator with experience of translation in the social sciences field was included in the second round of the translation. The following steps were observed during the multi-stage translation procedure: 1. Iterative back-translation, 2. contextual translation, 3. pilot version.

1. For *iterative back-translation*, the assessment scale was distributed to the whole group of translators, and then translated individually. Three of the six translations thus produced were translated back into English by different group members and then, in a third step, back again into German.

2. In the next round (*contextual translation*), in which the professional translator also participated, the task was to compare the translations with each other and to achieve a jointly translated version. In doing so, special attention was paid to the language use in the German health care context and to the general understandability of the language and format of the scale. Considering the background that the scale was to be applied by multiple professions, special care was taken that wording was common to all the different professional groups. Also, the format of the scale was adapted along these lines.

3. The translation was then followed by a *pilot study*, in which the German version of the CANE was tested by members of the translation group on five inhabitants of nursing homes and five elderly people living independently. What emerged in the following discussion was that no further changes were needed. In common with early applications in Britain, raters from different professional groups reported that the German version was easy to apply.

Consensus workshops

In the following stage, a first workshop was arranged, in which an enlarged circle of different professionals from the out-patient and in-patient sector took part. The main topic was the discussion on how the assessment scale could be used in clinical work with elderly patients. The following questions were discussed: Is the scale principally relevant and helpful in practical work? Do the items appear to be plausible? Is it applicable in the context of the German health care system? In this first workshop, the aspects considered to be relevant for use of the scale within the framework of the German health care system were: the functional perspective of the scale, the generalistic, multidimensional format designed for persons with psychiatric morbidity, the conceptualisation as an assessment scale of use to multiple professions, and the integration of the relatives' perspective. There also was agreement about the plausibility of the items of the scale and that the principal needs of elderly persons were covered in the CANE. It was emphasised that the functional perspective on the impairments of elderly people was still a relatively new concept or way of thinking in German health care. As the planning of supporting services depends more upon the functional status of a person and less directly on the diagnosis, the CANE was considered a helpful tool for health planning purposes. Since mostly a mixture of formal and informal support services was being used, the inclusion of the relatives' perspective was considered an important aspect.

A second workshop was organised to explore concrete possibilities for applying the CANE and the main topic was the discussion on where the assessment scale could be used. With the de-institutionalisation of care and support for old people, towards more differentiated out-patient services, the task of integrated treatment and care planning will become more and more important. It makes sense to use a single systematic and standardised tool to assess patients moving between in-patient and out-patient services and also to provide information for all the separate services operating in the out-patient sector.

The scale could be used as part of the *Integrierte Behandlungsplanung* (integrated treatment planning programme) or in *Geriatrische Rehabilitation* (geriatric rehabilitation), i.e. case management and coordination of different services for a patient. With the changes in the health care system, the question of quality management is gaining in importance, and treatment and support standards should be planned and supervised with appropriate control mechanisms. Assessment by means of the CANE was seen to have an important role in this process.

First results of a study with the CANE

In the following, we report first results from a study in two nursing homes in Germany using the CANE. A further study in the out-patient sector is forthcoming. The sample consisted of elderly inhabitants of two large nursing homes (96 and 200 inhabitants), situated on the outskirts of a university town (90 000 inhabitants) in the Frankfurt area. Both nursing homes belonged to long-established, church-affiliated German charity organisations. Nursing home 1 was built 1984 and had 96 inhabitants, who lived in 32 one-bed apartments and 32 two-bed apartments. All apartments have their own bathroom. On each floor there is also a community room. A daily programme of different activities (memory training, exercises, singing, etc.) was offered. Catholic and Lutheran services were regularly held in the nursing home's chapel. The nursing home is located in a middle-class suburban area. Nursing home 2 was built in 1972 and completely renovated in 1995. It cared for 200 inhabitants, who lived in 154 one-bed apartments and 23 two-bed apartments. All apartments have their own bathroom. There are several community facilities and daily group activities such as memory training, a handicrafts group, a reading circle, exercises, singing, etc. Services were also regularly held in the nursing home's chapel. The nursing home is located in a suburban, upper middle-class area.

In addition to the German version of the CANE, the following standardised scales were applied. For screening of cognitive impairments and of dementia, the Mini-Mental State Examination (MMSE) (Folstein *et al*, 1975) was used. For evaluation of activities of daily life and capabilities in the area of self-care and mobility, the Barthel Index (Mahoney & Barthel, 1965; Wade & Collin, 1988) was applied. For rating of severity of cognitive and functional impairment the Global Deterioration Scale (GDS) (Reisberg *et al*, 1982; Ihl & Frölich, 1991) was used. As a measurement instrument for health-related quality of life, the SF–36 (Bullinger & Kirchberger, 1998; Ware *et al*, 1998) was used. Additionally, a set of questions regarding patients' psychosocial situation and their care needs was asked.

Except for eight persons, of 102 approached in both nursing homes, all interviewees and/or their legal representatives agreed to participate in the study. In all, 94 inhabitants were assessed, of whom 48 lived in nursing home 1 and 46 in nursing home 2. In the total sample, the average age was 85.6 years (range 65–102 years), with no difference in the age distribution between the two nursing homes. Most people were female (86.2%), only 13.8% were male: approximately the usual gender distribution in nursing homes. Most of the assessed home inhabitants were widowed (74.3%), only 10.8% were married, 10.6% were single and 4.3% were divorced. The average duration of residence in the nursing home was 33.5 months (*s.d.* = 36.5 months: range 1–153 months). As shown in Table 4.1, all needs for accommodation, food, household work (skills), self-care and physical health were met. In contrast, psychosocial needs such as daytime activities or company, which were common, were often unmet. Psychiatric symptoms and psychological distress, which occurred in around two out of three inhabitants, were frequently identified as not met.

Table 4.1 Levels of needs of 94 individuals as rated by staff

CANE item	No need		Met need		Unmet need		Not known	
	n	(%)	*n*	(%)	*n*	(%)	*n*	(%)
Accommodation	0	(0)	94	(100)	0	(0)	0	(0)
Household skills	0	(0)	93	(99)	1	(1)	0	(0)
Food	0	(0)	91	(97)	3	(3)	0	(0)
Self-care	0	(0)	94	(100)	0	(0)	0	(0)
Caring for someone else	0	(0)	94	(100)	0	(0)	0	(0)
Daytime activities	1	(1)	56	(60)	37	(39)	0	(0)
Memory	19	(20)	71	(76)	4	(4)	0	(0)
Eyesight/hearing/communication	36	(38)	52	(55)	6	(6)	0	(0)
Mobility/falls	16	(17)	70	(74)	8	(9)	0	(0)
Continence	15	(16)	77	(82)	2	(2)	0	(0)
Physical health	3	(3)	86	(92)	5	(5)	0	(0)
Drugs	1	(1)	78	(83)	15	(16)	0	(0)
Psychotic symptoms	35	(37)	40	(42)	19	(20)	0	(0)
Psychological distress	22	(23)	52	(55)	10	(11)	10	(11)
Information	61	(65)	33	(35)	0	(0)	0	(0)
Deliberate self-harm	92	(99)	2	(2)	0	(0)	0	(0)
Inadvertent self-harm	51	(54)	40	(43)	3	(3)	0	(0)
Abuse/neglect	93	(99)	0	(0)	0	(0)	1	(1)
Behaviour	50	(53)	36	(38)	8	(9)	0	(0)
Alcohol	92	(98)	2	(2)	0	(0)	0	(0)
Company	1	(1)	69	(73)	23	(25)	1	(1)
Intimate relationships	31	(33)	47	(50)	16	(17)	0	(0)
Money/budgeting	2	(2)	92	(98)	0	(0)	0	(0)
Benefits	65	(69)	28	(30)	0	(0)	1	(1)
Carer's need for information	83	(88)	7	(7)	1	(1)	3	(3)
Carer's psychological distress	60	(64)	24	(26)	1	(1)	0	(0)

In the application of the CANE as well as in the workshops, some small methodological and practical questions occurred. Some raters felt that it would be better if 'needs' were registered in the first question instead of 'no needs'. Also, as the items took a more general perspective of the functions needed in daily life, a section should be added for registering more detailed information about the individual patient. An important feature of the CANE is the inclusion of the carers' and the patients' views. A methodological problem may be inherent in the validity of the patients' ratings, as patients with dementia tend to overestimate their capabilities and underestimate their needs. It was suggested that it would be useful to have a manual with details and examples on how to make decisions in some rating situations. This would become more important as the CANE becomes more widely used, especially as raters may have little training. We therefore compiled a (preliminary) manual in German with examples and criteria for rating.

The results of the CANE assessments were in accordance with the situation in German nursing homes, where the proportion of severely dependent inhabitants has been increasing and nursing activities have been primarily focused on physical health, while psychosocial needs very often cannot be given the appropriate time and attention (Weyerer *et al*, 1995; Richter *et al*, 2000).

Standardised assessment and evaluation of health needs becomes more and more important with the building up of more complex service structures for elderly people (Bach *et al*, 1995; Hamid *et al*, 1995). In contrast to Britain (Wing, 1990; Thornicroft *et al*, 1992), standardised needs assessment in psychiatry is still a rather new concept in Germany. Up to now, there have also been very few assessment instruments for older people in Germany (e.g. RAI; Morris *et al*, 1990; Garms-Homolova *et al*, 1996). Alternative methods have included rather time-consuming test batteries composed of sets of individual psychometric scales for diagnosing functional status and capabilities (*Geriatrisches Basisassessment*; Nikolaus & Specht-Leible, 1992), but these did not give information about resource needs (Nikolaus, 2001). There has been an emerging need for coordination of different community services and case management. In addition, the requirements of the *Integrierte Behandlungsplanung* (integrated treatment planning programme) as well as programmes such as *Geriatrische Rehabilitation* (geriatric rehabilitation) demand comprehensive yet quick assessments. Although only preliminary conclusions can be drawn from this ongoing study, the CANE proved to be a useful assessment tool in a typical German health setting. The scale was easy to administer and registered relevant psychosocial and health needs of elderly people.

Obtaining the German CANE

The German version of CANE can be obtained from the Department of Social Psychiatry, Hanover Medical School, Carl-Neuberg-Str., 30625 Hanover, Germany.

5 The needs of older people living in sheltered housing

Elizabeth Field, Mike Walker and Martin Orrell

Summary

Eighty-seven residents of three sheltered accommodation schemes for people over 60 years old were interviewed about their health, social networks and any needs they might have: environmental, physical, psychological or social. They were asked who, if anyone, met these needs: family, friends, health, social or voluntary services. Overall, 61% of psychological needs identified were unmet, as were 52% of social needs, 33% of physical needs and 19% of environmental needs. Activity limitation, somatic symptoms, dementia and depression were all associated with higher numbers of needs, and particularly unmet needs. Residents with private, restricted support networks had most unmet needs, while those with locally integrated or wider, community-focused networks had the least. Health and social care services need to be aware that individuals who are isolated, or who have physical disabilities or mental health problems, are more likely to have unmet needs.

Introduction

In the UK, more older people live in sheltered housing than in residential/nursing home care. Around 6% of older people live in the 0.54 million sheltered housing units in Britain (Age Concern, 1998). There is a considerable body of research into institutional care, but very little is known about the health, social support and needs of people in sheltered accommodation. Accurate identification of needs is an essential prerequisite to planning and providing services (Kamis-Gould & Minsky, 1995) to meet health, social and housing needs, and so improve well-being and quality of life.

Sheltered housing in Britain comprises groups of about 30 or more self-contained flats or bungalows, although some are bed-sitters. Facilities vary, but generally there is a common room, a laundry, an alarm or communication system for residents to summon help in an emergency and a warden (sometimes resident on site) who makes a daily check on all residents. Wardens also have responsibility for cleaning and maintenance of the property and helping to organise social activities (Williams, 1986). Sheltered housing schemes are usually situated in established neighbourhoods near public amenities and transport links in order to facilitate independent living.

Dependency appears to be lower in sheltered residents compared to people in residential homes or continuing care wards (Harrison et al, 1990). Walker et al (1998) found people living in sheltered housing were more likely to use health and social services resources. Logistic regression analysis suggested that the higher service use could not be entirely accounted for by the greater disability or the higher rate of people living alone. Elderly supported public housing residents in the USA appear to be more at risk of having to move out if they have unmet needs for mental health care (Holshouser, 1988). Untreated psychiatric symptoms were the most frequently cited reasons for residents of public housing for older people being asked to leave or being refused renewal of their lease. This was most likely to happen to those with few family members or friends, and poor social skills (Barker *et al*, 1988).

Older people's support networks have been classified into five types following longitudinal research on ageing (Wenger, 1994). Different network types are distinguished on the availability of local close kin, the level of involvement of family, friends and neighbours and the level of interaction with the community and voluntary groups (Wenger, 1994, 1997). Private restricted networks are associated with greatest risk, locally integrated networks with least risk (Wenger, 1997). A study in a community mental health team for older people found low levels of social support were associated with high levels of need (Wilcox *et al*, 1995). The amount and type of social support provided and whether the needs of a person in sheltered housing are met depends in part on personal factors, for example men and those over 75 were significantly less likely to receive assistance from friends living elsewhere (Kaye & Monk, 1991). Many needs of married people may be invisible as they are met by their spouses' usual activity such as cooking, company and intimacy. The amount and type of social support provided and whether needs are met also depends in part on the type of support network (Wenger & Shahtahmasebi, 1991). The present study was part of a survey of 89 residents of three sheltered accommodation schemes in Harlow (Field *et al*, 2002).

Aims

1.   To identify the met and unmet needs of sheltered housing residents.
2.   To identify demographic, health and social factors associated with unmet needs
3.   To test the following hypotheses: that residents with depression, dementia, and/or activity limitation will have more unmet needs; and that residents with a private restricted network will have more unmet needs than those with other networks.

Method

Selection of the sheltered housing schemes

In order to select schemes that had sufficiently different environments, but together were broadly representative of the range of council-run sheltered accommodation schemes in Harlow, we developed an environmental questionnaire to be completed by the wardens. Questions were adapted from the Multiphasic Environmental Assessment Procedure (MEAP; Moos & Lemke, 1992) and included questions about the residents, the physical environment and unit policies. Sixteen questionnaires were returned (84%). Two were excluded as most questions were left unanswered. The results of the remaining 14 questionnaires were entered into a hierarchical cluster analysis using SPSS for Windows Release 6.0 (SPSS, 1993). Schemes were chosen from the groups on the basis of their being representative of their group, of sufficient size (20+ residents), and qualitatively different from the other two chosen schemes according to their description in the warden questionnaire. The aim was to obtain an adequate sample size of around 90 residents that was broadly representative of the range of schemes in Harlow. One of the larger groups was characterised by schemes consisting of bungalows, a relatively large number of couples (compared to single residents), decisions often made by residents, few meetings and an intolerance of difficult behaviour. The other was characterised by mainly consisting of flats and decisions being made by the staff. It is interesting to note that these appear to correspond to some extent to Category 1 and Category 2 sheltered housing, respectively (Ministry of Housing and Local Government, 1969). The unclustered scheme chosen shared some characteristics with each of the other two clusters, but was characterised by an emphasis on social activity with an active residents committee and newsletter. All three schemes had one resident warden and no other staff.

Procedure

Once permission had been sought from the wardens of the three schemes, all 96 residents were contacted by a letter, which explained the study and informed them that someone would call in person in the next few weeks to invite them to participate. Residents away for several months or who did not speak English were excluded (7). Of the remaining 89 residents who were approached, two declined and 87 (98%) agreed to be interviewed. Each consenting resident (87) was seen once in their own home, and semi-structured interviews were conducted.

Measures

Camberwell Assessment of Need for the Elderly (CANE: Reynolds *et al*, 2000)

This assesses met and unmet needs in older people from the three perspectives of the client, the carer, and the staff involved. It covers a range of health and psychosocial needs and help received from carers and services. It has very good validity and reliability, and predicts levels of dependency.

Practitioner Assessment of Network Typology (PANT: Grant & Wenger, 1993)

This is a short, eight-question instrument that assesses the individual's support network according to three main features: availability of local close kin; level of involvement of family, friends and neighbours; and the level of interaction with the community and voluntary groups. Networks are then characterised either into one of 5 main types (family dependent, locally integrated, locally self-contained, wider community focused and private restricted) or into a combination of two types.

Short-CARE (Gurland *et al*, 1984)

This was developed from the Comprehensive Assessment and Referral Schedule (CARE) but it is quicker to administer. It is a semi-structured interview developed for older people and has scales measuring: cognitive impairment, depression, sleep problems, somatic problems, subjective memory impairment and activities of daily living. There are also diagnostic scales for depression and dementia.

Client Service Receipt Inventory (CSRI) (Beecham & Knapp, 1992)

This was adapted to the evaluation context and the local care settings. It recorded facility characteristics, living circumstances, service use, benefit receipts, informal care inputs (where relevant), and socio-demographic data.

Demographic and other data

Residents were asked for information regarding socio-economic variables such as age, years of education, previous occupation, financial status, ethnicity and whether they live alone.

Data analysis

Parametric tests were used where the data met the requirements of a normal distribution or homogeneous variances, otherwise non-parametric tests were used e.g. Mann–Whitney (U) or Kruskal–Wallis (H). A logistic regression analysis was carried out in order to investigate the relationship between unmet needs and other factors.

Results

Residents

The mean age of residents was 80 years (s.d.=7.0) and 68% were female. There was no significant difference in the mean ages or gender ratio between the three schemes. All the residents interviewed were of White British ethnic origin. Thirty-one residents (36%) were married and living with their spouse, the remainder, who all lived alone, were widowed (49%), divorced (13%) or single (2%). Men were more likely than women to be married and less likely to be widowed ($\chi^2(2)=10.7$, $P=0.01$). More men (16; 57%) were married than women (25%). The proportions of people living alone differed between the three schemes ($\chi^2(2)=5.9$, $P=0.05$). Scheme A had the most people (79%), followed by B (70%). In scheme C, there were actually more couples (53%) than people living alone. The great majority of residents (84%) left school at the age of 14, after 9 years of education. The length of residency in the schemes ranged widely from 1 month to 16 years, with a mean of 5 years 2 months (s.d.=4 years 4 months); however, there were no significant differences between the schemes (Kruskal–Wallis $H(2)=2.6$, $P=0.27$). Length of residency correlated with age ($r=0.36$, $P<0.001$). Locally integrated social networks were most common (35, 41%), followed by locally self-contained (15, 18%), private restricted (14, 17%), family dependent (12, 14%) and wider community focused (9, 11%). The distribution of network types was similar across the three schemes (Field *et al*, 2002).

Needs

The vast majority of residents (79, 91%) had at least one need (mean=4.9, s.d.=3.8), 25 (29%) had over six needs and two people actually had 14 needs. Eight residents (9%) had no known needs. The range in the number of needs per resident was similar in each scheme. Residents had a mean of 1.5 (s.d.=1.9) unmet needs, and most residents (51, 60%) had at least one unmet need, 27 (31%) had two or more unmet needs, and one person had 9 unmet needs. There were no significant differences between the three sheltered schemes in their total number of needs ($F(2,84)=0.06$, $P=0.9$), the number of met needs ($F(2,84)=0.1$, $P=0.9$), or the number of unmet needs (Kruskal–Wallis $H(2)=2.6$, $P=0.3$). In total, 426 needs were identified, of which 300 (70%) were being met and 126 (30%) were unmet. Numbers of met needs and unmet needs per resident correlated to some degree ($r=0.34$, $P<0.001$).

Types of need

Table 5.1 shows that all 24 needs for help covered by the CANE were found in at least one resident. The percentages of residents with each need and the percentages with each need unmet were remarkably similar across the three schemes in almost all cases. The only difference was in needs relating to accommodation; no one in scheme A reported an unmet need for adaptations to their home, whereas eight (27%) in scheme C did (e.g. needs for bath adaptations, a shower or improved wheelchair access).

Physical health needs were almost always met, 64 (93%) of the 69 residents with this need were receiving appropriate treatment. Most needs relating to medication use were also met. Other common needs such as looking after the home, shopping and cooking, managing money and self-care were also usually met. The most common unmet needs were mobility (17%), eyesight and hearing (12%), company (14%), information regarding treatment (12%), and psychological distress (12%). The last three were more often unmet than met. Other less common needs were also more often unmet than met: claiming benefits; continence; accommodation; memory; and problems with intimate relationships.

Daytime activity was an unmet need for seven (40%) of the 15 residents with the need. None of the four residents with an alcohol problem were receiving help. Overall, 22 psychological needs were unmet (61%), as were 35 social needs (52%), compared to 46 physical needs (33%) and 23 environmental needs (19%).

Who was meeting the needs?

Most people (58%) received some help from their family (Table 5.2). Over half the residents (51%) received help from family with shopping and over a quarter (26%) help with housework. Single residents were more likely to receive help from family members than were married residents ($\chi^2(1)=4.2$, $P<0.05$). Some needs were predominantly met by family, some by services and others by both (Table 5.1). Most help with needs for managing money, shopping and cooking was provided by family. They

Table 5.1 Residents' needs and where their help comes from

				Residents receiving help from			
	Residents with unmet needs[1]	Total with needs[2]	Unmet needs	Family & friends only	Services only	Family, friends & services	No one, despite need
Need	*n* (%)	*n* (%)	%	*n* (%)	*n* (%)	*n* (%)	*n* (%)
Environmental needs							
Accommodation	7 (8)	12 (14)	58	0 (0)	9 (75)	0 (0)	3 (25)
Looking after home	5 (6)	41 (48)	12	20 (49)	16 (39)	4 (10)	3 (7)
Food and shopping	0 (0)	39 (45)	0	26 (67)	6 (15)	7 (18)	0 (0)
Money	1 (1)	14 (16)	7	11 (79)	3 (21)	0 (0)	0 (0)
Benefits	9 (10)	14 (16)	64	0 (0)	3 (21)	4 (29)	7 (50)
Caring for someone	1 (1)	2 (2)	50	1 (50)	0 (0)	0 (0)	1 (50)
Physical needs							
Physical health	5 (6)	69 (80)	7	0 (0)	57 (83)	11 (16)	2 (3)
Drugs	2 (2)	15 (17)	13	4 (27)	8 (53)	1 (7)	2 (13)
Eyesight/hearing/ communication	10 (12)	32 (37)	31	2 (6)	16 (50)	9 (28)	5 (16)
Mobility/falls	15 (17)	44 (51)	34	15 (34)	9 (20)	15 (34)	9 (20)
Self-care	6 (7)	25 (29)	24	6 (24)	13 (52)	2 (8)	6 (24)
Continence	8 (9)	16 (19)	50	1 (6)	9 (56)	1 (6)	5 (31)
Psychological needs							
Psychological distress	10 (12)	17 (20)	59	8 (47)	4 (24)	3 (18)	6 (35)
Memory	7 (8)	8 (9)	88	1 (13)	1 (13)	0 (0)	6 (75)
Behaviour	0 (0)	1 (1)	0	0 (0)	1 (100)	0 (0)	0 (0)
Alcohol	4 (5)	4 (5)	100	0 (0)	1 (25)	0 (0)	3 (75)
Deliberate self-harm	1 (1)	3 (3)	33	0 (0)	2 (67)	0 (0)	1 (33)
Inadvertent self-harm	0 (0)	2 (2)	0	1 (50)	0 (0)	1 (50)	0 (0)
Psychotic symptoms	0 (0)	1 (1)	0	0 (0)	1 (100)	0 (0)	0 (0)
Social needs							
Company	12 (14)	23 (27)	52	11 (48)	1 (4)	10 (43)	9 (39)
Intimate relationships	7 (8)	12 (14)	58	6 (50)	0 (0)	3 (25)	6 (50)
Daytime activities	6 (7)	15 (17)	40	1 (7)	8 (53)	1 (7)	5 (33)
Information	10 (12)	15 (17)	67	1 (7)	7 (47)	0 (0)	7 (47)
Abuse/neglect	0 (0)	2 (2)	0	0 (0)	1 (50)	1 (50)	0 (0)

1. This includes those receiving help which is inadequate to meet their need.

2. Includes both met and unmet needs.

Table 5.2 Number of residents receiving help from family and friends

Activity	Help received from	
	Family	Friends
Laundry	14 (15%)	4 (5%)
Shopping	45 (51%)	3 (4%)
Finances	12 (13%)	0 (2%)
Housework	23 (26%)	3 (3%)
Bathing	5 (6%)	0 (0%)
Other, e.g. gardening	12 (13%)	8 (9%)
Any sort of help	51 (58%)	12 (14%)

also provided more of the help with psychological distress and relationships. Most residents receiving help with company and mobility were receiving the help from family, with some receiving additional help from services. Residents tended to receive help with looking after the home either from family or services, but not both. Help with daytime activity, continence, and information about health was usually provided by services only. Help with self-care and with drugs was also mainly provided by services but some received help just from their family. Most residents receiving help with physical health, eyesight and hearing were receiving help from services, with some receiving additional help from family. Most residents (67%) had visited their general practitioner in the preceding 3 months and 28% had seen a district nurse in the past month. Many (49%) had attended hospital out-patient appointments in the past year. Few residents had seen a community psychiatric nurse, psychologist, occupational therapist or physiotherapist in the past 3 months and few had attended a day hospital or day centre. Home help provided personal care or cleaning services to 29% of residents, but few received meals on wheels (Table 5.3).

Table 5.3 Services received by residents in the time period given

Services received	Number of residents seen	Contacts of those receiving service	
		Mean	Range
In the preceding month			
Home help[1]	25 (29%)	15.6	4–56
Other regular help	5 (6%)	2.3	0.5–4
Meals on wheels	4 (5%)	23	8–28
Lunch club	10 (12%)	4.7	3–8
Day centre	3 (3%)	4.7	2–8
Day hospital	3 (3%)	6.3	1–16
District nurse	24 (28%)	2.1	1–8
In the preceding 3 months			
GP	58 (67%)	1.7	1–6
Occupational therapist	7 (8%)	3.3	1–16
Community psychiatric nurse	3 (3%)	5.7	1–12
Physiotherapist	2 (2%)	5.0	4–6
Psychologist	1 (1%)	3.0	3
In the preceding year			
Social worker	13 (15%)	1.4	1–4
Hospital out-patient appointment	42 (49%)	4.4	1–16

1. Personal care and/or housework

Table 5.4 Comparison of unmet needs between residents with and without diagnoses of depression, dementia, serious activity limitation or somatic symptoms

	No. of unmet needs of residents		
	Diagnosis/problem (*n*=20) Mean (s.d.)	Not a problem (*n*=64) Mean (s.d.)	Mann–Whitney (*U*)
Depression (*n*=20)	2.9 (2.5)	1.1 (1.4)	350**
Dementia (*n*=7)	3.2 (3.0)	1.3 (1.7)	145*
Activity limitation (*n*=46)	2.2 (2.1)	0.7 (1.3)	470***
Somatic symptoms (*n*=31)	2.4 (2.2)	1.0 (1.5)	496**

*$P<0.05$, **$P<0.01$, ***$P<0.001$

Factors associated with needs

Single residents (i.e. those living alone) had significantly more met needs (mean $M=4.0$, s.d.$=3.0$) than married residents ($M=2.5$, s.d.$=1.9$) ($U=625$, $P<0.05$), but there was no difference between single ($M=1.6$, s.d.$=2.1$) and married ($M=1.1$, s.d.$=1.4$) residents in the number of unmet needs ($U=823$, $P=68$). Single people received family help with significantly more needs than married people did ($t(84.02)=2.5$, $P<0.05$ unequal variances). There were no relationships between age, gender or length of residence and number of either met or unmet needs.

A diagnosis of depression predicted high levels of unmet needs ($P<0.001$) (Table 5.4). Less than one in four people were depressed, but they accounted for 46% of all unmet needs and 75% of those with depression had one or more unmet needs. Unmet needs were also significantly more frequent in those with either a diagnosis of dementia or clinically significant levels of activity limitation or somatic symptoms.

Residents with no confidant were more likely to have at least one unmet environmental need ($\chi^2(1)=6.18$, $P<0.05$ Fishers exact test, two-tailed) and at least one unmet psychological need ($\chi^2(1)=4.6$, $P<0.05$ Fishers exact test, two-tailed). Those who said they had nobody to help if they became ill were more likely than those with a potential carer to have at least one unmet social need ($\chi^2(1)=9.7$, $P<0.01$ Fishers exact test, two-tailed), as were those who reported often feeling lonely ($\chi^2(2)=33.0$, $P<0.001$). Seventy-six per cent of residents who said they did not see their relatives as often as they would like had unmet needs. They were more likely to have at least one unmet environmental need ($\chi^2(1)=4.7$, $P<0.05$), at least one unmet social need ($\chi^2(1)=8.9$, $P<0.01$) and overall had significantly more unmet needs ($\chi^2=8.68$, $P<0.003$). The small minority (8, 10%) who were very unhappy living in sheltered housing had more needs (met 7.4 v. 4.9: unmet needs 2.1 v. 1.5).

Needs and social networks

The 14 residents with private restricted support networks all had one or more unmet needs (compared to half of those with other network types) (Table 5.5). They also had significantly more unmet needs (mean$=3.0$, s.d.$=2.4$) than the 71 residents with other network types (mean$=1.2$, s.d.$=1.7$) (Kruskal–Wallis $H(1)=12.5$, $P<0.001$). Those with private networks also had significantly more unmet social needs (Kruskal–Wallis $H(1)=9.0$, $P<0.005$) and more unmet physical needs (Kruskal–Wallis $H(1)=9.9$, $P<0.005$). The groups with wider community focused networks or locally integrated networks had the fewest unmet needs.

Table 5.5 Types of need among residents with different support networks

Needs	Private	Family-dependent	Self-contained	Wider community	Locally integrated focused	
	(14)	(12)	(15)	(9)	(35)	
	Mean (s.d.)	Mean (s.d.)	Mean (s.d.)	Mean (s.d.)	Mean (s.d.)	K–W[1]
Unmet	3.0 (2.4)	1.8 (2.7)	1.4 (1.5)	0.6 (0.7)	1.0 (1.4)	$H=14.4$ $P=0.006$
Met	2.0 (2.2)	1.3 (1.9)	1.1 (1.8)	0.3 (0.5)	0.7 (1.0)	$H=5.9$ $P=0.2$

1. K–W, Kruskal–Wallis test

Multivariate analysis of unmet need

A backwards stepwise selection procedure was used to select variables following logistic regression analysis. As a result of this procedure, seeing relatives enough ($P=0.043$), having a private network ($P=0.002$), dementia score ($P=0.005$) and depression score ($P=0.03$) correctly classified 79% of the sample according to whether they had any unmet needs.

Discussion

The present study had an excellent response rate (98%) and the use of cluster analysis to choose three schemes that differed from one another suggests we have a representative sample of sheltered schemes with wardens. The sample was homogeneous with respect to ethnicity, education, socio-economic status, age and housing provider.

Such a wide-ranging needs assessment has not previously been carried out in sheltered housing. Butler et al (1983) reported similar levels of needs for help with shopping, housework and mobility, to those found in the present study. The present study found that on average sheltered residents had considerably fewer needs than had been found in residential care or nursing home residents from Harlow and the surrounding area (Martin et al, 2002). However, there was some overlap between the most in need in sheltered housing and the least in need in residential care. A greater proportion of sheltered (than residential care) residents (80%, 41%) had a need relating to physical health (usually prescription medication) or a sight/hearing need (37%, 21%).

Almost all residential or continuing care residents (96%) had one or more unmet need (Martin et al, 2002), whereas only 59% of sheltered housing residents did. Common unmet needs experienced by residents in both sheltered housing and residential care included mobility, company, psychological distress, and daytime activity. Common unmet needs in sheltered housing but not residential care included sight/hearing (12%) and information about treatment (12%). Many residents of residential care had an unmet need for help with their memory (85%), but no one with this need had it met. In sheltered housing only one of the 8 with this need had it met.

Increasing age was not associated with increasing numbers of needs or unmet needs. However, residents with depression, dementia and serious activity limitation were much more likely to have more unmet needs. This supports findings by Badger (1998) that depression is a significant predictor of need for mental health services and financial assistance. Depression, activity limitation and somatic symptoms were also all significantly associated with having at least one unmet social need. Logistic regression analysis found that depression scores, dementia scores, having a private support network and not being satisfied with frequency of contact with relatives were the only predictors of residents having one or more of their needs unmet. This suggests that isolated people in sheltered accommodation with mental health problems are particularly likely to have unmet needs.

Many residents (58%) in the present study were receiving family help, (e.g. 51% with shopping and 26% with housework). Single residents received help from their family with more needs than married people did, but they did not receive more help from services (Field *et al*, 2002), which supports previous findings that adult children and other close family are more involved when there is no spouse present (Wenger, 1997). As expected, those with a private network required formal services for the greatest number of needs and those with a locally integrated network for the least number of needs. This fits in with previous findings that older people with private restricted networks were over represented on social services caseloads (Wenger, 1994, 1997).

Psychological and social needs were often unmet, and loneliness was frequently reported by sheltered housing residents. Assessment of the current level of social participation in a unit and the barriers preventing participation when it was desired would be of great benefit and enable barriers to be tackled. People may not attend for social reasons, e.g. too many women and too few men, class differences (Young, 1993) or different interests. Disability may also make it difficult, for example wheelchair access, deafness (Woolrych, 1998) or cognitive impairment. Interventions to raise participation in activity with recently bereaved or disabled older people have shown that increased engagement significantly decreases distress (Reich & Zautra, 1991). It would be particularly important to monitor participation and to check why regular attendees stop attending. Woolrych (1998) said that the common rooms were underused and suggested they be made available for outside use such as a luncheon club for older people. Butler and colleagues (1983) found places where this was happening and in these schemes residents were generally in favour. In schemes where this did not happen, opinion was more divided. There are certainly potential benefits for residents with more local activities, although this needs to be carefully managed.

Training wardens in dealing with difficult group dynamics is another potentially useful area of input. Resident groups are a potentially complex mix of people and sensitive support of the residents committees (where in existence) is important. Considerable bad feeling arose in one of the schemes studied when some residents said they did not want the more disabled residents to come to activities and so set up a club off site which those disabled residents were unable to walk to. Splits in resident groups have also been reported elsewhere (Young, 1993).

Group interventions, while valuable, are not the way to meet all social and psychological needs. Projects such as Kindred Spirits help isolated older people by putting them in touch with an other who shares a similar interest (Jewell *et al*, 1997). Wardens could put interested residents in contact with others who share the same interests, which would help address the common unmet needs for company and activity. As Rook (1998) puts it: 'friendships may emerge more easily from shared activities and projects than from interactions focused overtly on friendship formation', and so this may also help intimacy needs. Although never a goal over time, Kindred Spirits found that those people who had made contacts to share interests with, became more interested in meeting in groups (Jewell *et al*, 1997). Making acquaintances with shared interests could mean residents become more likely to attend social events in the common room, thus having individual and group contact which may help meet their needs even more comprehensively. Others ideas for wardens include facilitation of taxi share schemes and joint shopping trips for those wanting more social contact, or lacking the confidence or finances to go alone.

Private restricted support networks can be associated with long-standing personality problems, and are common on social workers' caseloads. This study found that private support networks and diagnoses of depression and dementia were variables associated with having unmet needs of various types. Mental health problems were common in sheltered residents but mental health staff alone cannot meet the psychological needs of this community. However, perhaps mental health staff should provide consultancy services to wardens and sheltered housing providers as well as expanding training in primary care and training wardens in identifying needs and equipping them with the skills and knowledge to help residents access appropriate services (e.g., health, housing or social services). Jackson & Mittelmark (1997) suggested screening older people for unmet needs when they come into contact with services, such as primary care, day centres and emergency services.

Butler *et al* (1983) found that few residents had had the warden's role explained and suggested this would be useful for residents. Family and service providers would also benefit from such information as wardens in the present study commented that the expectations placed on them by those outside were often beyond their job description and may lead to needs being unmet. In such situations, wardens had to knowingly leave needs unmet or do more than they were employed, or even allowed, by their employer to do.

Further research

The present study highlights several areas in need of further research: the determinants and consequences of met and unmet need, particularly social and psychological needs, and the longitudinal investigation of the interactions over time between different types of unmet need and of interactions between unmet need and network type. Needs are also likely to change over time as people become ill or recover from illness or other life events befall them. Exploration of the impact of unmet needs on the development of other needs would be of interest, e.g. an unmet mobility need could lead to psychological distress or need for company. Associations have also been found between unmet needs and transportation problems, as these make it difficult to meet personal needs and access community services (Jackson & Mittelmark, 1997). Woolrych (1998) found that some residents in sheltered housing were housebound and isolated because of unmet needs. Understanding the links with network type would hopefully produce ways of supporting the different networks so they function well and meet the needs of older people. A residents' support network has a large influence on service use (Wenger, 1997) and a further exploration of associations between network type, who meets needs and the type of help wanted from the warden would be useful.

It would also be important to determine the relationships between needs and networks, and environmental factors, such as the layout and location of the scheme, the type of housing (e.g. flats or bungalows), access, lighting, public rooms, activity level, policies concerning allocation, resident participation in organisation, and local policies on dealing with problem behaviour and dependency. These studies would be useful to town planners, architects, the local council and those managing sheltered housing schemes. The relationship between needs and people's initial decision to move in would also be of interest to service planners and providers in housing, health and social services.

Conclusion

The present study aimed to explore needs and investigate those factors associated with unmet needs. Residents of sheltered housing were generally found to have the majority of their physical and environmental needs met, but psychological and social needs, although less frequently reported, often remained unmet. Residents with depression, dementia, clinical levels of activity limitation or somatic symptoms had the highest numbers of unmet needs, as did those with private networks. These findings have implications for the practice of those working in sheltered housing and their management, as well as for professionals working in mental health and social services. There is a need for further research, but the present results have highlighted the frequency of unmet psychological and social needs. This should be the first step in helping to meet more of the needs of older people in sheltered housing.

6 Needs in continuing care settings

Mark D. Martin, Geraldine Hancock, Barbora Richardson, Peter Simmons, Cornelius Katona and Martin Orrell

Summary

This chapter looks at the met and unmet needs of elderly residents of nursing care and residential care settings. Thirty-four residents of a residential care home and 40 residents of two nursing care settings were assessed. The CANE was used to interview each resident and a respective staff member in order to obtain a profile of the resident's current met and unmet needs. The Clifton Assessment Procedures for the Elderly – Behaviour Rating Scale (CAPE–BRS) was completed by the staff member to indicate the participant's current level of dependency. In addition, the Mini-Mental State Examination was administered to participants and a DSM–IV diagnosis was recorded. The CANE ratings indicated a high number of needs in both continuing care settings, the level of dependency being proportional to the level of need. There was a core set of needs in both samples related to difficulties with accommodation, food preparation and self-care. Both settings were meeting these needs; however, residential care residents had a significantly greater level of unmet need for suitable daytime activities. The greatest predictor of type of setting was gender, and there were significantly more females in residential care. Controlling for gender, participants in nursing care had greater levels of dependency, particularly problems with apathy and social skills, as measured on the CAPE–BRS. It is possible that the greater level of social needs in nursing care residents had led to their placement in the more specialised nursing care settings. On the other hand, these settings might be left caring for a group of residents who, because of their specific needs, have been difficult to place into residential care. These findings have clinical implications for the future development of continuing care for older people. This study also highlighted that there is a substantial need for specialist services to address the unmet needs in these two types of continuing care settings, such as interventions for social disturbances in nursing care and suitable daytime activities in residential care. The CANE was a suitable instrument to evaluate the comprehensive nature of needs in the continuing care population. This chapter concludes by outlining further research being conducted into needs-based assessment and treatment in the continuing care population. It is based on an earlier paper (Martin *et al*, 2002).

Background

The population of elderly persons has been steadily increasing over the past decades (Department of Health, 2001). Better living standards, nutrition and health care have led to individuals living longer. As individuals reach old age (over 65) and very old (old-old) age (over 85), however, the chances that they will require additional health and social services increases (Impallomeni & Starr, 1995). In an effort to reduce costs and the pressures on services, health and social services have emphasised that elderly individuals should largely have their needs met in the community (Department of Health, 2001). This emphasis on community care has much to commend it, such as encouraging continued involvement in the community and maximising individual independence. On the other hand, increased community care provision and the increases in the very elderly population has meant that there are a large number of elderly people who are very dependent and frail when they enter continuing care institutions. This increase in demand for continuing care for this highly dependent population has occurred at the same time as the closure of many long-term care wards (Lam *et al*, 1989).

There has therefore been pressure on residential care and nursing homes to accept more dependent people (Simmons & Orrell, 2001). There is a common view that nursing care settings provide care for a select group of highly dependent elderly people, who because of their special medical and/or psychiatric needs, have been found to be difficult to place elsewhere (Bollini *et al*, 1986; O'Driscoll, 1993). These people with special needs include many individuals with dementia, a mental illness that involves a complex mix of psychological, social and physical changes that many community and residential care services find difficult to manage (Aronson *et al*, 1992; Chester & Bender, 1999). However, the population in residential care has also become increasingly frail and more recently there has been a debate regarding whether residential and nursing care settings may be providing care for older people with similar levels of dependency rather than two distinct groups.

Although there is evidence to suggest that the current group of elderly people living in continuing care settings are now more dependent than they had been previously (Janzon *et al*, 2000), the actual profile of needs and whether these needs were being adequately met is not known. In addition, it is suggested that pressure on these institutions to meet the high level of need in this elderly population can lead to detrimental effects on the residents and home staff, such as reliance on medication for behavioural problems in residents, staff burnout, over-use of untrained assistants, and under-resourced and supported homes (i.e. lack of support from psychiatric or specialist medical services; Audit Commission, 2000). Whether these settings can adequately meet individual needs has been recognised as a major factor in effective, efficient and comprehensive health care delivery (Leese *et al*, 1998; Department of Health, 2001; Walters *et al*, 2001).

In order to measure an individual's needs, new assessment instruments have been developed that differ from the traditional assessments of disability (Tracey, 1986; Brewin *et al*, 1987; Slade & Thornicroft, 1995). These developments in needs assessment tools allow, for the first time, an evaluation of the specific social, physical and health needs of individuals in these continuing care settings. Measurement instruments using a definition of need as a remediable deficit distinguish these scales from those assessing levels of disability in that they can assess an individual's met and unmet needs and can therefore be directly used to develop care plans. The Camberwell Assessment of Need for the Elderly (CANE) is one such tool, which has been shown to be a valid and reliable way to comprehensively measure the met and unmet needs of older individuals in a variety of settings (Reynolds *et al,* 2000; Walters et al, 2001; Ashaye *et al*, 2003).

The ability to directly measure met and unmet needs in ongoing care populations could provide a detailed description of remediable problems present in individual residents living within these institutions. Furthermore, a detailed assessment of individual needs could gauge how well different long-term care settings are addressing the needs of their residents and how residential and nursing care residents may differ. This study aimed to describe and compare needs (met and unmet) and levels of dependency in residential and nursing care settings.

Method

Participants

Participants were recruited from one residential care home and two specialist elderly mentally ill nursing care settings (a hospital-based continuing care ward and a health-funded private nursing home) within the local catchment area of west Essex. All residents in residential care and nursing care were placed with respect to the eligibility criteria for placement into continuing care outlined by the Department of Health (1995b). To summarise these criteria, participants in residential care had sufficient social or personal care needs that they could no longer live in their own homes in the community. Participants in nursing care settings had ongoing needs that required nursing interventions that could not be provided for in their own homes. In addition, those in the nursing care homes had specialist mental health needs, requiring them to live in a setting that could provide mental health care and meet their physical dependency needs. Participants were included for selection if they had resided in the care home for over one month. Thirty-four residents of the residential care home were randomly selected (using a random number sheet) and agreed to take part in the study. All 40 individuals from the nursing care settings agreed to participate.

Procedure

All interviews were conducted in a quiet room away from communal areas within the homes. General demographic information was collected from all participants (i.e. age, gender and length of stay). The CANE (Reynolds et al, 2000) and the Mini-Mental State Examination (MMSE; Folstein et al, 1975) were then administered to participants by a trained assessor. The participant's keyworker was identified from the nursing notes and this staff member was interviewed using the CANE. The staff member then completed the Clifton Assessment Procedures for the Elderly – Behaviour Rating Scale (CAPE–BRS; Pattie & Gilleard, 1975) concerning the person's behaviour over the previous week. The CAPE–BRS is a rating scale designed to measure the level of dependency and behavioural function of older people. It assesses a wide range of behaviours and activities of daily living divided into four sections: physical dependency, apathy, communication difficulties and social disturbance. A DSM–IV diagnosis was also recorded, based on the interviews and the participant's nursing notes.

CANE data for each participant was based upon ratings made by a trained rater using all information gathered. The two additional areas in the CANE designed to assess carer's needs were not used in the present study. Data were analysed using SPSS version 10.0 for Windows. Differences between residential and nursing care homes were assessed using standard parametric tests for two independent samples. If the assumption of homogeneity of variances was violated, however, equivalent non-parametric tests were undertaken. The P-value for significance was set at 0.05 unless otherwise stated.

Results

Demographics

There were 29 males and 45 females in the total sample. The nursing care homes had even numbers of males ($n=20$) and females ($n=20$), while the residential care home contained more females ($n=25$) than males ($n=9$), producing a significant difference between the two types of care settings ($F(1,72)=4.4$, $P<0.05$). The mean age of participants was 80.6 years (s.d.$=8.5$), and women (mean$=82.5$, s.d.$=8.2$) were significantly older than men (mean$=77.5$, s.d.$=8.2$), $t=2.6$, $P<0.05$. However, a t-test revealed no significant difference in participants ages between the residential care (RC) (mean=82.5, s.d.=8.9) and nursing care (NC) (mean=78.9, s.d.=7.8) groups. The average length of time participants had lived in the facilities was 26.4 months (s.d.=25). A *t*-test of the length of stay between the residential care setting (mean=30.5, s.d.= 28.4) and the nursing care settings (mean=22.9, s.d.=21.6) was not significant, indicating that the average length of time participants had resided in the homes was 2 to 2.5 years. Sixty participants had dementia (27 RC, 33 NC) and 13 of these also had a comorbid affective disorder. In addition, five residential care residents had an affective disorder and one nursing care resident had schizophrenia.

MMSE scores were available for 58 (78%) participants (mean=5.9, s.d.=8.2). The RC (*n*=23, mean=10.4, s.d.=8.9) residents had significantly less cognitive impairment than the NC (*n*=35, mean=2.9, s.d.=6.2) residents (*t*=3.8, *P*<0.05).

Dependency

The mean CAPE score for the total sample was 19.7 (s.d.=6.0), indicating very high levels of dependency. A *t*-test of CAPE scores between the two home settings revealed that the NC (mean=22.1, s.d.=5) residents were significantly more dependent than the RC (mean=16.8, s.d.=5.9) residents (*t* (72)=4.2, *P*<0.001). Table 6.1 indicates that the NC residents were significantly more impaired on the apathy, communication difficulties and social disturbance sub-scales of the CAPE than the RC residents. The difference in resident's physical dependency ratings between the two settings was less than for the other sub-scales and was not statistically significant. Using a weighting system (met need=1, unmet need=2), the level of residents' needs was positively correlated with their level of overall disability on the CAPE–BRS (Pearson one-tailed correlation *r*=0.25, *P*<0.05).

Assessment of needs

The average number of needs identified (met and unmet) for all participants was 14.2 (s.d.=2.3). There was no difference between the number of needs in RC (mean=14.1, s.d.=2.1) and NC homes (mean=14.4, s.d.=2.4). The average number of met needs was 11.7 (s.d.=2.1) for the total sample and there was also no significant difference in the number of met needs between the RC (mean=11.5, s.d.=1.9) and NC (mean=11.9, s.d.=2.2) homes. The average number of unmet needs was 2.5 (s.d.=1.5) for the total sample. Again, there was no significant difference in the number of unmet needs between the RC (mean=2.6, s.d.=1.4) and NC (mean=2.5, s.d.=1.6) homes.

Table 6.1 CAPE sub-scale results between residential care and nursing care settings

Sub-scale of CAPE (maximum score)	Residential care Mean (s.d.)	Nursing care Mean (s.d.)	*t*-test, d.f.=72
Physical dependency (12)	7.59 (2.87)	8.35 (2.27)	1.27
Apathy (10)	6.53 (2.53)	8.6 (1.66)	4.22**
Communication difficulties (4)	1.08 (1.46)	2.38 (1.55)	3.65**
Social disturbance (10)	1.26 (2)	2.73 (2.73)	2.49*
Total	16.8 (5.9)	22.1 (5)	4.19**

* *P*<0.05; ** *P*<0.001

Table 6.2 Frequency (%) of identified and unmet needs in residential care (RC) and nursing care (NC) settings

CANE areas of need	Identified needs		Unmet needs	
	RC	NC	RC	NC
Accommodation	34 (100)	40 (100)	0 (0)	0 (0)
Looking after the home	34 (100)	40 (100)	0 (0)	1 (3)
Food	34 (100)	40 (100)	0 (0)	1 (3)
Self-care	34 (100)	40 (100)	0 (0)	3 (8)
Caring for someone else	0 (0)	3 (8)	0 (0)	3 (8)
Daytime activities	32 (94)	32 (82)	18 (53)*	3 (8)
Memory	29 (85)	38 (95)	29 (85)	32 (80)
Eyesight/hearing/communication	7 (21)*	7 (18)	3 (9)	3 (8)
Mobility/falls	28 (82)	20 (50)	7 (21)	13 (33)
Continence	23 (68)	32 (80)	21 (0)	1 (3)
Physical health	14 (41)	21 (53)	1 (3)	1 (3)
Drugs	32 (94)	34 (85)	0 (0)	0 (0)
Psychotic symptoms	4 (12)	10 (26)	2 (6)	3 (8)
Psychological distress	14 (41)	18 (45)	8 (24)*	2 (5)
Information	3 (9)	3 (8)	0 (0)	0 (0)
Deliberate self-harm	1 (3)	1 (3)	0 (0)	0 (0)
Inadvertent self-harm	24 (71)	37 (93)*	3 (9)	2 (5)
Abuse/neglect	9 (26)	39 (98)***	1 (3)	0 (0)
Behaviour	14 (41)	23 (58)	5 (15)	13 (33)
Alcohol	0 (0)	0 (0)	0 (0)	0 (0)
Company	23 (68)	27 (68)	8 (24)	5 (13)
Intimate relationships	13 (38)	10 (27)	3 (9)	5 (14)
Money/budgeting	34 (100)	33 (87)	0 (0)	0 (0)
Benefits	34 (100)*	5 (14)	0 (0)	0 (0)

*P<0.05; *** P<0.001

Table 6.2 shows the breakdown of individual needs identified by the CANE. The most common needs (seen in more than 75% of individuals) were accommodation, food, household activities, safety (accidental self-harm), self-care, personal finances, memory and daytime activities. Over half of the total sample had needs connected with claiming their benefits, continence, mobility, behaviour, company, and vulnerability to abuse or neglect from others. Table 6.2 also shows that 25% of residents had identified needs in areas of physical health care, intimate relationships and psychological distress. Fisher's exact test was used to examine the differences in needs identified between residential care and nursing care homes. This test showed that residential care residents had a greater number of needs for assistance with mobility $\chi^2=8.4$, $P<0.05$ and with their benefits, $\chi^2=53.5$, $P<0.001$. On the other hand, nursing care residents had more met needs for assistance with safety in terms of accidental self-harm, $\chi^2=6.09$, $P<0.05$, and for protection from abuse or neglect from others, $\chi^2=40.69$, $P<0.001$.

Table 6.2 also shows the frequency of unmet needs for the two types of settings separately. It can be seen that the majority of needs had been met (i.e. the difference between identified and unmet needs), with the exception of memory, which was unmet in 82% of the total sample. Between 24% and 28% of the total sample also had unmet needs in areas of daytime activities, mobility and behavioural issues. A Fisher's exact test of the differences in frequency of unmet need between RC and NC homes revealed that residential care residents had more unmet needs for both daytime activities $\chi^2=18.15$, $P<0.001$, and psychological distress, $\chi^2=5.40$, $P<0.05$.

Relationship between disability, need and home type

Having identified that some factors differed between care homes, including some demographic variables (e.g. gender and age), a logistical regression was performed to assess whether certain variables could be used to predict placement in either of the two care facilities. Type of home (residential or nursing care) was the dependent variable, whereas gender, age, total unmet needs and total CAPE score were independent variables. This analysis revealed that gender of participants ($F=5.1$, $P<0.05$) and CAPE dependency scores ($F=16.3$, $P<0.001$) were still significant predictors of care setting when the number of unmet needs and age were controlled for. Initially, the Mini-Mental State Examination was not added as an independent variable due to the low number of scores available, however, a separate logistical regression was undertaken using the same variables, but with the addition of participants' Mini-Mental State Examination scores. The addition of the scores into the logistical regression did not change the outcome of the original calculation. Having established that some CAPE scores, particularly the social disturbance sub-scale, differed between settings more than the physical dependency sub-scale on the CAPE a second logistic regression was performed. This analysis entered each CAPE sub-scale score separately. The analysis revealed that gender was still a significant predictor of home type ($F=4$, $P<0.05$), but that the CAPE sub-scales of apathy ($F=18.4$, $P<0.001$) and social disturbance ($F=8.2$, $P<0.05$) could also predict home type. Residents with problems in these areas were more likely to live in the nursing care home.

Discussion

The aim of this study was to describe and compare the needs and dependency level of a group of residents in residential and nursing care homes. The results showed that both residential and nursing care residents had similar rates of met and unmet needs. Nursing care residents, however, were shown to have greater levels of dependency as indicated on the CAPE–BRS and Mini-Mental State Examination. More specifically, nursing care residents had greater social disabilities, rather than physical dependencies.

This study has limitations in that results were based on a relatively small sample of elderly residents. However, the settings draw participants from the same catchment area, making them appropriate groups for comparison. There was also a large discrepancy in the gender ratio between the nursing and residential care populations that may have biased the results. It is possible that this may have been related to potentially higher levels of behavioural disturbance in males in the nursing care setting. It is noted, however, that the proportion of females in residential care in the wider elderly community is greater than males, so this discrepancy may reflect a genuine imbalance of gender in continuing care populations (Lam *et al*, 1989) rather than a bias in the sampling.

Previous literature had suggested that old-age care facilities were dealing with an increase in the number of frail and dependent residents (Chester & Bender, 1999; Janzon *et al*, 2000). Indeed, in 1986 Bell and Gilleard reported a mean CAPE–BRS of 10.2 for 13 individuals who entered continuing care, a 9-point difference compared to residential and nursing care residents in this study. This suggests that residents on average in both settings required more assistance than residents had done previously.

Very frail elderly people have, in the past, resided in nursing care homes. In this study, nursing care residents had a greater level of overall dependency than the residential care group, as well as greater levels of cognitive impairment. On closer inspection, the nursing care group had more problems with social disturbance and apathy. This result fits with original suggestions that nursing care residents come to live in NHS-funded facilities because of difficulties in finding appropriate placements within the community (Bollini *et al*, 1986; O'Driscoll, 1993). On the other hand, this difference could also be a factor of the type of care provided, such that the social difficulties in nursing care were a product of this particular environment. The results of the present study are cross-sectional in nature and as such they cannot suggest what could have led to participant's social problems in nursing care settings. Future research would do well to investigate residents' pathways into care facilities using longitudinal research techniques to clarify their needs and dependency over the course of their stay in continuing care.

Both populations had a high rate of dementia and Mini-Mental State Examination results indicated that nursing care residents had more severe cognitive impairments than residential care residents. This difference in cognitive impairment and possible dementia could account for some of the observed differences in other needs. For example, the problems of unsteady gait, which give rise to the higher rates of need for mobility in residential care, may be less of an issue in advanced dementia as individuals become less mobile in nursing care. Another possible effect of advanced illness may be the decreased need for regular daytime activities. There may also be decreased capacity for social relationships in individuals with more advanced dementia, as reflected in the CANE items intimate relationships and company. In a similar way, the risk of harm from others may be higher in nursing care, owing to the decreased ability of people with severe dementia to protect themselves, which, together with the higher background level of behaviour disturbance, makes them a particularly vulnerable group of individuals in need of protection.

The CANE results indicated that residential and nursing care homes had similar levels of identified needs overall. However, two differences in individual need were noted. First, residential care residents had more frequent need for assistance with managing their money and benefits than nursing care residents. This difference may be due to the fact that nursing care residents have special status as elderly mentally ill in-patients in continuing care funded by the National Health Service (NHS) and, unlike their residential care counterparts, do not pay for their accommodation. Secondly, nursing care residents had more frequent need for assistance with risk of accidental self-harm and abuse/neglect. These types of behavioural difficulties are generally regarded as requiring specialist assessment and intervention (e.g. Aronson *et al*, 1992), which may be why individuals with these safety needs reside in nursing care homes where there is a higher level of qualified staff to provide this type of assistance. Both facilities, however, were effective at identifying and meeting the specialist needs of the majority of their residents.

Certain needs remained unmet in both residential and nursing care settings, such as memory, daytime activities, behaviour and psychological distress. It may be that these needs had not previously been identified, or that access to suitable interventions was problematic (e.g. unwillingness by the resident to accept an intervention for psychological distress or the home unable to develop an activities programme). Certain needs may have been complex (e.g. mobility problems affecting an individual's ability to go to a previous day club, thus affecting their company needs). Homes may not have had the skills or resources to provide the appropriate interventions (e.g. lack of trained staff to met participants' memory needs). A further possibility is that implementing solutions for some needs may take precedence over finding solutions for other needs. For example, if someone has very disturbed behaviour, they might not be able to participate in the care home's activities programme, even though staff agree that such activities might help them in the future. If some or all of these reasons for not meeting individual needs are supported, it is likely that both residential and nursing care facilities suffer from the same problems (i.e. scarcity of resources or trained staff).

The CANE showed that all care residents had a wide range of needs (social, physical, and psychological). This finding indicates the need for a comprehensive assessment instrument that can assess the relevant needs for all residents (Audit Commission, 2000). Nursing care residents had more disabilities and cognitive problems, especially in terms of social problems, and needed more assistance in order to keep themselves safe. The nursing care facilities were meeting these needs adequately for most residents. Residential care residents had more identified needs in areas concerning money and benefits – again, the residential care home was able to met these needs for the majority of individuals.

Both facilities, however, particularly the residential care home, had difficulty meeting residents' needs for more specialist help, such as behaviour problems, memory and suitable daytime activities.

In conclusion, the concept of need is useful in exploring the effectiveness of care settings in providing for their residents. The data presented here provide a coherent picture of two continuing care settings. Rates of unmet need are substantial, and further research is required to confirm this finding and to explore the reasons why particular needs are not being met in these long-term care settings.

Further research

A project is currently underway to investigate the needs of people with dementia living in residential care and to explore ways of meeting their needs. A pilot study designed to test the feasibility of the method has been completed with 20 residents of long-term care homes in the London area. Data from this pilot study show that residents frequently had a moderate to severe level of dementia (Mini-Mental State Examination mean=9.09, s.d.=3.89), and dependency (CAPE–BRS mean=15.75, s.d.=4.45). The average number of unmet needs was 2.9 (s.d.=2.36). The most frequent unmet needs were for daytime activities (n=10, 50%), continence (n=9, 45%), eyesight/hearing (n=6, 30%) and mobility (n=5, 25%).

Feedback regarding individual residents' unmet needs and suggested interventions were given to one of the two homes involved in the pilot. The staff at this home, as well as the resident and carer (where appropriate) were supported by a clinical researcher (GH) to met the individual unmet needs identified by the CANE. A 3-month follow-up was conducted by a second clinical researcher, blind to the original condition of the two homes. Data from this follow-up indicated that the level of unmet need had been reduced from baseline levels. The main study is now currently underway, funded by a grant from the Wellcome Trust. This study aims to document the needs of 260 people residing in 26 long-term care facilities from several sites within the UK, including London, Bangor and Manchester. Interventions to meet these unmet needs will then be suggested to 50% of the homes. This study aims to gain a comprehensive picture of the needs of this population, while also providing some relevant data about which interventions are best able to meet their needs. Research that focuses on individual needs in different care settings will help services to establish effective care programmes that cater to the needs of their residents and can promote well-being and quality of life for older people.

7 Needs of liaison psychiatry referrals from general hospital wards

Mohan Bhat, Suki Greaves and Martin Orrell

Summary

Older people admitted to wards in general hospitals often have a combination of medical, psychiatric and social problems. Managing their care requires a comprehensive assessment and a well-conducted team approach. Psychiatric problems such as dementia, delirium and depression are common in general hospital in-patients, and may lead to referral for a psychiatric liaison assessment. Patients referred for liaison assessments are more likely, therefore, to have complex or multiple needs that may be more effectively assessed using a systematic approach such as the CANE. A feasibility study was conducted using the CANE as part of a psychiatric liaison assessment. Forty-four older in-patients were assessed and were found to have an average of 4.3 unmet needs. Unmet needs were common not only for psychiatric problems but also for physical problems, particularly for mobility and continence. The results emphasised the importance of comprehensive assessment in identifying unmet needs in order to improve clinical care in general hospitals.

Introduction

The National Service Framework for Older People (Department of Health, 2001) has emphasised that clinical practice should become more person-centred to assess the individual needs of the patient and their carer. In-patient wards, both psychiatric and medical, are settings that require comprehensive assessments of the often complex and multiple needs of the older patient. The Camberwell Assessment of Need for the Elderly (Reynolds et al, 2000) can provide a good framework for the assessment of these complex needs within these settings.

Standard 2 of the National Service Framework for older people states that the NHS and social services should aim to treat older people as individuals and enable them to make choices about their own care. To facilitate this objective, it recommends a single assessment process, which is aimed at improving standards, decreasing inconsistency and bringing about uniformity in assessments across localities and services used by older people. CANE is one of the tools listed by the Department of Health for comprehensive needs assessment.

The provision of psychiatric care for older people with physical illnesses presents a number of special problems. Older people frequently present with a combination of physical illnesses, mental disorders and chronic disabilities in the context of a changing social situation. This often leads to difficulties in obtaining a comprehensive assessment and therefore problems with coordinating their care and management. There is a need for coordination of general medical, psychiatric and social services. It is generally agreed that a comprehensive approach with a high level of mutual trust and respect is needed to set up a psychiatric liaison service and a simultaneous desire on the part of the geriatric and psychiatric services to establish strong lines of communication. This objective has, however, proven to be difficult to establish (Wattis *et al*, 1981).

A large proportion of patients on acute wards in general hospitals are elderly and these patients have an extensive range of needs, often due to the high degree of comorbid medical and psychiatric problems. It has been estimated that up to 30% of patients aged over 65 years on hospital wards have dementia (Johnston *et al*, 1987; Pitt, 1991*a*). Prevalence rates for delirium are also high, ranging from 10% to 61%, depending on stage of hospitalisation and type of ward (Gustafson *et al*, 1988; Rockwood, 1989). Pitt (1991*b*) reviewed the prevalence studies of depression in medical wards, and found a range of between 5% and 40%. These figures emphasise the high prevalence of mental disorders in general hospital wards and the need for a comprehensive assessment tool in the acute hospital setting.

As early as 1959, Querido showed that team assessments were more accurate at predicting individual outcome than clinical forecasts based on patients' physical illness and, as a consequence of these findings, advocated the use of multidisciplinary assessment of needs in hospital settings. However, nearly 30 years later, Johnston *et al* (1987) investigated a group of patients on general hospital wards and found that those with a psychiatric disorder had a greater length of stay due to problems of placement. They argued that these problems had arisen because the needs of these patients had not been adequately assessed. Slaets *et al* (1997) compared 'usual care' with 'interventionary care' (comprising a multidisciplinary joint treatment approach by an old age psychiatry team) in a group of elderly medical patients. They found that those receiving interventionary care had fewer admissions to nursing homes, better overall improvement in physical functioning, and a shorter stay in hospital compared with the 'usual treatments' groups. Cole *et al* (1991) found that elderly medical and surgical patients who had had a psychiatric assessment, were more likely to show a reduction in the severity of their confusion, anxiety, depression, abnormal behaviour and functional disability, and were also discharged home more rapidly compared with controls (who did not receive a psychiatric assessment). These studies demonstrated the benefits of comprehensive assessments that involve mental health services. Indeed, Goldberg (1985) had suggested that one of the reasons for the non-detection of psychiatric problems in patients on general hospital wards is that many clinicians were not confident of their ability to make a psychiatric assessment. Lastly, the environment on general hospital wards often does not encourage patients to discuss their other problems and it has also been suggested that many patients do not provide cues, although they will describe their problems if asked. Coordination of medical care with any psychosocial care is likely to result in better outcomes and more effective use of resources (Feldman *et al*, 1987).

Older people often hold a perception that mental illness is associated with a lack of 'moral fibre' and this, in turn, leads to a natural reluctance to describe themselves as ill (Wenger, 1988). Elderly people also exhibit a tendency to minimise their health problems in order not to fit the negative stereotype of old age (Sidell, 1995). Walters *et al* (2001) used CANE to assess the needs of older people in a community-based sample and help-seeking behaviour in response to identified needs. They showed that the majority of older people and their carers do not seek help for a variety of reasons, often related to feelings of resignation and a low expectation of the services available. Problems such as incontinence were minimised and memory problems were attributed to age-related changes. They also found that sometimes the older person simply lacked information about what assistance was available or who to approach.

The CANE as an assessment tool in the ward setting

The CANE works well as a tool for use within a multidisciplinary team, where the diverse areas of a patient's needs can be assessed using the skills of the various professionals. Traditionally, hospitals have been viewed as places where decisions are made about treatment plans, as access to various agencies is relatively easier and quicker. Assessment using the CANE aims to be person-centred, and therefore includes the views of the user as well as the staff and family carers. An assessment of this type can be effectively used to match the services with the individual needs identified. The structure of the CANE is user-friendly, particularly within the context of the busy ward setting. The rating process replicates formal clinical decision-making, and also provides scope and encourages discussion about various points of view, while also addressing complex needs and risk areas. Since the CANE also involves speaking to the carers, it helps promote clear communication between carers and ward staff. The involvement of carers also helps to identify their areas of need, such as psychological distress and information that might not have been considered.

The feasibility of the CANE was investigated in a small sample of older individuals referred for a psychiatric consultation. The sample was drawn from the liaison psychiatric referrals from three different general hospitals in north-east London. One hospital was a rehabilitation unit, with 115 beds for acute/rehabilitation patients. Another hospital was a district general hospital with 454 acute beds. There were 144 acute beds for older people in the third hospital, with an extra 24 during the winter months. The average length of stay in these hospitals was 12–14 days. There were also 20 beds allocated to specialist rehabilitation wards. Patients were excluded from the study if the psychiatric assessment was incomplete due to severe physical illness, excessive drowsiness or coma.

Upon receiving a referral for a liaison psychiatry assessment from the medical wards, the nursing staff on the ward were given a scheduled appointment day and time, and were asked to inform the patient and their nearest relative or carer of this appointment. After the study was explained to patients and their carers, and formal consent was obtained, the CANE was used to assess the needs of these patients. It was completed using additional interviews with the staff (i.e. nurses, medical personnel, occupational therapists or physiotherapists) involved in the care of the patient and by reviewing the relevant medical notes. Wherever possible, carers were also interviewed for a collateral history and for their opinion about the needs of their family member or friend. Based on this information, the unmet needs of the patient were identified and fed back to the ward team along with a care plan designed to address the unmet needs. The patient's met needs identified by the CANE assessment were also relayed back to the ward team.

Forty-four elderly patients were assessed. Patients had a mean of 4.2 unmet needs. The frequencies of unmet needs are shown in Table 7.1. Common unmet needs included; memory (57%), mobility (43%), incontinence (34%), looking after the home (32%), psychological distress (32%), self-care (30%) accommodation (25%), inadvertent self-harm (22%), food (20%), and daytime activities (20%). Overall, only 31% (57 of 183) of the unmet needs were psychiatric (memory, psychological distress, psychotic symptoms, behaviour, deliberate self-harm) and many unmet needs were for social or physical problems.

All needs that had been identified and assessed by the team and were receiving appropriate interventions were regarded as met needs. The most frequent met need was for physical problems. This was to be expected, as staff on the general wards focused on identifying and treating physical illness. The most frequent psychiatric unmet needs were psychological distress and memory. In many cases, however, need for assistance with memory problems had not been identified by the ward team and tended to be minimised by the team and the patient. Thus, these results suggest that the CANE was able to identify a large number of unmet needs in these patients that had not previously been recognised by the ward staff.

It is acknowledged that the results collected thus far were from a relatively small sample. This study also did not provide information about the unmet needs of patients who did not receive a psychiatric assessment, and it was likely that we saw a highly selected group with more complex problems requiring specialist assessment. In addition, it was likely that if they had not been assessed, some of the unmet needs would have been recognised by the ward team and appropriately managed. Having said this, the study found that many of the unmet needs were not psychiatric, suggesting that they could have been picked up or dealt with by the ward team. Lack of knowledge regarding the

Table 7.1 Unmet needs of acute hospital patients at initial assessment

Section of the CANE	Frequency (%)	
1 Accommodation	11	(25)
2 Looking after the home	14	(32)
3 Food	9	(20)
4 Self-care	13	(30)
5 Caring for someone else	0	(0)
6 Daytime activities	9	(20)
7 Memory	25	(57)
8 Eyesight/hearing/communication	3	(7)
9 Mobility/falls	19	(43)
10 Continence	15	(34)
11 Physical health	7	(16)
12 Drugs	4	(9)
13 Psychotic symptoms	7	(16)
14 Psychological distress	14	(32)
15 Information	0	(0)
16 Deliberate self-harm	8	(18)
17 Inadvertant self-harm	10	(22)
18 Abuse/neglect	1	(2)
19 Behaviour	3	(7)
20 Alcohol	0	(0)
21 Company	8	(18)
22 Intimate relationships	1	(2)
23 Money/budgeting	2	(5)
24 Benefits	0	(0)

availability of other services (i.e. memory clinic, day hospital facilities and voluntary agencies) and the tendency to minimise some of the needs was highlighted by patients, carers and staff in the present study. Other factors may also have worked against the needs being identified. These include pressures on staff time, changing staff, inexperience in dealing with some needs (particularly psychological), and lack of knowledge and awareness of the local services. In addition, attitudes of both patients and staff may have been influential.

Using the data from this preliminary study, it has been demonstrated that the use of the CANE in an in-patient setting is feasible. The CANE proved useful as an assessment tool that encouraged holistic health and social care interventions directed at individual unmet needs, and also promoted user and carer involvement in the process of assessment and treatment. The CANE was also responsible for highlighting strengths and inadequacies in services offered by different in-patient wards within the hospitals, particularly for those patients with mental health problems. The tool was used to feed back to ward staff possible gaps in their services, including the need for more psychosocial interventions and staff training. It has been shown in earlier studies that an increased knowledge about psychiatric disorders and the potential benefits of treatment can result in physicians' increased confidence in dealing with the needs of their older patients (Anderson & Philpott, 1991). This study has highlighted the importance of the liaison psychiatry service and the need to offer local training about common mental health problems to medical and nursing staff working in general hospitals. A follow-up study is in progress to look at outcomes and patient needs 4 months after initial assessment.

8 The needs of long-term day hospital attenders

*Juanita Hoe, Martin Orrell, Jan Lambert
and Richard Prettyman*

Summary

The National Service Framework for Older People (NSF–OP) has identified psychiatric day hospitals as an important part of service provision (Department of Health, 2001). Nevertheless, there is considerable debate as to their effectiveness, and the *Forget-Me-Not* report (Audit Commission, 2000) noted that many people had attended for a year or more. This study aimed to investigate the needs of those older people attending day hospitals for a year or more and identify their unmet needs. The highest ratings for unmet need identified using the Camberwell Assessment of Need for the Elderly (CANE) were memory, psychological distress and daytime activities. No association was found in relation to unmet needs and length of day hospital attendance; however, the length of contact with the psychiatric services was positively associated with long-term day hospital attendance.

Introduction

Day hospitals for older people with mental health problems have attracted increased scrutiny and debate, with their purpose and design being called into question (Baker & Byrne, 1977; Arie & Jolley, 1982; Campbell *et al*, 1983; Ball, 1993; Beats *et al*, 1993: Rosenvinge, 1994; Audini *et al*, 2001). One issue has been whether long-term use of day hospital services might be important for successfully maintaining older people with mental illness in the community, or their needs could be met elsewhere, such as in day centres or other non-health settings. Time-limited assessment and treatment was defined as 'best use' of day hospitals and long-term attendance (over a year) as being 'ineffective use' and a result of inadequate alternative arrangements (Audit Commission, 1999a). The Health Advisory Service's *Standards for Mental Health Services for Older People* (Finch & Orrell, 1999) recommended that day hospitals focus on assessment and treatment and the *Forget-Me-Not* (Audit Commission, 2000) report stressed that attendance should be time limited and needs led.

The existence and organisation of day hospitals has continued to provoke much discussion, owing to a lack of clarity and consensus regarding their function and model of service delivery (Cooper, 1997). Consistency does exist, however, with day hospitals being clearly identified as providing assessment, treatment and rehabilitation. The duration of time over which this care should be has provided the greatest amount of discussion (Arie, 1974; Pearce, 1982; Vaughan, 1985; Murphy, 1991; Jolley & Arie, 1992; Fasey, 1994; Howard, 1994; Jolley, 1994). Vaughan (1985) declared that day hospitals do not function at their optimum, are under-utilised and lack focus. Murphy (1994) also argued that day hospitals are inadequate, rigid and extravagant, suggesting patients' needs could be met elsewhere and the buildings put to more effective use. In addition, long-term day hospital attendance has been found to contain a high element of social care that could possibly be met within alternative day-care settings (Kitchen *et al*, 2002). Cooper (1997) reiterated the argument that day hospitals are 'under-utilised and expensive', but acknowledged a lack of conviction that day centres could provide equally good-quality day hospital care.

Fasey (1994) argued that day hospitals offer a respite-type service and that patients' needs could be met within alternative environments, such as day centres. Day hospitals were viewed as costly, overstaffed and a waste of resources. However, Fasey's argument focused on the social aspect of day hospital services and did not reflect the therapeutic value of the setting. Instead, the review mainly focused on patients with dementia and failed to acknowledge the range of psychiatric illness encountered. In contrast, Howard (1994) argued that the long-term monitoring of clients with enduring mental health needs in the community is a particular advantage of day hospitals and allow a more rapid and effective response during times of crisis. In addition, he saw day hospitals as helping to reduce the need for patients with chronic illnesses to be admitted into institutional care and as providing ongoing rehabilitation.

More recently, the *National Service Framework for Older People* stated that mental health day hospitals should 'offer intensive assessment and treatment to people with functional disorders and dementia, including aftercare following in-patient admissions and rehabilitation and support for older people with long term mental illness' (Department of Health, 2001: 104). This statement raised the possibility that in some cases, long-term day hospital care might be appropriate.

Literature review

A review of the literature identified studies that measured the benefits of mental health (Table 8.1) and geriatric day hospitals. An early study by Gilleard (1987) assessed day hospital patients with dementia 3 and 6 months after admission. He found that levels of carer burden did not diminish over this time, but that day hospital care significantly reduced carer distress and helped maintain patients in the community, regardless of whether the presenting problems were resolved. In another study comparing day hospital and day centre attenders with dementia, Warrington & Eagles (1996) found that there were higher levels of cognitive impairment, greater apathy and more communication deficits in day hospital patients than in the day centre attenders. In both settings, there were similar levels of challenging behaviour and carer stress. A German study investigated the outcome of day clinic treatment for late-life depression, including antidepressants and therapeutic and social activities (Bramesfeld *et al*, 2001). While approximately half the sample showed no response, the other half demonstrated a significant reduction in depressive symptoms, along with improvements in cognitive performance and social functioning.

Ashaye *et al* (2003) undertook a randomised controlled trial using the CANE to assess needs and measure the efficacy of day hospital services for older people with mental health problems. The study included 112 new patients experiencing a range of mental health problems, and measured the level of met and unmet needs on admission and at 3-month follow-up. Current day hospital practice was found to be effective in assessing and meeting the needs of patients, with over two-thirds of initially unmet needs becoming met over the course of the study. Use of the CANE structured the needs assessment, identified more needs in comparison to clinical assessment and was useful in determining interventions for unmet needs. The needs of longer-term attenders were not included, as the focus was on patients newly referred to the day hospital.

An evaluation of 10 day hospitals (Kitchen *et al*, 2002) indicated a strong focus on social care within some settings. Reasons for this included inappropriate referrals, lack of multidisciplinary staff and inadequate resources. A possible reason for the high level of social care was the inconsistent

Table 8.1 Published studies demonstrating the benefits of day hospital care

Study	Design	n	Organic or functional?	Methodology and rating scales	Outcome
Bergmann *et al*, **1978**	Prospective study to examine the viability of elderly patients with dementia in the community	83	Organic	Psychiatric assessment, medical examination, social work assessment re-evaluated at 3 & 12 months	Family support is the most important factor influencing patient's viability in the community
Macdonald *et al*, **1982**	Prospective study to examine the effect of day and residential care	134	Organic	Informant interview, patient interview, CARE–OBS & Depression scale, PADL, BAS repeated at 9 months	Care setting has no effect on mortality or change in dementia scores. Improvement in dependency measures is associated with day centre care
Gilleard *et al*, **1984**	Prospective study to examine the impact of psychogeriatric day hospital care on carers	129	Organic & functional	Carer interview, GHQ, strain, social interaction and problem checklist scales, retrospective diary, repeated at 3 & 6 months	Increased length of day hospital attendance is associated with increased carer satisfaction.
Currie *et al*, **1995**	Comparison study to investigate the severity of dementia and dependency in day hospital and day centre attenders	128	Organic	CRBRS, MMSE	As characteristics of attenders are similar, day centres could undertake the work of day hospitals.
Warrington & Eagles, 1996	Comparison study of cognitively impaired day hospital and day centre attenders and their carers	60	Organic	MMSE, CAPE–BRS, HADS, RSS, carer questionnaire	Day hospitals and day centres are equally effective at relieving stress and psychiatric morbidity in carers.
Furness *et al*, **2000**	Comparison of day hospital and day centre attenders – carer profile, carer stress, unmet need	129	Organic & functional	Client and carer interview, MMSE, GDS, BDI, IQCODE, MOUSEPAD, CSI	Similarities and important differences exist between all categories of day care: – higher level of cognitive impairment in day centre attenders; – day hospital patients with dementia had more psychotic symptoms and behavioural problems; – severity of depression greater in voluntary sector day care.
Bramesfeld *et al*, **2001**	Prospective study on the outcome and effect of day clinic treatment in patients with late-life depression	44	Functional	MMSE, HADS, CIRS, Barthel ADL INDEX, IADL, social situation scale – Hochbetagter QOL – Munchner Lebensqaualitats Dimensionenliste, measured at 12 weeks, repeated at discharge, 6 & 12 month follow-up	Day clinics can meet the specific needs of patients with late-life depression, maintaining life in the community, self-care ability and social contact.
Ashaye *et al*, **2003**	Randomised contolled trial to measure the efficacy of day hopital services using a structured needs assessment	112	Organic & functional	CANE, CAPE–BRS, HoNOS	Day hospital practice was effective in assessing and meeting the needs of patients. Use of structured needs assessment identified more needs in comparison to clinical assessment and helped plan interventions.

manner in which the provision of day hospital care was organised. Furness *et al* (2000) also noted the influence and impact of local provision and the accessibility to adequate day centre care.

A systematic review of 12 day hospitals (Forster *et al*, 1999, 2001) found that geriatric day hospitals provided effective care, but had no clear advantage over other mainstream elderly medical care settings. A randomised controlled trial, which compared the outcome of geriatric day hospital care with day centre therapy, found similar reductions in functional impairment and carer strain in both settings (Burch *et al*, 1999), but those receiving day centre care were less satisfied and less compliant with treatment (Burch *et al*, 2000). The similarity and crossover of roles could also indicate a potential reduction in the need for day hospital services and the potential for day centres to provide long-term care for mental health needs (Vaughan, 1985; Murphy, 1994; Audit Commission, 2000; Department of Health, 2001).

The current political emphasis is on ensuring 'best value' from services, through the 'most economic, efficient and effective means available' (Audit Commission, 1999*b*), requiring performance frameworks to incorporate both cost and quality. Competing demand for resources means service evaluation should not only reflect clinical effectiveness, but must examine cost and efficiency, the aim being to deliver services in the most efficient and effective way (Department of Health, 1998). Early evaluations of day hospital services were undertaken within geriatric and psychiatric services. A 5-year follow-up review by Greene & Timbury (1979) described the increasing role of day hospitals as maintaining people with dementia at home prior to admission into long-term care. Less effective functions were avoiding admission, speeding up discharge or delaying long-term care. A high turnover was observed for patients with organic disorders, with higher numbers of functionally ill patients attending for longer than a year.

The cornerstone of high-quality care was considered to be 'proper assessment of need and good case management' (Department of Health Social Services Inspectorate, 1990), with services organised and outcomes measured on the basis of the needs identified. The Care Programme Approach (CPA) emphasised that systematic assessment of health and social needs is essential, but has offered little guidance on methods for measuring need or its definition (Department of Health, 2000). Effective assessment of older people with mental health needs was discussed in the *Forget-Me-Not* report (Audit Commission, 2000), which criticised the unnecessary repetition of multiple assessments by various professionals. The report advocated use of assessment tools such as the Camberwell Assessment of Need for the Elderly (Reynolds *et al*, 2000), which reflects the measurement of complexity, risk, and can be used across disciplines. Further guidance on the single assessment process (Department of Health, 2002) stressed that agencies should work together to provide person-centred, effective and coordinated assessment and care planning. Again, use of the CANE was cited as a possible tool that could generate this type of information.

The review of relevant literature and guidance regarding day hospital services and attendance criteria (Department of Health, 2001) clearly indicated the demand for a systematic and logical investigation. This study aimed to investigate characteristics and needs of older people who had attended mental health day hospitals on a long-term basis (a year or more). This definition was based on criticisms made regarding the inappropriate use of day hospitals for patients attending for longer than this period (Audit Commission, 1999*a*).

Method

The sample population was made up of day hospital patients who had attended for over a year, from three NHS mental health care day hospitals for older people. A further day hospital was used for the pilot study. Patients with concurrent admissions to the in-patient services were excluded as the continuity of their attendance was interrupted. Ethical approval was obtained from the Leicestershire Health Authority Research Ethics Committee and informed consent was sought from both patients and carers.

Day Hospital A was the base for the pilot study, which was conducted to assess the feasibility of the full study and to carry out training for the interviewers. The three day hospitals in the main study were Day Hospital B and Day Hospital C, which both offered 40 places per day, and Day Hospital D, which provided 25 places daily. All were one-storey, purpose-built facilities and able to accommodate the needs of older people with varying levels of mental and physical dependency. They were all organised around similar philosophies and models of care provision, offering multidisciplinary assessment and treatment to older people with both functional and organic mental illness. Catchment areas covered rural, urban and inner-city populations, with access to a varied but similar level of day care resources and provision within the statutory and voluntary organisations (Furness *et al*, 2000).

Instruments

Camberwell Assessment of Need for the Elderly (CANE)

The CANE was used as outlined elsewhere in this book (also see Reynolds *et al*, 2000).

Mini-Mental State Examination (MMSE)

As a high proportion of patients attending day hospitals have dementia (Corcoran *et al*, 1994. Furness *et al*, 2000), the MMSE was included as a brief test of cognitive function (Folstein *et al*, 1975).

Geriatric Depression Scale (GDS)

Depressive illness was considered the most prevalent mental health problem within older people and the most predominant functional disorder within old age psychiatric day hospitals (Corcoran *et al*, 1994). The GDS provided a screening tool for detecting depression in older people, with a predominant focus on the thought processes and emotional symptoms of depressive illness (Yesavage *et al*, 1983).

Clifton Assessment Procedures for the Elderly – Behaviour Rating Scale (CAPE–BRS)

The CAPE–BRS measured behaviour and functional ability and was used to rate levels of dependency (Pattie & Gilleard, 1979). The CAPE–BRS has been found to be a reliable and valid screening tool, which can predict service use and outcome (Little & Doherty, 1996) and has been associated with long-term attendance in day centre settings (Audit Commission, 2000).

General Health Questionnaire (GHQ–12)

The GHQ–12 gave a screening measure of distress and possible psychiatric illness (Goldberg, 1978). The instrument has been shown to have good reliability and consistency across studies, in the assessment of carer's psychological health and the impact of caring (Morris *et al*, 1988, cited in Levin, 1997).

Procedure

A survey was initially undertaken to determine the number of patients with the required length of attendance using computerised records containing patient activity and data. This was then confirmed with the individual day hospital managers and through double-checking the information records held manually. The initial survey identified 111 long-term day hospital patients. Initial requests for participation were made by post, the letters being sent out from the day hospital manager. As replies were received, individual respondents were approached and times arranged for structured interviews to take place. Where no response was received either follow-up telephone calls were made to carers, or the patient was approached directly. J.H. interviewed subjects at Day Hospital's C and D and J.L. interviewed subjects at Day Hospital B; neither was directly involved in the care of the patients they saw.

Data was obtained through the completion of relevant questionnaires and examination of medical notes. Diagnostic classifications followed the criteria outlined in DSM–IV (American Psychiatric Association, 1994). The CANE was undertaken with patients where possible and their 'named nurse'. An overall rating was then applied by the interviewer, based on the information obtained from the patient, staff member and medical notes.

Results

A total of 59 patients were available and eligible for inclusion in the study, 51 agreed to participate (85%) and eight refused (16%). Of the 51 patients, four were from Day Hospital D (8%), 20 were from Day Hospital C (39%) and 27 were from Day Hospital B (53%). The local area encompassed rural districts (28%), urban areas (47%) and inner-city areas (26%). There were 14 males (28%) and 37 females (73%), with a mean age of 75.8 (s.d.=6.0) years (range 61–89). Most subjects (49; 96%) were of White British or European descent; six did not have English as their first language (12%), although all had a good understanding of spoken English. There were 20 married patients (39%), four were single (8%), six divorced or separated (12%) and 21 were widowed (41%). Twenty-three patients lived alone (45%) and two lived in residential care homes (8%).

Fourteen subjects had a primary diagnosis of dementia (28%) and 37 had a functional illness (73%), including 23 with depression (45%). Mean scores included the Mini-Mental State Examination (MMSE) (21.6; s.d.=8.6), Geriatric Depression Scale (GDS) (5.8; s.d.=4.2) and Clifton Assessment Procedures for the Elderly (CAPE) (9.3; s.d.=7.5). Six participants with dementia were too severely

Table 8.2 Frequency of service use and details of distribution

Variable	Category	Patients	
		n	%
Level of day hospital attendance	Once weekly	24	47
	Twice weekly	18	36
	3 times weekly	5	10
	Alternate weeks	4	8
Has additional care package	Yes	39	77
	No	12	24
	Day centre attendance	17	33
	Receiving homecare	13	26
	Respite care	7	14
	CPN involvement	20	40
	Social worker involvement	12	24
Other services	District nurse	2	4
	Supported housing	1	2
	Laundry	1	2
	Mobile meals	2	4
	Support group	1	2

CPN, Community psychiatric nurse.

affected to complete the GDS. Of the 26 patients with carers (51%), six (12%) refused permission for their carers to be contacted and four carers (8%) did not return their questionnaires, hence only 16 of 26 possible GHQ scores (62%) were included. The mean GHQ score for carers was 4.4 (s.d.=3.2).

The length of contact with psychiatric services ranged from 1.5 to 62 years (mean=21.5; s.d.=18.6), though this contact was not necessarily continuous in nature. The mean length of attendance at the day hospital was 38.9 months (s.d.=22.2, range 12–99 months). Sixteen subjects had had previous admissions to hospital on three or more occasions (31%), with an equal number never having been admitted as in-patients (31%). Only five subjects had had a previous day hospital admission (9.8%). Table 8.2 shows the current services used by participants.

The level of attendance at the day hospital was calculated, with 47% attending weekly, 35% twice weekly, and 10% on 3 days per week. Four subjects (8%) had attendance arranged for alternate weeks, in preparation for discharge from the day hospital. Three-quarters of the study population received an additional package of care (77%), in conjunction with their attendance at the day hospital.

The number of met and unmet needs were recorded for each area of the CANE. Table 8.3 shows the frequency of met and unmet needs, as rated by interviewees. The mean total number of needs was 9.45. Several areas of the CANE were rated as 'no need', including caring for someone else, accommodation, benefits, deliberate self-harm, and alcohol. The most common met needs were drugs (71%), psychological distress (65%), food (63%) and physical health (61%). The most frequent unmet needs were memory (20%), psychological distress (18%) and daytime activities (14%). There was no unmet need in the following areas: caring for someone else, information, behaviour and benefits. In addition, 23 patients (45%) were rated as having no unmet needs. There were also no unmet needs for carer information, but some unmet need for carer psychological distress (10%).

Table 8.3 Frequency of patients with met and unmet need as assessed by the CANE

Variable	Met need		Unmet need	
	n	(%)	*n*	(%)
1 Accommodation	1	(2)	4	(8)
2 Looking after home	28	(55)	2	(4)
3 Food	32	(63)	2	(6)
4 Self-care	24	(48)	4	(8)
5 Caring for someone else	2	(4)	0	
6 Daytime activities	22	(43)	7	(14)
7 Memory	12	(24)	10	(20)
8 Eyesight/hearing	8	(16)	5	(10)
9 Mobility/falls	24	(47)	6	(12)
10 Continence	13	(26)	3	(6)
11 Physical health	31	(61)	5	(10)
12 Drugs	36	(71)	2	(4)
13 Psychotic symptoms	16	(31)	3	(6)
14 Psychological distress	33	(65)	9	(18)
15 Information	7	(14)	0	
16 Deliberate self-harm	4	(8)	1	(2)
17 Inadvertent self-harm	10	(20)	4	(8)
18 Abuse/neglect	8	(16)	4	(8)
19 Behaviour	7	(14)	0	
20 Alcohol	3	(6)	1	(2)
21 Company	30	(59)	3	(6)
22 Intimate relationships	13	(26)	6	(12)
23 Money	30	(59)	5	(10)
24 Benefits	1	(2)	0	
Mean total number of needs	**7.57 (s.d.=3.23) (range 3–14)**		**1.71 (s.d.=2.37) (range 0–11)**	

Table 8.4 Level of unmet need in relation to other continuous variables assessed

Variable	Unmet needs	Mean	Standard deviation	F ratio (Levene)	P	95% CI
Number of years contact	None	30.2	20.5	10.1 (.01)	<0.001	21.1–39.3
	1+	14.4	14.1			8.8–20.0
MMSE	None	25.4	4.2	8.5 (.000)	<0.05	23.5–27.3
	1+	18.8	9.9			15.0–22.5
GDS	None	4.3	3.3	5.9 (.04)	<0.05	2.8–5.8
	1+	7.2	4.6			5.2–9.2
CAPE	None	4.6	3.5	21.4 (.001)	<0.001	3.0–6.1
	1+	12.8	7.8			9.9–15.8

Predictors of unmet need

An analysis of variation (ANOVA) was used to investigate which factors were associated with having one or more (1+) unmet needs. Patients with no unmet needs (Table 8.4) had significantly longer duration of contact with psychiatric services, less cognitive impairment, less depression and lower dependency than those with one or more unmet needs. There was no relationship between the presence of unmet needs and age, level of attendance at the day hospital or GHQ score.

Table 8.5 shows that a diagnosis of dementia and having a carer are both significant predictors of unmet need. No other demographic factors or services received were associated with unmet need, although receiving an additional care package tended to be more common in those with unmet needs ($P=0.059$).

When the difference between day hospitals was compared a higher mean for unmet need was noted for Day Hospital B (2.1), compared with Day Hospital C (1.15) and Day Hospital D (1.5). This difference appeared to be related to patient characteristics and diagnosis. Day Hospital C was observed to have greater means for length of service contact (35.3 years, s.d.=18.3), age (78.6 years, s.d.=6.0) and MMSE (25.7, s.d.=3.3) scores, but lower dependency scores CAPE (7.1, s.d.=5.6), suggesting a population with more chronic functional illness than Day Hospitals B and D.

Discussion

This study found that just over half of all long-term day hospital attenders continued to have one or more unmet needs. Almost a quarter of these needs related to psychiatric problems (e.g. memory,

Table 8.5 Demographic characteristics and association with unmet need

Variable	Categories	No unmet needs		Has 1+ unmet needs		Mantel–Haenszel (FET)	P
		n	(%)	n	(%)		
Diagnostic category	Organic	1	(2)	13	(26)	0.001	0.0001
	Functional	21	(41)	16	(31)	(n/a)	
Carer	Yes	7	(14)	19	(37)	0.02	0.002
	No	15	(29)	10	(20)	(n/a)	
Additional care package	Yes	14	(28)	25	(49)	0.6	0.059
	No	8	(16)	4	(8)	(n/a)	

psychological distress). These were also the most common unmet needs found by Ashaye *et al* (2003) on admission to day hospital. A further 20% of unmet needs comprised physical problems (particularly mobility and sensory problems). This suggests that although a maximum duration of day hospital attendance of 1 year is a feasible target, many patients do have chronic and/or recurrent problems that might not be easy to address.

In the Ashaye *et al* (2003) study of new day hospital patients, the new attenders had a mean of 3.5 unmet needs and at 3-month follow-up this fell to 1.2 unmet needs. Our long-term group therefore had 0.5 more unmet needs than the Ashaye *et al* group, assessed 3 months after admission. This could be interpreted as reflecting the day hospital's ability to meet the needs of patients over a longer period of time. What is of concern is the apparent increase in the mean value for unmet needs over this time. It is possible that the high level of unmet needs in the present sample reflected the complexity of needs for those patients requiring longer-term attendance, or indicated inconsistencies in practice within various day hospital settings.

It was considered that the population of patients attending a day hospital for a long period of time were doing so because of the nature and severity of their mental health problems. As the CANE identified a high level of met need for psychological distress, this could be considered to demonstrate the effectiveness of the day hospital in meeting the specialist mental health needs of these patients. The Furness *et al* (2000) study (which used the same day hospitals as the present study) had identified higher levels of psychotic symptoms and challenging behaviour for day hospital patients in comparison to day centre attenders. In the current study, it was apparent that there was a low incidence of patients with psychotic symptoms and behavioural problems, and patients with these types of needs may not have required day hospital attendance on a long-term basis. One role of day hospitals may be supporting patients prior to admission into long-term care (Bergmann *et al*, 1978; Greene & Timbury, 1979), which might have been the case for some patients in this study.

A service had been established specifically for patients with mild-to-moderate dementia at Day Hospital B. Where there was an unmet need for memory, this was associated with a diagnosis of dementia secondary to a functional disorder, and suggests a need for widening the availability of specialist therapeutic resources, such as memory retraining and anti-dementia medication. This area of unmet need for memory was also apparent in patients who suffered from severe cognitive deterioration, and was accompanied by factors such as inadvertent self-harm and increased dependency. For these patients, the future plan of care was to move into a continuing care type setting, and one patient was placed in a nursing home just before the study was completed. Many of the patients with unmet needs were progressing towards discharge, but a factor that impeded some patients was the lack of an appropriate alternative day care setting, particularly in the area covered by Day Hospital B (Furness *et al*, 2000). On the other hand, the inner-city areas and some rural districts were well resourced, having good social services and voluntary agency day care provision.

A frequent objection to long-term day hospital care is that it mostly meets social care needs (Fasey, 1994), and this has been described as a source of frustration for day hospital staff trying to provide assessment and treatment (Kitchen *et al*, 2002). Although a social element is inherent within the therapeutic milieu provided by day hospitals, the great majority of needs for daytime activities and company were met and only one-third of patients had additional day care. However, anecdotal information was provided by staff and some patients of their refusal to attend other day care. This issue was frequently identified as a barrier to discharge, and many staff commented on the inability of day centres to meet the current needs of their patients. For some of those patients interviewed, particularly those without unmet needs, a transfer of care over to a day centre setting was indicated as the future plan of care.

The frequency of attendance at the day hospital was measured as high (twice or three times weekly) or low (once per week/fortnight), with a high level of attendance at the day hospital being associated more with unmet needs. Nevertheless, for the total duration of day hospital attendance, no meaningful association with unmet needs was identified. In contrast, the length of contact with the psychiatric services for those without unmet needs was double that of patients with unmet needs. Again, this finding demonstrates the efficacy of services in meeting the needs of patients, through providing ongoing contact and care. For those patients with functional illnesses, the length of service contact was possibly indicative of enduring mental health problems, and, indeed, higher scores for depression were associated with unmet need. However, this relationship might also suggest a degree of institutionalisation.

Interestingly, the GHQ scale undertaken with carers was noted to have greater mean scores for the group of patients with no unmet needs. This might be due to carer burden in relation to service use and the care package provided – further examination of how needs are met, and by whom, is required. This information could be obtained through the CANE assessment, but was not analysed for this investigation.

While approximately three-quarters of participants in this study had a care package in addition to day hospital attendance, most did not require complex or elaborate additional packages of care. During the study, inconsistencies were evident in the documentation within the medical and nursing notes. There was a lack of consistent use of rating scales in these notes, which were supposed to assist teams in determining diagnostic and mental health needs. However, during the study, it was noted that the named nurses had an excellent knowledge of their patients, which enabled prompt and thorough responses for each area and few areas were 'not known'. This insight was probably due to the long-standing nature of patients' attendance at the day hospital.

The main limitation of this study was that, being a cross-sectional survey, no conclusive evidence of association can be stated at this time. Clearly the day hospitals demonstrated an effective setting for meeting the needs of these patients, but it was difficult to determine which factors of day hospital care were most influential in maintaining the mental health of this patient group.

Conclusion

The results indicate a need to review the current definition for long-term attendance of 1 year or over, as it is evident that attendance is needed and continues well beyond this time for many patients. Having said this, the majority of patients with functional disorders had no unmet needs, suggesting that at least some of them could possibly be transferred to other facilities. What was also recognised was the value of day hospitals in supporting older people with mental illness and maintaining their mental well-being, through long-term attendance. It is obvious that a review of the admission and operational criteria for day hospitals should be undertaken, with a common philosophy and consistent model of care delivery agreed. A priority is also the need to clarify the criteria for defining and identifying needs, which may require a much wider debate.

The reasons why needs continue to be unmet in the long-term day hospital population requires exploration in order to identify the factors reflecting and influencing those needs. The CANE successfully identified the needs of the study group and could be of value in predicting the future needs of patients through monitoring the number of their unmet needs. Overall, the CANE was effective in identifying the needs of patients attending the day hospital on a long-term basis and determined that those needs, both met and unmet, were appropriately dealt with within the day hospital setting. This is an area that could be of considerable benefit to old age psychiatric services and should be explored further. A closer examination and comparison of the data with the Ashaye *et al* (2003) study may prove advantageous, particularly for identifying associations with unmet need. Alternatively, undertaking a longer-term prospective cohort study of day hospital attenders, that follows the pathways of care offered to patients and measures their outcome, may be of further interest and would provide answers to the questions raised within this investigation.

9 Identifying and managing the needs of older people attending psychiatric day hospitals

Olakunle Ashaye, Gill Livingston and Martin Orrell

Summary

The Care Programme Approach (CPA) was designed to coordinate the assessment and care planning of older people attending mental health services. The resultant CPA meeting includes professionals of various disciplines, carers, relatives and the patients, leading to completion of a CPA form. The Camberwell Assessment of Need for the Elderly (CANE) is a structured needs assessment instrument that was also identified as suitable for identifying the needs of older people using its comprehensive, structured and person-centred approach. Little is known about the comparison between the traditional CPA assessment and the structured CANE tool for assessing needs. We aimed to compare the profile of needs generated by these two approaches, and also to compare the suggested and completed interventions recommended by these two approaches after 3 months of day hospital attendance. All 112 new patients admitted to two day hospitals over 1 year were assessed by routine clinical methods (CPA) and using the CANE. The CANE identified more met and unmet needs in patients than the multidisciplinary team CPA assessments, particularly in the areas of unmet need for daytime activities, company, suitable information for patients and information for carers. The information generated from 50% of individual CANE assessments was fed back to keyworkers and day hospital teams (experimental condition); for the rest of the patients their CANE assessments were not disclosed and they continued with usual care (control condition). This feedback of needs identified by the CANE did not correspond to a increased number of interventions completed to meet patients needs at follow-up. It was concluded that the CANE was good at identifying met and unmet needs, and that day hospital patients may benefit from the use of standardised assessment instruments in ensuring a more comprehensive coverage of their needs.

Introduction

The National Health Service and Community Care Act 1990 required Local Authority Social Services and District Health Authorities to agree, coordinate, publish and implement joint care plans and make individual assessments of need for community care services. The care programme approach (CPA) was created to provide a standardised approach to assessment and care planning by which the Act could be realised (Audit Commission, 2000). Across England and Wales, the CPA has enabled the needs of individual patients to be identified in detail; however, the collection of this information is often unstructured and unsystematic. These CPA meetings included professionals of various disciplines, carers, relatives and patients, discussing and agreeing upon completion of a CPA form, indicating identified needs and the proposed care management plan. Over the next 2 years, the CPA is due to be complemented by the single assessment process (SAP) (Department of Health, 2001), which aims to coordinate the assessment of treatment of an individual's needs across health and social services. This SAP may involve the use of more standardised and formal needs assessment instruments, such as the CANE (Camberwell Assessment of Need for the Elderly; Reynolds *et al*, 2000), to allow structured and comprehensive assessments of individual needs.

The current practice of CPA meetings, in which multidisciplinary team members, clients and their families meet, may provide a suitable forum for needs to be discussed, and interventions planned and implemented. These needs can also be identified using a comprehensive and standardised tool for needs assessment, such as the CANE. For example, in order to meet a specific individual need, a care plan could involve collaboration between different professionals.

Day hospitals should be flexible and needs-led in approach, acting as centres for training and liaison with other professionals and carers (Rosenvinge, 1994). The process and outcome of day hospital care should be subject to audit and research. These objectives will ensure that the hospitals are sensitive to the needs of the local population and that appropriate resources are best used to meet those needs. The current scientific evidence on day hospital care still leaves the question of its effectiveness unanswered. This is likely to remain the case until randomised controlled studies of day hospital care, using standardised instruments to measure outcome, become available. Such studies need to be extended to include comparison with alternative forms of care, such as that provided by community mental health teams.

In the study reported here, the outcome in terms of identified needs using CPA was compared with needs identified using the CANE (Ashaye *et al*, 2003). In addition, the interventions carried out in routine day hospital practice were identified and compared with those suggested following the use of the CANE.

Method

All new admissions to two day hospitals for older (65 years and over) psychiatric patients over a period of 1 year were approached for interview within 2 weeks of admission. The first hospital (A) covered rural and urban populations of Essex and Hertfordshire. The second (B) was an inner-London psychiatric day hospital for older people, with a catchment area covering two London boroughs. Before beginning the study, approval from the local ethics committees was obtained. Visits were made to both hospitals to familiarise staff with the study and to develop a strategy on the best times to see new referrals. All the responsible consultants of both day hospitals were contacted, given information on the study, and their permission obtained to carry out the study on the patients under their care. Each patient was introduced to the investigator by day hospital staff and informed consent was obtained.

The CANE assessments were completed on two occasions by a psychiatrist (O.A.), first on admission and then after 3 months in the day hospital or at the time of discharge. Three months was taken as the period to reassessment because in many cases it allows sufficient time for assessment and treatment and gives enough time for the hospitals' multidisciplinary reassessment meetings following admission.

The CPA process entailed a multidisciplinary team (MDT) assessment, usually involving a nurse and a psychiatrist, and sometimes a social worker, occupational therapist, or clinical psychologist. Then a CPA meeting was held following initial assessments. This meeting involved patients, their family members and staff, and during the meeting appropriate needs and interventions were identified.

All patients were randomly placed into one of two conditions, an experimental (CANE) or control (CPA) condition. Randomisation was done by placing numbers 1 to 120 in separate envelopes. After completing each assessment and identifying the required interventions, an envelope was picked blindly. Those patients with odd numbers were allocated to the experimental group and those with even numbers were allocated to the control group. In the experimental group, the keyworkers of patients received a written summary of the results of the CANE assessment, defining areas of unmet need and identified interventions for each. They were expected to discuss this information with other members of the multidisciplinary team. A copy of the list of unmet needs and suitable interventions was also placed in patients' case notes, so that team members could have direct access to it.

In the control group, a summary of the CANE results and suitable interventions was prepared, but not fed back to the staff. They relied on the current day hospital practices of assessment to identify needs. For both the experimental and control groups, usual practice was maintained including the usual treatment and the CPA, in which multidisciplinary meetings were held to facilitate the design and review of individualised care plans. During these meetings, a CPA form was completed by the keyworker highlighting each professional's role, along with a list of identified met and unmet needs. A list of needs identified by the staff was obtained from the hospital records of the different professionals involved in patient care and CPA forms. The format of the list was the same as the 26 items listed in the CANE.

For both groups, 3 months after the initial assessments or at discharge if it occurred earlier, assessment using the CANE was completed again and the interventions undertaken were recorded.

Analysis

The independent *t*-test was used to analyse parametric data. In the case of categorical data, the marginal homogeneity test was carried out. This test is an extension of the McNemar test for binary to multinomial responses and tests changes using the χ^2 distribution.

Results

There were 112 new admissions to both hospitals over the 1-year period. They consisted of 54 patients from Day Hospital A and 58 patients from Day Hospital B. All patients admitted to the hospitals agreed to take part in the study and were assessed. The new admissions had a mean age of 76.4 (s.d.=7.1) years, and there were 72 females (64.3%) and 40 males (35.7%). Almost all patients (108; 96.4%) were living at home and the remaining four were either in residential care or hospital. In terms of ethnic origin, 107 patients (95.5%) were of White British or European descent. The rest were of either Asian (1), Black African (1) or of Caribbean descent (3). A large proportion of patients (52; 46.4%) were widowed, 39 (34.8%) were married, 13 (11.6%) were either divorced or separated and eight (7.1%) were single. Nearly half (55; 49.1%) of the patients lived alone, 41 (36.6%) lived with a spouse or partner, 10 (8.9%) lived with other relatives and six lived with others (four in long-term care and two with friends). In terms of past psychiatric history, 58 patients (49.1%) had never been admitted to a psychiatric in-patient unit, 23 (20.9%) had been admitted only once and 5 (4.5%) had been admitted 10 or more times, mostly losing count of the actual number of previous admissions.

In both hospitals, depression was the most common diagnosis (Table 9.1). However, Day Hospital A had a much higher proportion of patients with dementia. Day Hospital B, in contrast, had more frequent diagnoses of schizophrenia or alcohol-related problems. There were no significant differences

Table 9.1 Distribution of diagnoses among the patients by hospital

Diagnosis	Day Hospital A		Day Hospital B		Both hospitals	
	n	(%)	*n*	(%)	*n*	(%)
Depression	32	(55)	33	(61)	65	(58)
Dementia	24	(41)	11	(20)	35	(31)
Schizophrenia	2	(3)	6	(11)	8	(7)
Anxiety	–		1	(2)	1	(1)
Alcohol misuse	–		3	(6)	3	(3)

Table 9.2 Mean number of needs identified by CANE *v.* CPA on admission (*n*=112)

	CANE (s.d.)	CPA (s.d.)	*P*[1]
Total	8.9 (3.3)	5.6 (2.8)	<0.0001
Unmet needs	3.5 (2.0)	2.9 (1.7)	<0.0001
Met needs	5.4 (3.1)	2.8 (2.6)	<0.0001

1. *P*, probability in paired *t*-test.

between the two day hospitals in terms of the mean number of met/unmet needs identified by either the CPA or CANE.

Assessing needs

The CANE identified a significantly higher total number of unmet and met needs in patients from both day hospitals than the multidisciplinary team assessments and CPA meetings. Table 9.2 shows that the CANE identified nearly twice the number of met needs than the CPA meetings.

Table 9.3 compares individual unmet/met needs identified by the CANE and the CPA. The most frequent problems identified by both assessment strategies were for psychological distress, company,

Table 9.3 The distribution of met and unmet needs identified by CANE and CPA (*n*=112)

Needs	Met needs, *n* (%)		Unmet needs, *n* (%)		*P*[1]
	CANE	CPA	CANE	CPA	
1 Accommodation	2 (1.8)	3 (2.7)	15 (13.4)	12 (10.7)	0.38
2 Looking after the home	71 (63.4)	41 (36.6)	9 (8.0)	6 (5.4)	<0.001
3 Food	77 (68.8)	46 (41.1)	3 (2.7)	3 (2.7)	<0.001
4 Self-care	65 (58.0)	35 (31.3)	5 (4.5)	5 (4.5)	<0.001
5 Caring for someone else	5 (4.5)	1 (0.9)	0	3 (2.7)	0.56
6 Daytime activities	14 (12.5)	9 (8)	65 (58.0)	38 (33.9)	<0.001
7 Memory	20 (17.9)	12 (10.7)	40 (35.7)	47 (42)	0.43
8 Eyesight/hearing/communication	20 (17.9)	11 (9.8)	4 (3.6)	4 (3.6)	0.13
9 Mobility/falls	34 (30.4)	18 (16.1)	3 (2.7)	2 (1.8)	<0.01
10 Continence	21 (18.8)	7 (6.3)	5 (4.5)	6 (5.4)	0.04
11 Physical health	58 (51.8)	34 (30.4)	4 (3.6)	7 (6.3)	0.01
12 Medication	34 (30.4)	10 (8.9)	7 (6.3)	3 (2.7)	<0.001
13 Psychotic symptoms	14 (12.5)	11 (9.8)	12 (10.7)	17 (15.2)	0.24
14 Psychological distress	26 (23.2)	9 (8)	64 (57.1)	72 (64.3)	0.9
15 Information	3 (2.7)	1 (0.9)	30 (26.8)	4 (3.6)	<0.001
16 Deliberate self-harm	20 (17.9)	9 (8)	3 (2.7)	5 (4.5)	0.07
17 Inadvertent self-harm	17 (15.2)	1 (0.9)	4 (3.6)	6 (5.4)	0.01
18 Abuse/neglect	5 (4.5)	3 (2.7)	0	0	0.32
19 Behaviour	8 (7.1)	1 (0.9)	19 (17)	20 (17.9)	0.46
20 Alcohol	2 (1.8)	0	9 (8)	9 (8)	0.69
21 Company	6 (5.4)	2 (1.8)	58 (51.8)	43 (38.4)	<0.01
22 Intimate relationship	1 (0.9)	0	16 (14.3)	7 (6.3)	<0.01
23 Money	57 (50.9)	26 (23.2)	1 (0.9)	1 (0.9)	<0.001
24 Benefits	19 (17)	16 (14.3)	0	1 (0.9)	0.8
A Carer's need for information	0	2 (1.8)	9 (8)	0	<0.01
B Carer's psychological distress	8 (7.1)	6 (5.4)	6 (5.4)	3 (2.7)	0.14

1. *P* determined using the marginal homogeneity test.

memory and daytime activities. The CANE identified significantly more patients with unmet needs than the CPA in the areas of daytime activities, company, information for patients and intimate relationships.

Interventions

The most frequent suggested interventions following the use of the CANE were day centre referral, review of medication, introduction to suitable social groups, multidisciplinary team assessment, supportive psychotherapy, and information for patients on diagnosis and treatment. Medication review, multidisciplinary team assessment, day centre referral, supportive psychotherapy, introduction to suitable social groups, and information for carers and patients on diagnosis and treatment were the most frequent interventions completed (Table 9.4).

Chi-squared tests were used to compare the experimental and control groups across individual suggested interventions completed. The suggested intervention of housing support showed a significant difference in the proportion of suggested interventions completed ($\chi^2=7.15$, df (2), $P<0.05$), indicating a greater proportion of completed interventions in the experimental group. In the introduction to social groups, there was also a significant difference ($\chi^2=12.89$, d.f.(2), $P<0.01$), indicating a greater proportion of these suggested interventions were completed in the experimental group. For the other suggested interventions, there were no significant differences between the experimental and control groups.

Table 9.4 Frequency distribution of suggested interventions completed by feedback condition

Intervention	CANE			CPA		
	Suggested	Completed		Suggested	Completed	
	n	*n*	(%)	*n*	*n*	(%)
Day centre referral	31	21	(68)	32	15	(47)
Review of medication	29	24	(82)	27	27	(100)
Introduction to suitable social groups*	34	17	(50)	18	6	(33)
MDT assessment	20	18	(90)	22	22	(100)
Supportive psychotherapy	18	17	(94)	18	18	(100)
Information on management	16	9	(56)	10	3	(30)
Referral to clinical psychologist	9	5	(55)	6	3	(50)
Provision of information for carer	8	7	(88)	8	8	(100)
Housing support*	9	9	(100)	4	2	(50)
Provision of home care	4	3	(75)	6	3	(50)
Address alcohol-related problems	3	2	(66.7)	5	1	(20)
Liaise with GP/district nurse over physical health	5	3	(60)	3	2	(66.7)
Referral to other specialities and departments	4	1	(25)	2	1	(50)
Anger management	2	1	(50)	4	2	(50)
Marital counselling	2	2	(100)	3	3	(100)
Anxiety management	0			3	1	(33.3)
Bereavement counselling	0	0		2	1	(50)
Meals on wheels	2	1	(50)	1		0
Community psychiatric nursing visit	0	0		1	1	(100)
Respite care	2	2	(100)	1	1	(100)
Power of attorney or receivership	1	1	(100)	0	0	

*$P<0.05$ using the chi-squared test to compare the CANE and the CPA.

Table 9.5 Mean (s.d.) number of interventions suggested by the CANE and the CPA

	CANE	CPA	P^1
Number of suggested interventions	3.5 (1.7)	2.8 (1.5)	0.02
Number of completed interventions	2.3 (1.3)	1.9 (1.1)	0.07

1. P determined using the independent t-test.

In both the experimental and control groups, about two-thirds of the suggested interventions had been completed at follow-up (Table 9.5). Using the analysis of covariance to correct for differences in the suggested number of interventions, there were no significant differences in the number of completed interventions between the experimental and control groups ($F=0.028$, $P=0.86$). There were also no significant gender differences in the number of suggested or completed interventions or between those patients with a diagnosis of depression and dementia.

Day centre referral, introduction to suitable social groups, and information for patients on diagnosis and treatment were the three most frequent interventions yet to be carried out at the time of follow-up assessment. In 26 instances, reasons were given for suggested interventions not having been implemented. The most frequent reasons for failure to carry out suggested interventions were admission to hospital (9), patient refusal (8) and self-discharge (7). There was a similar distribution between the experimental and control groups. In 47 instances, there were no recorded reasons for suggested interventions not being completed. Discussions with staff revealed that in cases where reasons were not recorded, the main reasons were that the patients were not ready to proceed with suggested interventions or that there was a lack of suitable resources.

Discussion

This is the first study to compare structured needs assessment in older people with the current practice of multidisciplinary team assessments and CPA meetings in day hospitals. The main finding was that the CANE identified more unmet needs in patients than the CPA. In terms of individual needs, the CANE appeared to be better at identifying the unmet needs of daytime activities, information for patients and carers, intimate relationships and company. Furthermore, the tendency for the CPA not to record met needs led to an inaccurate assessment of needs and interventions for some individuals. It may have been that the CPA did not flag up unmet needs for daytime activities because all new patients would be attending the day hospital activities. The finding that the CPA often overlooked needs for social support and information for patients and carers, however, was more of concern. Services such as day hospitals need to be aware of these common, but often unmet, needs. In addition, many physical needs were frequently not recorded in the CPA process, suggesting that better documentation and a more structured and comprehensive assessment, such as that offered by the CANE, might be more accurate and helpful.

Depression was the most frequent diagnosis made among the patients of both day hospitals. In comparison, the 5-year review of new admissions to a day hospital for older people by Greene & Timbury (1979) found that the majority of new patients had organic disorders, with affective disorders as the most frequent functional disorder identified. The difference in this study may reflect the current emphasis of day hospitals being for treatment rather than social care, and the growth in the number of community mental health teams and dementia day care centres.

Older patients have special needs relating to cognitive decline, psychiatric problems coloured by social adversities and life events, proness to physical problems and lower utilisation and accessibility of services (Hamid *et al*, 1995). As a result, it is important to have a systematic assessment procedure and reliable documentation of the needs for older people with mental health problems. In a survey of the care needs of a population with dementia, Gordon *et al* (1997) identified that the most common needs were assistance with mobility (48%), personal care (70%), domestic tasks (75%) and behaviour (57%). All these needs were identified as among the 10 most frequent needs using the CANE in this study. Among carers, Gordon *et al* (1997) also noted that 23% felt they were not coping, 47% felt they had practical problems caring and 51% found care upsetting. The results in this study involving new day hospital attenders revealed much lower levels of carer distress (12%). However, carers still played a major role in meeting needs in this study, especially in the areas of food, self-care, looking after the home, finances, mobility and sensory impairment.

Kay (1989), in a review of the literature, identified musculoskeletal disease as the most common physical cause of dependency in older people. Dependency, which is the inability to perform self-care activities of daily living without the regular help of another person, could be a consequence of both physical and psychological disorders. In this study, the CANE identified needs resulting from physical health problems, cognitive impairment and psychological distress as among the most frequent needs in new day hospital patients.

Many of the unmet needs in this study reflected the importance of social issues in the care of older people. As a result, some of the most frequent interventions suggested were social in nature, such as day centre referral, introduction to suitable social groups, supportive psychotherapy and psychology referral. Depression is common in older people (Copeland *et al*, 1987) and it is important that services are also geared towards meeting their social needs. Day hospital activities such as support, individual work and group work can play a significant role in meeting the needs of those with depression.

Other interventions suggested included medication review and multidisciplinary team assessments, which were also core needs observed by Hamid (1997) in homeless, older men living in hostels. Multidisciplinary day hospitals with regular review meetings are well equipped to carry out these functions. A review of the interventions generated in this study using the CANE indicated that day hospitals can address the range of social, psychological, physical and medication needs of their patients.

In this study, being in the experimental group, which included a detailed list of unmet needs and interventions being both given to staff and placed in the case notes, did not result in a higher rate of suggested interventions being completed. We also found that both the experimental and control groups had around two-thirds of their presenting unmet needs met at follow-up (Ashaye *et al*, 2003). For two of the interventions, housing support and introduction to suitable social groups, the proportion of suggested interventions completed was greater in the experimental group. This may have made a difference in the outcome of the need for company, with a lower proportion of patients reporting an unmet need at follow-up in the experimental group.

Looking at the list of interventions, many patients required agencies or services external to those available within the day hospitals. Staff suggested that inability to meet all needs identified at initial assessment could be due to the lack of resources in the community to carry out some of the suggested interventions, and the follow-up assessment period being too short for all interventions to be implemented.

A limitation that could have compounded outcome was the fact that although key workers were given feedback on CANE assessments in the experimental group, actual use of this feedback could not be verified other than by verbal assurances of the staff involved. In addition, staff were exposed to the systematic approach adopted by CANE needs evaluation and the proposed interventions during the course of this study. This information and exposure may have resulted in contamination between the experimental and control groups due to the staff indirectly being trained to have a more comprehensive approach to needs assessment and case planning.

This study was carried out with 3 months' follow-up of patients from two different day hospitals in both experimental and control conditions. Possibilities for further research could include a longer period of follow-up to observe the long-term impact on outcome of day hospitals care. Potential contamination of staff exposed to the use of structured needs assessment was highlighted as a limitation of this study. To reduce the risk of such contamination, a multicentre study should be undertaken, in which several day hospitals are randomly allocated to the experimental and control groups rather than the practice used in the current study of randomising individual patients from the same day hospital into the two groups.

This study found that the CANE was superior to CPA in identifying unmet needs. However, this structured assessment of needs and feedback did not seem to make a difference to individual outcome in terms of unmet needs addressed or interventions implemented at 3 months' follow-up. In the UK, the introduction of the single assessment process (Department of Health, 2001) should encourage services to use tools like the CANE, which can both comprehensively assess need and assist in care planning.

10 Using the CANE for service evaluation: the needs of people with younger-onset dementia

Bob Hammond, Martin Walter and Martin Orrell

Summary

Younger adults with dementia often miss out on the services they need because dementia services are aimed at an older, frailer population and mental health services for younger adults are not generally suitable for the needs of people with dementia. With the formation of a large mental health National Health Service (NHS) Trust, there was an identified need to review and evaluate services for younger people with dementia. The service included mapping the current service provision, identifying centres of good practice, and assessing the needs of people with younger-onset dementia and their carers.

Many people with younger-onset dementia had unmet needs, particularly for mobility, psychological distress and day care, which needed to be flexible, stimulating and active according to the individual's abilities. Carers often needed help with psychological distress and had different information needs to older carers. In addition, services were not well coordinated and interprofessional working needed to improve. The results suggested that a specialist, peripatetic and interdisciplinary service was required. This would include an information and advice service, and staff training.

Introduction

Younger-onset dementia remains rare; Harvey (1998) indicated that in the age range 30–64 years, there was a prevalence of 67.2 cases per 100 000 population (including those with comorbid learning disability and dementia). The comparative rarity of the disorder has often meant that specialist services are few and far between. This is unfortunate, since people with younger-onset dementia often have complex needs that cannot be easily met by standard services.

Lloyd (1993) identified that carers will often reject services they feel are inappropriate to the needs of the individual, which can be seen in the frequent rejection, from people caring for a younger person with dementia, of services and facilities designed for older people. Butterworth (1993) showed that the mixing of younger people with dementia with older people often caused distress for both groups. At the same time, there has been an acknowledgement of the expertise available in older peoples' services in recognising and diagnosing dementia, and in delivering appropriate advice and information to individuals (Furst & Sperlinger, 1992; Husband & Shah, 1999). O'Donovan (1999) concluded that services need to be more age-appropriate, having identified that younger people would benefit from a more 'socially active club-like' approach, providing activities related to their own hobbies.

There can be significant difficulty in obtaining a diagnosis for a younger person with dementia (Furst & Sperlinger, 1992; Lloyd, 1993), and Luscombe *et al* (1998) found that diagnosis took an average of 3.4 years to reach, after having consulted, on average, 2.8 professionals. Luscombe *et al* (1998) also found that 59% of working carers had to reduce their working hours or stop working following diagnosis, while 89% faced financial problems. Penfold (1998) emphasised the issues of changing employment and found that not enough detail was paid to the financial needs of carers. In a comparative study of carers of younger and older people with dementia, carer burden was found to be significantly higher in the younger group (Freyne *et al*, 1999).

Owing to the unique nature of issues and problems caused by dementia in the younger person, the plight of these individuals may be overlooked. With the recognition of large numbers of people in the Liverpool area with younger-onset dementia, a charter was produced by a group of carers who recognised a lack of support and services for this group. This work was reproduced in the booklet *The Younger Person with Dementia* (Alzheimer's Disease Society, 1993). The charter asked for full informed medical assessment, recognition of the need for specialist services, access to services on at least a sub-regional basis, access to welfare benefits, retrospective reinstatement of rights and benefits and appropriate training, and information in order to provide adequate services to this group of patients.

Our aim in this investigation was to review and map current services that existed in four London boroughs and to make recommendations concerning services available for people with young onset dementia. The hypothesis was that the needs of the younger person with dementia (under the age of 65) and their carer were not being met by current services in the area. The service review had five components:

1. A review of literature to identify needs of people with younger-onset dementia, and descriptions and evaluations of services.
2. An inspection of existing services in other areas to identify good practice.
3. An interview with managers in the new trust to map current service provision for younger people with dementia.
4. An assessment of needs of people with younger-onset dementia.
5. A survey of carers' needs.

Method

The amalgamation of three existing NHS trusts to form the North East London Mental Health Trust provided an opportunity to review services for younger people with dementia across the area. Issues included equity of service provision, quality of services and ability of the services to meet the needs of the client group. The study employed a questionnaire, designed particularly for the study, to interview service managers, the Camberwell Assessment of Need for the Elderly (CANE) to establish whether needs were being met in the client group and a carer's questionnaire from the Audit Commission 'Forget-me-not' report (2000) to identify barriers and other difficulties within the service.

Assessing good practice

Three organisations were identified from the database of the Alzheimer's Society (2000), and one from a circular sent to the project manager, advertising a new service. All four offered a specialist approach for the younger person with dementia. Between them they offered assessment, day care, residential care, respite and continuing care, and they used a mix of health service, voluntary sector and private sector provision. The four organisations studied were the Peaceful Place, Counselling and Diagnosis in Dementia, Maple Lodge and the Jasmine Centre.

The Peaceful Place

This was a day centre operating across three sites in the Southend area. The service was particularly aimed at the more active person with dementia, and provided activities such as table tennis, snooker, arts and crafts. A minibus was also part of the service, used to pick up the clients and for trips out.

Counselling and Diagnosis in Dementia (CANDID)

CANDID was a counselling, diagnosis and information service, based at the National Hospital for Neurology and Neurosurgery, Queens Square, in London. There were 2000 people on the CANDID database, the majority of whom were under the age of 65. One of its main roles was to support people who attended the specialist dementia clinic at Queens Square, in leading up to and being given a diagnosis.

Maple Lodge

Maple Lodge nursing home offered specialist nursing care for people with younger-onset dementia. This was a new service, based in St Neots in Cambridgeshire. When visited there were no clients with younger-onset dementia; however, the manager outlined the philosophy and plans for the service, working towards active care plans for this client group.

The Jasmine Centre

This service, based in Westgate in Kent, offered specific residential care and some day care for younger people with dementia. Flexibility was offered with different groups cared for in the part of the service that best met their needs, as there were different units in the building. The clients were allowed to personalise their surroundings with personal effects and the building was largely secured by keypad doors.

Service evaluation

Thirteen interviews were conducted with managers of specialist services within the larger trust area. These were identified through contacts made with nursing management staff across the trust. Services provided were a mixture of day services, assessment and long-term care. The interview included collecting information on the numbers of younger people with dementia, present costs of services, types of services offered and how the service manager thought services could develop to better meet the needs of this group.

The CANE was used to assess the needs of people with younger-onset dementia. Participants were identified through service managers, who identified people from their case loads. The local consultant psychiatrists were also asked identify suitable clients from their case loads. These clients were invited to participate via written invitation sent to their main carer. The main professional who was involved in their care was used to establish initial contact with individuals. The project manager (B.H.) followed up these initial contacts with a telephone call, to ascertain whether the carer was willing to participate. The process involved speaking to carers and professionals involved with the person, and on one occasion to the person with dementia themselves. After gathering all relevant information, the researcher made an overall assessment as to whether or not the needs of the person with dementia were being met.

A questionnaire adapted from the national study by the Audit Commission (2000) was also administered to carers. This questionnaire was designed to establish whether the carer had experienced any barriers to the provision of services for themselves or for the younger person with dementia. This questionnaire covered the services received by the client group and other pertinent issues such as possible delays between onset and diagnosis, and whether carers had to change their work commitments as a result of their caring role.

Results

Thirty-five people with younger-onset dementia were identified and contacted. However, three declined to be interviewed, giving a response rate of 91%. The age of the group ranged from 53 to 65 years, with a mean age of 59.9 years. Fifteen of the group were male and 17 female. Ten of the group resided in long-term care facilities. Table 10.1 shows the number of met and unmet needs as measured by the CANE.

Many participants (27; 84%) had unmet needs for daytime activities; some were left for long periods during the day (when the carer was frequently working), many were bored, or the activities they participated in needed to be more vigorous, and more in line with the individual's own hobbies and interests. There were also a large number of unmet needs for company (23, 72%), including

Table 10.1 Comparison of needs that were met and unmet (total *n*=32)

	No need		Total needs identified		Unmet needs		Total needs unmet
	n	(%)	*n*	(%)	*n*	(%)	%
Accommodation	16	(50)	16	(50)	10	(31)	62.5
Looking after the home	3	(9)	29	(91)	7	(22)	24.1
Food	1	(3)	31	(97)	8	(25)	25.8
Self-care	4	(13)	28	(88)	5	(16)	17.9
Caring for someone else	32	(100)	0	(0)	0	(0)	0
Daytime activities	0	(0)	32	(100)	27	(85)	84.4
Memory	0	(0)	32	(100)	25	(79)	78.1
Eyesight/hearing/communication	27	(84)	5	(16)	1	(3)	20
Mobility/ falls	4	(13)	28	(88)	14	(44)	50
Continence	14	(44)	18	(57)	8	(25)	44.4
Physical health	22	(69)	10	(31)	7	(22)	70
Drugs	3	(9)	29	(91)	8	(25)	27.6
Psychotic symptoms	18	(56)	14	(44)	6	(19)	42.9
Psychological distress	8	(25)	24	(75)	15	(47)	62.5
Information	25	(78)	7	(22)	4	(13)	57.1
Deliberate self-harm	27	(84)	5	(16)	1	(3)	20
Inadvertent self-harm	7	(22)	25	(78)	7	(22)	28
Abuse/neglect	15	(47)	17	(53)	5	(16)	29.4
Behaviour	20	(63)	12	(38)	3	(9)	25
Alcohol	29	(91)	3	(9)	1	(3)	33.3
Company	1	(3)	31	(97)	23	(72)	74.2
Intimate relationships	26	(81)	6	(19)	5	(16)	83.3
Money/budgeting	0	(0)	32	(100)	3	(9)	9.4
Benefits	18	(56)	14	(44)	6	(19)	42.9
A Carer's need for information	16	(50)	16	(50)	14	(44)	87.5
B Carer's psychological distress	5	(16)	27	(85)	22	(69)	81.5

people whose carer worked for long periods of time and those with dementia either lacked company or needed more varied company. In all, 25 (78%) had unmet needs for memory, including more stimulation and occupation-type activities. Some people appeared appropriate for anti-dementia drugs but were not being prescribed them. Many participants identified a need regarding mobility, including 14 (44%) whose need was unmet. Being unable to use public transport was a major issue, considering the long distances to be travelled across the larger trust. Twenty-four individuals (75%) had psychological distress needs, such as depression or significant distress and for 15 (47%) this need was unmet. Some carers said they had identified that the person they were caring for had an element of depression, but felt they were not always taken seriously when they attempted to seek help. In terms of intimate relationships, although only six participants (19%) identified this as a need, five of these rated the need as unmet (16%). Carers described situations in which the dementia had caused major problems within their relationship, for which they received little assistance.

Table 10.2 shows the met and unmet needs of those people with dementia in long-term care. Again, memory and daytime activities were common unmet needs, but it is interesting to note that for 40% their accommodation was considered inappropriate for their needs, indicating the high level of need for specialist long-term facilities for people with young-onset dementia.

Table 10.2 Met and unmet needs of people in long-term care (total $n=10$)

	No need		Total needs identified		Unmet needs		Total needs unmet
	n	(%)	*n*	(%)	*n*	(%)	%
Accommodation	0	(0)	10	(100)	4	(40)	40
Looking after the home	0	(0)	10	(100)	0	(0)	0
Food	0	(0)	10	(100)	2	(20)	20
Self-care	0	(0)	10	(100)	1	(10)	10
Caring for someone else	10	(100)	0	(0)	0	(0)	0
Daytime activities	0	(0)	10	(100)	8	(80)	80
Memory	0	(0)	10	(100)	7	(70)	70
Eyesight/hearing/communication	10	(100)	0	(0)	0	(0)	0
Mobility/falls	0	(0)	10	(100)	3	(30)	30
Continence	1	(10)	9	(90)	1	(10)	11
Physical health	6	(60)	4	(40)	2	(20)	50
Drugs	1	(10)	9	(90)	0	(0)	0
Psychotic symptoms	6	(60)	4	(40)	2	(20)	50
Psychological distress	2	(20)	8	(80)	4	(40)	50
Information	9	(90)	1	(10)	0	(0)	0
Deliberate self-harm	8	(80)	2	(20)	0	(0)	0
Inadvertent self-harm	1	(10)	9	(90)	0	(0)	0
Abuse/neglect	3	(30)	7	(70)	1	(10)	14
Behaviour	5	(50)	5	(50)	0	(0)	0
Alcohol	9	(90)	1	(10)	0	(0)	0
Company	0	(0)	10	(100)	4	(40)	40
Intimate relationships	7	(70)	3	(30)	3	(30)	100
Money/budgeting	0	(0)	10	(100)	0	(0)	0
Benefits	7	(70)	3	(30)	2	(20)	67
A Carer's need for information	7	(70)	3	(30)	2	(20)	67
B Carer's psychological distress	4	(40)	6	(60)	3	(30)	50

Carers' needs

Sixteen carers (50%) identified information as a need, and 14 of these carers (44%) said this need was presently unmet. Carers identified issues with regard to the legal and financial aspects of their support for the person with dementia. Twenty-seven carers (84%) identified psychological difficulties in caring, including 22 (69%) whose needs were unmet. Most of the carers found looking after someone to be difficult, with many considering themselves to be very stressed, and some were on antidepressants.

A carers' questionnaire, the results of which are detailed in Table 10.3, was administered at the same time as the CANE. A total of 33 carers were able to complete this: 31 of the 32 in the CANE study, along with a further 2 whose charges had recently passed the age of 65 (the latter had been recognised by the managers of services and contacted by post). All carers identified that the person they were caring for was forgetful and confused, yet two carers said they had not been told the diagnosis. Of the 31 that had been given a diagnosis, 52% had been told Alzheimer's disease and 23% were simply told 'dementia'. The onset of dementia was estimated to be an average of 6.6 years ago (range 1–17 years), and the mean time since diagnosis was 4.2 years (range 0–12 years). This leaves a gap of 2.4 years on average between the onset as recognised by the carer and the point when a diagnosis was made. Nearly two-thirds (61%) of carers said they had not been told how problems were likely to develop. Just over a third (39%) of carers did not know about Enduring Power of Attorney, and

Table 10.3 Carer's views on services and information provision (total *n*=33)

Question	Yes	
	n	%
Is your relative or friend forgetful or confused?	33	100
Have you been told what is wrong with your relative or friend?	31	94
Were you told how problems were likely to develop?	13	39
Do you live with your relative or friend?	20	61
When your relative or friend first become forgetful were they examined by a doctor?	18	55
Has a doctor or nurse checked their condition since then?	30	91
Has anyone asked if you need any help?	18	55
Have you been told what help is available?	21	64
Have you been told how to get help?	22	67
Have you been told whether any help would have to be paid for?	16	49
Were you told about any allowances or benefits that could be claimed?	19	58
Have you been introduced to someone you can contact when you have a worry or problem?	22	67
Have you been told how to complain or put forward any views about the help you get?	6	18
Have you ever heard about 'enduring power of attorney'?	20	61
Has anyone ever formally assessed your needs as a carer?	8	24
Do you know how to obtain a place in a care home?	11	33
Can you get help to have a break from caring?	17	52

82% were not aware of how to complain about or comment on services they were receiving. Many carers (76%) said they had not had their own needs assessed as a carer. Four carers (12%) had had to reduce working hours and nine (27%) had had to give up work due to their caring commitments.

Discussion

Younger-onset dementia remains rare, yet using Harvey's (1998) prevalence rate of 67.2 cases per 100 000, it was estimated that in the area covered by this study there would be 208 people with the disease. However, this study found far fewer people and the number of people found for inclusion was much lower than the estimates provided by managers of local services.

The main issues identified by the managers, which would enable them to take their services forward, revolved around networking with other agencies and the need to set up a specialist service, aimed at providing appropriate day care and respite. Indeed, the issue of a specific service was also raised by carers, especially for day care and respite. Both groups recognised that younger people with dementia have special and complex needs, and that sharing with other groups did not always meet these needs. Day services needed to be different from services offered to older people, and in particular they needed to offer more strenuous activities, such as swimming and trips out, and activities should be matched to people's interests. Some element of organisation and support was also required to enable people with dementia to carry out activities they wanted to do, including those connected to their hobbies.

Findings from the present investigation were similar to those found by Luscombe et al (1998), in that there was a consistent delay in receiving a diagnosis for younger people with dementia. A specialist service could raise the profile of younger people with dementia within the area and encourage earlier diagnosis, which might then enable access to appropriate services. The CANE and the carer's questionnaire also identified needs for carers, which included legal and financial advice.

Conclusion

The main recommendation from this study was that a comprehensive specialist service is needed for younger people with dementia. This service needed to draw on existing partnerships with health, social services and the voluntary sector. The service should also include long-term care, respite care, day care, assessment, outreach work, advice, information and carer support. A number of options were considered, taking into account current services and potential costs.

There were a mixture of teams that presently offered a service across the trust investigated. The proposal would be for these teams to identify an individual to take a lead within that team for younger clients. These keyworkers would then form a virtual team, including a consultant psychiatrist, community psychiatric nurses, social services (senior practitioner), occupational therapist, and a clinical psychologist with linked staff from each borough within the trust. A manager would be required, and other therapists such as art, music, and speech and language therapists would also be beneficial.

A number of current services in the area had people with younger-onset dementia as their main focus: a specialist community psychiatric nurse, an in-patient ward and a day club. It was recommended that these services be an integral part of the peripatetic team. Staff within them would meet as a team and hold development sessions, including training and support. The meetings would naturally facilitate networking activity, and team members could act as a resource for their own professional teams on any issues regarding younger people with dementia.

This study showed that the day care activities were not meeting the needs of younger people with dementia and that a different approach needed to be considered. A group of individuals needed to be built up to provide this type of service, both in formal settings associated with a particular venue and, as it was also important for the service to be mobile and flexible, in visits to clients' homes, nursing homes and hospital wards. The services needed to be open to providing a wide range of activities for people with dementia.

Advice and information services have traditionally been available through the voluntary sector, and groups such as Age Concern and the Alzheimer's Society had been identified as providing good quality advice and information. The Alzheimer's Society also has a national worker specifically for this group and their potential contribution needed to be considered. Alternatively a member of staff from each area could specialise in young people with dementia or someone could be employed to provide an information service across the whole trust. The study showed that better information needed to be provided for legal and financial issues, and specific courses for carers of younger people with dementia should be considered a priority.

The lack of services to help sustain this group in the community had meant that there had often been a need to prematurely move clients into long-term care. Existing services should be reviewed to establish whether they could better meet the needs of this group and help them to remain in the community. Many of the present residents of the specialist in-patient ward had been there for many years and were suffering from advanced dementia. Some of these residents could be discharged to more appropriate settings, such as specialist nursing homes. The role of the ward could then be reviewed, perhaps to provide brief in-patient assessment, respite admissions and stimulating daytime activities for younger people with dementia.

We found that although the numbers of younger people with dementia were small, they had unmet needs – particularly in the areas of daytime activities, memory and support for carers. Problems with mobility, accommodation and psychological distress were also common. This review of services indicated that a better integrated specialist service was required. Though a longer-term solution requires significant funding, some progress could be made with a review of current service provision and a re-engineering of existing resources.

11 CANE instruction manual

Geraldine Hancock and Martin Orrell

Introduction

The Camberwell Assessment of Need for the Elderly (CANE) is a comprehensive needs assessment tool suitable for use in a variety of settings. The CANE has been successfully used for older people in primary care, sheltered accommodation, residential care homes, nursing homes and in mental health services for older people, including acute and long-term day hospital attendees. Lastly, CANE has been used to evaluate the complex needs of medical in-patients with psychiatric problems. Research into the use of the CANE in these settings has shown that an elderly person's needs are not automatically met once they have been assessed by a health or social care professional. In addition, older people, for a number of reasons, do not necessarily seek assistance when their needs are unmet (Walters et al, 2001). The CANE is a comprehensive and sensitive needs assessment instrument that can highlight these multiple and changing needs of the elderly person (see Reynolds & Orrell, 2001).

Background

The Camberwell Assessment of Need for the Elderly was developed from the original Camberwell Assessment of Need (CAN; Phelan et al, 1995). The CAN is a psychometric instrument designed to assess needs in individuals with long-term mental health needs. This instrument comprises 22 areas of need and gathers relevant information about these areas from the patient him/herself, carers and staff. The CAN was designed to provide detailed information about an individual's met and unmet needs, to provide data for service provision and to develop individual care plans. The CAN has been shown to have good reliability and validity, and is easy to use in a range of professional disciplines (Phelan et al, 1995). It also identifies needs as met or unmet (Slade et al, 1998). Although the CANE had a similar rationale and many similar items as the CAN, it was further developed to reflect the specialist needs of the elderly population.

This alteration of the CAN was undertaken by Reynolds et al (2000), who recognised that the older population with mental disorders was difficult to assess using previous methods, and that no adequate instrument was available to fully assess their particular needs. Using the CAN as a template, the research team completed an extensive development process to meet the special needs of the elderly population. This process entailed running focus groups involving service users, carers and various health care professionals. A modified Delphi process was then used to refine the specific items on the instrument. This process involved sending questionnaires to various elderly health care specialists, asking them to rate and comment on the instrument. This Delphi process was then further discussed and refined at a consensus conference involving various elderly care voluntary organisations and relevant professionals.

The final draft was called the CANE, and its reliability and validity were subsequently established (Reynolds et al, 2000). Test–retest and interrater reliability information was collected using data from

40 service users, 53 staff members and 18 carers in the London area. Reliability was reported to be very high with an average of $r=0.85$ for interrater staff ratings. Correlations of total number of needs identified by staff was also adequate (0.99 and 0.93 for interrater and test–retest respectively). Validity was assessed in various ways, such as face validity during the Delphi process.

Translations and cultural sensitivity

The CANE has been translated into the following languages for use in research and clinical settings: Swedish, Welsh, German, Hindi, Italian, French, Spanish, Portuguese, Turkish, Norwegian and Dutch. The areas of need assessed by the CANE, and the specific prompts provided in each section, have been translated and used in these countries without substantial alteration from the English version. The ease with which these translations were produced indicates that the CANE is an appropriate instrument for measuring needs in different cultures, owing to the fact that it uses local knowledge, including the administrator's knowledge and experience of the culture of those individuals they are assessing. It is noted, however, that scientific investigation of the reliability and validity of the CANE in these countries has only been reported in Spain (Mateos *et al*, Chapter 3) and Germany (Dech & Machleidt, Chapter 4). Please contact the authors for further information concerning these translations and use of the CANE in countries outside the UK.

Training

Although the CANE is not based on any specific diagnostic framework, the instrument is intended to form the basis of a complete clinical assessment of need. Therefore, the rater must have a detailed knowledge of the elderly in terms of their physical health, mental health and psychosocial needs. The rater will generally be a professional able to make assessments of need in the elderly (i.e. a social worker, medical doctor, psychiatrist, clinical psychologist, occupational therapist or psychiatric nurse). The ideology underpinning the CANE is complex as the rating process replicates formal clinical decision-making, therefore specific training in these concepts is useful. In addition, the rater is encouraged to undergo brief training (approximately 4–5 assessments) to ensure the reliability of individual ratings. Where several staff in a service are using the CANE it is a good idea for them to have opportunities to meet and discuss complex cases and how to rate their needs.

Description

The CANE consists of 24 sections, plus 2 sections aimed at assessing carer needs:

1. Accommodation
2. Looking after the home
3. Food
4. Self-care
5. Caring for someone else
6. Daytime activities
7. Memory
8. Eyesight/hearing/communication
9. Mobility/falls
10. Continence
11. Physical health
12. Drugs

13. Psychotic symptoms
14. Psychological distress
15. Information
16. Deliberate self-harm
17. Inadvertent self-harm
18. Abuse/neglect
19. Behaviour
20. Alcohol
21. Company
22. Intimate relationships
23. Money/budgeting
24. Benefits
A. Carer's need for information
B. Carer's psychological distress

Information is recorded separately via interviews with the carer, staff and patient over all of these 26 areas. Each item is rated based on information gathered about the user during the 2 months prior to the interview. The CANE takes approximately 10–30 minutes, with each interviewee (i.e. formal carers, staff and patients), depending on the number and complexity of needs identified.

Definitions

Need: A need is a situation in which there is a significant problem, for which there is an appropriate intervention that could potentially help or alleviate the problem. See Section 1 below for definitions of met need and unmet need.

Staff: A formal carer or keyworker who is familiar with the individual's clinical condition. More than one staff member can be interviewed to get a consensus on these ratings.

Carer: An individual who usually provides care on at least a weekly basis. This person is usually not paid for their care work, but may be paid by the user or the user's family (e.g. a family member, a neighbour or a friend).

Rater: The mental health professional conducting the assessment. The clinician should use all available information to rate areas on the CANE.

Informal services: Family, friends or neighbours who give assistance, but are usually not paid for their services. This section could include privately funded unskilled assistance, such as a neighbour helping with the gardening.

Formal services: These services are provided by health care, social care or other agencies and may include physiotherapy, home care or personal care. Usual formal supports for the elderly include paid carers, long-term wards, formal respite, day care centres, hospitals, residential homes and day hospitals. Other formal supports can include voluntary agencies, such as organised church groups, Age Concern or befrienders.

Administration

General instructions

Inform the interviewee that you would like to ask them questions about certain areas of the user's life that the user may have some difficulty with. Ask staff to review and bring any nursing or care notes with them to the interview in order to prompt their memory of needs and assistance given. Show the interviewee to a quiet, private and comfortable room. Start the interview by introducing yourself, explaining how long the interview will take, the purpose of collecting the information (e.g. in order to construct an individualised care plan based on their needs) and who will view the information they provide. Ask the interviewee if they have any specific queries or concerns before you begin. Begin by collecting a few details about the user, or you can start by summarising what you already know. Continue to complete any demographic information required in the first section.

Outline the interview procedure in general: 'I'm going to ask you about certain areas of your life that you might be having problems with. Then I'm going to ask you whether you are receiving any help from your friends or family with the problem, or from local services.' This explanation will provide some structure for the assessment. Next outline the first section: 'We will begin by looking at your home. Where are you living at the moment?' Continue along this line of questioning until all relevant information has been gathered. There is no set structure to the administration of the CANE, you may enquire about problem areas in any order, and you may revisit areas after collecting further information.

Section 1

This section aims to assess whether there is currently a need in the specific area. A need is defined as a problem with a potential remedy or intervention (see definitions above). Use the prompts provided on the record form to establish the user's current status with regard to the need area. Judgement of rating in this section should be based on normal clinical practice. The CANE is intended to be a framework for assessment, grounded in good professional practise and expertise. Although Section 1 in each problem area is the main section of interest to CANE administrators, it often cannot be rated until adequate information has been collected about the area. Indeed, some administrators have found it easier to rate Section 1 once information has been collected from the other Sections 2–5. When adequate information has been gathered, the rater should clearly be able to make a clinical judgement as to whether the area is a met need, an unmet need or is not a need for the person. Confusion with ratings can be avoided by not directly asking a closed question about whether there is a problem in a certain area, for example: 'Do you have any problems with the food here?' because the person can answer 'No'. This response may then be mistaken as a 'no need', whereas in fact it is a 'met need' because all food is provided by someone else.

No need: Score 0 there if there is no need in the area and go on to the next need area. In this situation, the user is coping well independently and does not need any further assistance. For example, the user has reported that they are successfully administering their own medication and do not have any problematic side-effects. Or the staff member reports that the user appeared to be comfortable in his/her home environment, and that no alterations to the building are needed or planned.

Met need: Score 1. A need is met when there is a moderate or serious problem that is receiving an intervention, which is appropriate and potentially of benefit. This category is also used for problems that would normally not be of clinical significance and would not require a specific intervention. For example, the user is receiving an assessment for poor eyesight, or a district nurse is overseeing the administration of medications each day.

Unmet need: Score 2 if the need is currently unmet. An unmet need is a significant problem requiring intervention or assessment, which is currently receiving no assistance or the wrong kind of help. The problem is unmet if it is regarded to be serious despite any help received. For example, a staff member reported that the user was incontinent of a large amount of urine every night, despite toileting twice during the night and the use of pads. Or a carer reported that the user has become very hard of hearing and has not received an assessment or suitable hearing aid.

Unknown: Score 9 if the person does not know about the nature of the problem or about the assistance the person receives, and go on to the next page/topic area. If the respondent gives a 1- or 2-point answer for Section 1 in any area, administer Sections 2–4. If the respondent gives a 0 or 9-point answer for Section 1, proceed to the next topic area.

If there is doubt as to whether the problem is mild, moderate or serious, consider whether the problem would normally warrant a clinical intervention. A mild problem probably would not need a clinical intervention, a moderate problem would and a serious problem would normally require immediate intervention. For example, occasional forgetfulness would not normally require a clinical intervention and would be considered a minor problem (no need). Frequent incontinence that disrupts the individual's lifestyle would be considered a moderate problem requiring a clinical intervention (unmet need). Imminent risk of neglect or abuse of an elderly person living in the community with an abusive sibling would be considered serious and would normally lead to an urgent intervention (unmet need).

Section 2

This section asks about assistance from informal sources during the past month. Informal sources are defined above to include family, friends or neighbours. Use the examples on the assessment form to prompt the interviewee. Score 1 when assistance is given very occasionally or is minimal. Score 2 when assistance is given more frequently or involves more time/effort (e.g. long periods of respite, family lives with the user and gives them full assistance with most tasks). Score 3 when assistance is very intensive and/or daily (e.g. the family lives with the user and gives them full assistance with most tasks). Score 9 if the interviewee is unsure of the level of assistance provided by these supports.

Section 3

Part 1 of this section asks whether the user receives any assistance from local services to help with the need. These formal supports are defined above to include paid carers, residential care, long-term wards, formal respite, day-care centres, hospitals, community nurses or other staff. Use the examples on the assessment form to prompt the interviewee. Score 1 for minimal support, occasional or light support. Score 2 for more regular assistance, maybe once a week or more significant support occasionally. Score 3 for specialist assistance, currently under assessment or intensive assistance. Score 9 if the interviewee is unsure of the level of assistance provided by these supports.

Part 2 of Section 3 asks what formal supports the interviewee feels that the user *requires*, using the same scale as in Part 1 of Section 3. This second part indicates under-met need, where the person is getting (Part 1) less than they require (Part 2), or over-provision of need, where the person is getting (Part 1) a higher level of service than they require (Part 2).

Section 4

Part 1 of this section asks whether the person feels that the user is receiving the right type of help with the problem. The answer to this question may have been obvious from the responses to the previous section, especially Section 1. However, if in doubt ask more specifically.

The second part of Section 4 asks about the user's satisfaction with the assistance they are receiving. Again, this may be obvious from prior responses, but it pays to ask specifically as a person's needs may be met, yet they are not satisfied with the help they are receiving (e.g. an individual in residential care who wishes to return home).

Section 5

This section is for documenting notes regarding the individual details of the assessment. This section should be used to document the problem and the details of the help the user receives and requires. Remember to document which informant is providing the information (i.e. U=user, S=staff, C=carer, R=rater/health professional). User perspectives on their expectations, personal strengths and resources should be noted here. Individual spiritual and cultural information should also be noted in this section. This information is vital for establishing an effective, individualised care plan.

Scoring

It is to be noted that scoring is a secondary aspect of the CANE, as its primary purpose is to identify and assess individual needs. The total CANE score is based on the rating of Section 1 of each of the 24 problem areas. The two areas (A and B) relating to carers' needs are not added into this total score. Count the total number of met needs (rated as a 1 in Section 1) out of a maximum 24. Count total number of unmet needs identified (rated as a 2 in Section 1) out of a maximum 24. Count total number of needs identified (rated as a 1 or 2 in Section 1) out of a maximum 24. The rater's (clinician's or researcher's) ratings are made based on all the information gathered throughout the assessment. Raters' ratings of Section 1 are most frequently used as the basis for total CANE scores.

Frequently asked questions

How do I rate a section when I know the information the interviewee is giving me is not correct?

This can commonly happen in cases where the interviewee has memory difficulties or is unsure of the details of the information they are giving. Rate what the interviewee is telling you about their perception of the problem under the respective individual headings (e.g. U=user, S=staff). You may prompt individuals with your own information (e.g. 'I thought you were getting some home help?'), but rate items based on the interviewee's information (e.g. a 9 for 'I don't know' or 0 for 'no problem'). Rate your own assessment under the R (rater) heading.

Can I skip questions I know are not relevant (e.g. when the user lives in a clean and comfortable residential home? Or when the people living in the home are not permitted to drink alcohol?)

Do not assume that because you do not know about a problem in a certain area this information is not useful. For example, it may appear to be satisfactory accommodation to you, but may be unsatisfactory to the user. It is noted that elderly people, in particular, often under-report problems because they do not think there is an effective solution or they rationalise that their problem is due to 'old age' (Walters *et al*, 2001).

What if I do not get all the information I need to complete the assessment from the interviewee?

Do not persist with an assessment if the interviewee is becoming fatigued or agitated. Rather, halt the assessment and continue again when the individual is ready. Try not to time assessments during activities in which the interviewee wishes to be involved, but rather book a time in advance to suit the person. Be aware that individuals fluctuate in their ability to cope with this type of assessment. Time the interview around the person's most attentive times (i.e. in the morning to early afternoon, rather than later in the evening). In addition, you can obtain supplementary information from clinical/social work notes to get a full and accurate picture and to allow you to complete the CANE.

If informants have responded differently to questions, how can I construct a care plan from the CANE?

The views of the user always need to be seriously considered when constructing a care plan. If views differ between informants, these differences in perception should be recorded. The final care plan should be negotiated between all relevant members of the care team, including the user.

Some definitions of need only consider a need to be unmet when there is a possible solution to the problem. Is a problem an unmet need if there is no treatment available?

The CANE is used to identify unmet needs for assessment or intervention even if no such treatment is currently available locally. This usually requires a judgement to be made, and this can be made after the assessment has been completed and any appropriate professionals have been consulted. In addition, this information may be useful for service provision and development (e.g. the development of memory clinics and activity programmes where they are needed but not currently available).

What if the person is refusing assistance to meet their needs (e.g. has refused any home care, offers of day hospital, or individual counselling)?

This is a difficult situation, but if the need still remains unmet it must be rated as a 2. Document all information regarding attempts to engage the user in appropriate treatment. Monitors may be put in place in order to prevent any possible crisis, in which case the unmet need (2) becomes a met need (1) (e.g. after attempts to engage the person in appropriate treatment are refused, an intermediate safety plan is established including further monitoring).

What if the person is too ill to engage in appropriate treatment (e.g. has no satisfactory activities or mobility because they are bed-bound or are being tube fed because of recent infection)?

If there is no clinically appropriate intervention to meet a need, then the area should be rated as a 1 (e.g. tube feeding). If significant need stills exists (e.g. suitable activities for people who are bed-bound), then the area should be rated as a 2.

Application of the CANE in long-term care facilities

The CANE is ideally suited for the assessment of needs in long-term care facilities. The majority of individuals in long-term care might prefer not to reside in care homes, but have come to live in the facilities because they could no longer function at home for a number of possible reasons. With the further development of community services, many elderly people are not entering long-term care facilities until they become very frail or have difficulty managing in the community. Therefore, most residents in these facilities have a high number of needs that they require the home to identify and meet.

The CANE is best used for assessment of residents who have lived in the care home for a period of time (e.g. over 1 month). This time gives the person the opportunity to settle into their new environment, and also allows staff to get to know the individual and find ways to adapt to their particular needs. CANE assessments of individuals in long-term care should involve speaking to all significant parties so that the most accurate assessment is possible. These people can include the individual themselves, a member of staff who knows the person well, and possibly a family carer. Permission should be sought from the individual themselves to obtain information from other sources. Many individuals in long-term care facilities may have carers in the community who can add valuable information to the CANE assessment, mainly because they have known the individual for some time before they entered long-term care. These external carers can offer the individual a range of support from occasional involvement in meetings, to regular involvement with care, providing emotional and physical support for the individual in the home (e.g. entertainment, activities and favourite foods). Usually if a carer is involved with the person at least weekly and knew the person before they came into care, they can provide valuable information, which can be particularly useful when individualising appropriate interventions and care plans.

All interviews should take place in a quiet setting, away from other residents, to ensure confidentiality and also to aid the interviewee's concentration by minimising other environmental stimuli. It is important to explain the aims and objectives of the CANE assessment to interviewees prior to initiating the interviews. In particular, staff might be protective of identifying unmet needs if they feel that it could reflect poorly on their job performance or competence. Additionally, the user and carer may be hesitant in identifying unmet needs if they feel the information is going to be poorly received by staff, and have potential detrimental consequences for user–staff relationships or have funding/placement implications. Clear communication of the purpose of the assessment and its implications will lead to a collaborative team approach to meeting needs.

On the other hand, some staff or carers might genuinely not recognise an unmet or over-met need. For example, an individual may be frequently incontinent of urine and be left to sit in wet clothing for long periods of time (an unmet need) or the individual may have all their self-care tasks completed for them by staff when they could manage some by themselves (an over-met need). Along similar lines, some areas on the CANE should not be discounted because interviewees might wrongly assume there is automatically 'no problem' in the area (e.g. for accommodation). Some prompting in this area can highlight needs specific for individuals that are unmet (e.g. not enough storage space in rooms, mobility problems and a room on the second floor, lack of wheelchair access or a damp room). For this reason, it is best not only to ask whether there is a problem in a certain area, but to enquire generally into an area and prompt for possible areas of need. It is important to remember to rate what each interviewee reports, then rate the clinician's or researcher's ratings after the interviews; unmet (or over-met) needs can be identified on the basis of clinical judgement and experience. In this way, the CANE is adept at illuminating previously unidentified problems, and picking up on significant problems for which interventions are available. Often, long-term care facilities have been struggling to manage a problem because they were unaware there was an appropriate solution to alleviate the situation.

For these reasons, every attempt should be made to explain the purpose of the assessment to the user and to gain their consent to administer the CANE. For people with moderate dementia and/or severe communication problems, assent rather that consent may be justified. An informal interview style can be adopted when interviewees have difficulties completing the entire CANE interview. In severe dementia, it may not be possible to get a 'user' rating. This might be the case, for example, if the individual becomes anxious or fatigued owing to impairments in language communication.

Such an advanced stage of dementia or another disability might preclude a need in a certain area in long-term care facilities. In this respect, some item areas might not be applicable. This is a rare situation in which information is known about the problem, but there is no longer a need owing to the nature of the individual's condition or because there is no known intervention for the problem. For example, if a person is bed-bound due to severe dementia, then their need for mobility would not be satisfactory, but if all efforts were being made to keep the person comfortable, exercised as appropriate and monitored to prevent pressure sores, then the area 'mobility' would be scored as 1 for a met need. Another example could be the need for information during severe stages of dementia, where the individual has not received and understood all relevant information, but the deficit in cognitive abilities means that the person would not be able to understand all information if it were given to them. If the person was, however, receiving assistance to understand a level of information about their condition that was appropriate for them, then this area would be rated as 1 for met need. A further example would be the area of 'caring for the home' when the person is too ill to look after any aspect of the home. This type of situation is infrequent, but due to the nature of the person's condition a score of 1 may be appropriate where this would not be the case for individuals without the condition.

Implications or interventions leading from the findings made during the CANE assessment need to be discussed with all relevant parties involved in the individual's care. This group must agree on priorities for intervention and changes made to care plans. This process of consultation is necessary if interventions are to be successful at changing these previously unidentified or unmet needs.

Specific need areas

These are some specific CANE areas for which additional assessment prompts and comments have been modified for the long-term care population.

Food

Establish that the user is getting the types of foods that they want or need or that he/she is permitted to assist where possible. For example, an individual may need culturally appropriate food on certain days. If this is not provided, this would be an unmet need. If someone wanted to assist with food preparation, such as peel some potatoes or carrots, and if they were assisted to do so with supervision from staff, this would be a met need.

Memory

People give many subtle and not-so-subtle prompts to help others with memory problems. Staff and carers often do not realise that they give prompts and assistance unless asked directly. More direct assessment could include questions such as: Do you help them find things they have lost or do you have to point out where things are? Are there clear signs around the home to help those with memory difficulties? Does the home have re-orientation activities or trained staff members that can use techniques to help with memory problems? Does the family bring in prompts, such as photograph albums and familiar objects, to help the person to reminisce?

Physical health

Particular physical illnesses are high-risk areas for the elderly and these should be enquired about specifically; for example, pain, oral health, foot care and tissue viability.

Need for information

As noted above, information should be pitched at the appropriate level of comprehension for the individual's needs as all individuals have the right to be involved as much as is possible in their own care. This may mean full information and access to information sources (e.g. clubs and books), or may mean very simplified information if the person has severe dementia.

Intimate relationships

Some interviewers have found this area of need difficult to ask about. The following prompts may be helpful: Do they have someone they can trust and talk to about things? Would someone give them physical touch and contact if they wanted/needed it? Who would they talk to about an important personal issue that they were concerned about?

Money/budgeting

Many long-term care facilities do not give money to individuals because of confusion and possible theft. Therefore, staff and residents often have little idea about a resident's financial status or ability to handle/budget money – however, check whether the individual can purchase the specific individual items they might need (e.g. clothes, shoes, food, cigarettes or toiletries).

Benefits

Many staff also know little about benefits received by residents. Speaking to home managers or nominated social workers can be helpful in gaining some clarification in this area.

Vignette 1 – William

William is an 89-year-old with dementia, who lives in a residential care EMI unit.

Interview with William

William was assisted to the interview room, with guidance from a carer. He verbally agreed to talk about his needs and said he was 'OK' with the information being used to help the home care for him (establish a care plan). William said he enjoyed 'working' in the home and that they fed him well. He said he assisted with the folding of laundry when asked, among other chores that help him to pass the day. Physically, William said he felt very well and was still able to wash and dress himself every morning. He said he was living in the home because his wife had died, but explained that his son knew most of the details. William reported to be happy at the home and that he thought he had enough to do with his day, walking down to see his son and working at the home. William said he was getting a good wage and was not in need of anything.

CANE Assessment Summary Sheet

User name <u>William</u>   Date of assessment   / / ____ _____

Ratings: 0 = no need 1 = met need 2 = unmet need 9 = unknown

Sections 2–4a show raters' overall ratings

	U	C	S	R	Section 2 Informal help	Section 3a Formal help	Section 3b Help needed	Section 4a Type of help	Section 4b User satisfaction
1 Accommodation	1	2	1	2	0	3	3	0	1
2 Looking after the home	1	9	1	1	0	3	2	1	1
3 Food	1	2	1	2	1	3	3	0	1
4 Self-care	1	1	1	1	0	1	1	1	1
5 Caring for someone else	0	0	0	0					
6 Daytime activities	1	2	1	2	2	1	2	1	1
7 Memory	1	2	2	2	1	1	2	0	1
8 Eyesight/hearing/communication	1	2	1	2	1	1	2	1	1
9 Mobility/falls	1	2	1	2	0	1	2	0	1
10 Continence	0	2	1	2	0	2	3	0	
11 Physical health	0	1	1	1	1	1	1	1	
12 Drugs	9	2	1	1	1	2	2	1	
13 Psychotic symptoms	0	0	0	0					
14 Psychological distress	0	0	0	0					
15 Information	9	2	1	1	0	1	1	1	
16 Deliberate self-harm	0	0	0	0					
17 Inadvertent self-harm	0	2	1	1	1	1	1	1	
18 Abuse/neglect	0	0	0	0					
19 Behaviour	0	1	2	2	1	1	2	0	
20 Alcohol	0	0	0	0					
21 Company	1	2	1	1	2	1	1	1	1
22 Intimate relationships	1	1	1	1	2	1	1	1	1
23 Money/budgeting	1	1	1	1	3	1	1	1	1
24 Benefits	9	1	9	1	3	2	2	1	
A Carer's need for information	9	1	2	2	0	0	2	0	
B Carer's psychological distress	9	0	2	2	0	0	2	0	
Met needs (Count the number of 1s in the column)	11	6	15	10					
Unmet needs (Count the number of 2s in the column)	0	11	2	8					
Total needs (Add number of met and unmet needs)	11	17	17	18					
Total level of help given, needed and level of satisfaction (add scores, rate 9 as 1)					19	27	32	12	11

Interview with Sandy, William's keyworker /carer

Sandy said William had come to the home 6 months ago, after struggling at home because his wife had died 9 months previously. Sandy reported that William needed minimal assistance every day to wash and dress himself. He ate well and was physically fit, only taking medication for constipation and heart problems. William's physical health was reviewed every 6 months by his general practitioner. William helped about the house, but otherwise sat in the same chair in the lounge room. He usually refused to leave the home, even when his son suggested they go for a walk. William's son Andrew visited for about 1 hour per week, but he was not involved in providing any physical care for William. Sandy felt that William would talk to the staff if he had any concerns and that he was close to one male staff member in particular. William's incontinence had worsened since coming into the home and he was frequently incontinent of large amounts of urine at night and often during the day. He occasionally hit out at other residents if they come close to him when he was talking to his son or he had asked them to go away. Staff could usually intervene rapidly to remove the other resident. William had had two falls in the past 3 months, both requiring hospital checks. Each fall had been when he had attempted to come down the stairs unassisted from his room to the dinning area. Sandy felt that Andrew was not aware of William's condition as he did not attend any meetings or appointments with him. She also felt that this was indicated by his insistence that William move home with him. Sandy also said that Andrew had been seen by other staff to become very upset when William had not recognised him and had on occasion tried to hit him.

Interview with William's son Andrew

Andrew said that he was unhappy with his father's present situation. Andrew said his father could no longer fit his clothes because he was being fed too much and was not getting any exercise. He said William was often without his hearing aid and glasses. Andrew thought that his father should be given 'new medication' to help his memory as well as have regular reviews in hospital.

Scoring of Vignette 1

William himself had little to say in the CANE interview. Andrew, on the other hand, mentioned many areas in which he felt his father had unmet needs. Staff felt they were meeting most of William's needs but the clinician-rater scored many items as 2, indicating that further assessment of some areas was needed.

Vignette 2 – Iris

Iris is a 67-year-old woman with a learning disability and schizophrenia who lived in a continuing care residential home.

Interview with Iris

Iris walked without assistance to the interview room. She reported that she had been living at the home for 4 years and enjoyed helping out the staff with certain residents. She said that she liked the food and her room, although she did not like her room-mate, whom she accused of stealing her money. She said that she would like to go out more, but was not allowed, and did not have enough to do with her day. She said plenty of people visited who she talked to. Iris said that she felt 'edgy' at night and liked to 'walk about'. She said that this helped her to keep the 'thoughts' out of her head. She said she did not like the medication she was given and wished to see someone for a check up of her physical health because sometimes she felt like things were crawling inside her.

CANE Assessment Summary Sheet

User name <u>Iris</u>   Date of assessment _____/_____/_____

Ratings: 0 = no need 1 = met need 2 = unmet need 9 = unknown

Sections 2–4a show raters' overall ratings

	U	C	S	R	Section 2 Informal help	Section 3a Formal help	Section 3b Help needed	Section 4a Type of help	Section 4b User satisfaction
1 Accommodation	1		1	1	0	3	3	1	1
2 Looking after the home	1		1	1	0	3	2	1	1
3 Food	1		1	1	0	3	3	1	1
4 Self-care	1		1	1	0	2	2	1	1
5 Caring for someone else	0		0	0					
6 Daytime activities	2		2	2	0	1	3	0	0
7 Memory	0		0	0					
8 Eyesight/hearing/communication	0		0	0					
9 Mobility/falls	0		0	0					
10 Continence	0		0	0					
11 Physical health	0		0	0					
12 Drugs	2		2	2	0	2	3	1	0
13 Psychotic symptoms	2		2	2	0	0	2	0	0
14 Psychological distress	2		1	2	0	0	2	0	0
15 Information	9		1	9					
16 Deliberate self-harm	2		1	2	0	0	1	1	0
17 Inadvertent self-harm	0		0	0					
18 Abuse/neglect	1		1	1	0	1	1	1	1
19 Behaviour	0		2	2	0	1	2	0	
20 Alcohol	9		9	9					
21 Company	1		2	2	0	1	2	1	1
22 Intimate relationships	1		2	2	0	1	2	1	1
23 Money/budgeting	1		1	1	0	3	3	1	1
24 Benefits	9		1	1	0	1	1	1	1
A Carer's need for information									
B Carer's psychological distress									
Met needs (Count the number of 1s in the column)	8		10	7					
Unmet needs (Count the number of 2s in the column)	5		6	8					
Total needs (Add number of met and unmet needs)	13		16	15					
Total level of help given, needed and level of satisfaction (add scores, rate 9 as 1)					0	22	32	11	9

Interview with Carmel, senior home care worker

Carmel said Iris did not need much assistance with daily self-care and appeared quite happy in the home. On occasion, however, Iris was reported to 'have a bad week' in which she would pace, shout at others and pick or dig at her skin, particularly at night. Carmel said that she would like her to go out more and have more to do, but that she needed assistance outside the home and no staff were available to help her. She said that Iris did not have many friends, mainly because she could be unpredictably aggressive towards others. She also did not appear to have anyone in whom she confided and did not keep friendships because of her style of social interaction.

Scoring of Vignette 2

Iris and Carmel appeared to agree on most of the items, although Carmel felt that Iris had needs for *company* and an *intimate relationship* that were unmet over the past month, whereas Iris felt she had enough contact with others. Iris had needs for social *company* and *daily activities* that may be more suited to her age and disabilities. Iris also had possible ongoing *psychotic symptoms* that appeared to affect her *behaviour* towards others, her own level of *psychological distress* and her tendency to *self-harm*, all of which are unmet and need to be reviewed. Iris's need for safety from *abuse/neglect* can be said to be met because she is supervised in the home and Carmel also thought that her need for safety from self-harm was also met within the home. Whether Iris was receiving the right type of *information* about her condition is unknown at the present time.

Application of the CANE in a day hospital environment

The day hospital provides assessment and treatment as a time-limited intervention or as ongoing monitoring through continuous attendance, with patients attending from the community, residential care or in-patient areas prior to discharge and receiving varying levels of support. As care packages are based on need identified through undertaking a full and comprehensive assessment, instruments that offer a broad and holistic approach to needs measurement, such as the CANE, are ideal for this setting. Where a multidisciplinary approach to care is offered, such as within the day hospital, the generic nature of the CANE means it can be implemented by any experienced discipline involved.

Day hospital patients' needs can be complex and difficult to assess from one environment. The range of topics within the CANE does, however, offer a global picture and helps identify areas of risk. While best practice would be to ensure a visit to the patient's home environment to help substantiate the information received, this information may be obtained through interviewing the carer or a professional familiar with the home setting (e.g. community psychiatric nurse; occupational therapist; or social worker).

The CANE involves the needs assessment being undertaken with the individual, their carer and a staff member, which can be considered to promote user and carer participation and encourage their involvement within the care planning process. The carer and staff assessments may be used to verify the patients' responses, or have their perceptions challenged. The structure of the CANE therefore ensures accurate assessments of the patients' needs are undertaken.

Implementing the CANE

The CANE may be used on admission with new patients; its structure allows for a broad range of needs to be measured. Using a systematic approach to assessment of need will ensure that those areas of unmet need are identified and will highlight the priorities for intervention. The CANE does not replace clinical assessments; should items such as memory, psychotic symptoms or psychological distress be identified as unmet needs, further in-depth and specialist assessments are still required. When assessing items regarding money/budgeting and benefits, if the information is not immediately available, then indicators that financial assessments have been undertaken could be the receipt of attendance allowance or home care services.

Alternatively, the CANE is a useful tool for reviewing the progress of patients who have attended the day hospital for a period of time, particularly those with chronic health problems. Repeated measurement of need at 6-monthly or yearly intervals allows an opportunity to acknowledge the needs that are met and the interventions that have been successful. An increase in the number of unmet needs at this stage may indicate either a deterioration in the person's well-being or a breakdown in the care package. This could also allow for future needs to be anticipated. When implemented within the day hospital, the depth of staff knowledge regarding their patients can be effectively demonstrated and readily consolidated using the CANE.

Ongoing risk assessment is of paramount importance and the items deliberate self-harm, inadvertent self-harm, abuse/neglect and behaviour allow for any significant risks to be identified in relation to harming self or others. When determining the presence of abuse/neglect, consideration should be given to financial abuse, coercion or intimidation, as well as physical, verbal or sexual abuse.

Where the day hospital assessment has been completed and the relevant treatment or intervention received, implementing the CANE may indicate areas of over-met need. This may be particularly evident when the level of support received is higher in comparison to that required, such as daytime activities or company. Over-met needs indicate a need to review the care package and consider or commence discharge planning.

Through effective listening when implementing the CANE unnecessary repetition can be avoided. If at the start of an assessment the patient identifies they have no family or close friends involved in their care, it is unlikely they will score within Section 2. In addition, references may be made to other items within responses, such that, when discussing psychological distress, details may be given of previous attempts at self-harm.

Vignette 3 – Harry

Harry was a 59-year-old gentleman with younger-onset dementia, who had attended the day hospital for the past 6 months. The dementia had progressed to an advanced stage and had resulted in a limited ability with comprehension and communication; therefore Harry was unable to participate in the assessment. A brief chat with Harry did identify that he enjoyed getting out of the house and that his wife did a 'wonderful job' of looking after him.

Interview with Carmen – Harry's wife

On interview with Harry's wife Carmen, areas of unmet needs and met needs were identified. Harry's existing care package included home care assistance with washing and dressing, both mornings and evenings, and attendance at the day hospital twice weekly and at a specialist day centre once a week. A volunteer from Age Concern sat with Harry once a week while Carmen attended a local evening class.

Despite having day care provision and access to respite services on request, Carmen was experiencing a high level of carer strain and became tearful during the interview. Carmen described difficulty with Harry being constantly 'on the go' and attempting to leave the house. Harry had wandered off on two occasions and had been brought back by the police, having been found attempting to cross

CANE Assessment Summary Sheet

User name Harry_____   Date of assessment ____/____/____

Ratings: 0 = no need 1 = met need 2 = unmet need 9 = unknown

Sections 2–4a show raters' overall ratings

	U	C	S	R	Section 2 Informal help	Section 3a Formal help	Section 3b Help needed	Section 4a Type of help	Section 4b User satisfaction
1 Accommodation		0	0	0					
2 Looking after the home		1	1	1	2	0	1	0	
3 Food		1	1	1	3	0	0	1	
4 Self-care		1	1	1	0	3	3	1	
5 Caring for someone else		0	0	0					
6 Daytime activities		1	1	1	2	2	3	1	
7 Memory		1	1	1	2	1	1	1	
8 Eyesight/hearing/communication		0	0	0					
9 Mobility/falls		0	0	0					
10 Continence		1	2	2	1	1	2	0	
11 Physical health		0	0	0					
12 Drugs		1	1	1	2	1	1	1	
13 Psychotic symptoms		0	0	0					
14 Psychological distress		2	1	2	2	1	2	1	
15 Information		0	0	0					
16 Deliberate self-harm		0	0	0					
17 Inadvertent self-harm		2	2	2	2	1	2	0	
18 Abuse/neglect		0	0	0					
19 Behaviour		2	2	2	2	1	2	0	
20 Alcohol		0	0	0					
21 Company		1	1	1	3	1	1	1	
22 Intimate relationships		0	1	0					
23 Money/budgeting		1	1	1	3	0	0	1	
24 Benefits		1	9	1	3	1	1	1	
A Carer's need for information		0	0	0					
B Carer's psychological distress		1	2	2	1	0	2	0	
Met needs (Count the number of 1s in the column)		10	10	9					
Unmet needs (Count the number of 2s in the column)		3	3	4					
Total needs (Add number of met and unmet needs)		13	13	13					
Total level of help given, needed and level of satisfaction (add scores, rate 9 as 1)					28	13	21	9	

a busy dual carriageway. A recent incident had also involved Harry becoming physically aggressive towards his son Peter, who had been clearing out the garden shed. Further concerns raised were bouts of 'sobbing' which were increasing in frequency. Harry was described as becoming extremely distressed and inconsolable at these times. Despite the high level of carer stress, Carmen expressed a wish to continue caring for Harry at home.

Interview with the staff member – Sophie

During the interview with Harry's named nurse at the day hospital, Sophie, it was reported that Harry attended the day hospital regularly, and appeared to recognise familiar faces and the environment. During his attendance, Harry spent the time constantly walking around the day hospital, although no attempts to leave had been noted. Sophie reported that Harry had been incontinent of urine on several occasions during his attendances at the day hospital and day centre. She had also witnessed episodes of lability, where Harry was observed crying and become frustrated when unable to explain why he was upset. Harry was reported to mix little with the other day patients, but could be engaged on a one-to-one basis in activities, enjoying simple repetitive tasks such as watering the garden, or sanding and painting the wooden craft kits. Harry also responded well to sensory work, particularly music and participating in sing-a-longs. A further concern for both day hospital and day centre staff was the increasing level of carer burden, Carmen having been observed to become tearful at a recent carer's support group and expressed how difficult it was to cope with Harry.

Scoring for case vignette

There are several areas of met need due to the existing package of care in situ and the support provided by his wife and family. This demonstrates the success of the existing interventions, but which may need modifying in response to the items now identified as unmet needs.

Application of the CANE in acute in-patient wards

The CANE was developed to assess the complex needs of older people in the community. With the developments in the fields of psychiatry and medicine for older people, in-patient wards have become an important point when a comprehensive assessment of the physical, psychological and social needs of the individual is required. The CANE can provide a good framework for the assessment of these complex needs in these settings. When using the CANE in an in-patient setting, the assessor should be aware of some important issues to consider.

Information gathering

Ideally, CANE is best suited for assessment of individuals who have lived in a particular place for a period of time (over 1 month). This is sometimes not be possible when assessing needs of patients on the medical wards because of the rapid turnover of patients and acute pressure for beds. In this case, one should also consider problems within the context of the period prior to admission.

Nurses on in-patient units work on a shift system, and hence there may be more than one nurse who knows the patient, or it might not be possible to speak to the staff member who knows the patient best. In this situation, it is important to look for information in the nursing and medical notes to complement the information gathered from speaking to staff. Medical notes are a key source of information. They can provide useful information about various observations of the patient, the progress of the patient during the stay in the hospital and, importantly, the care planned for the patient. Other particularly useful sources of information include occupational therapy, social work or clinical psychology assessments.

When getting information from relatives, one should be aware that the family member who visits the patient on the ward might not always be the best person to provide information about the patient prior to admission. Hence, efforts must be made to identify the person who could be the best source; sometimes it might be that the assessor has to speak to more than one individual. Patients on in-patient wards, particularly on the medical wards, are often acutely ill or very confused. In this scenario, the assessor will find that one has to rely on other sources of information or delay the assessment until a more appropriate time.

One of the important differences in the assessment of needs of an older person on the medical ward is that in some cases it may be difficult to estimate his/her current needs because of a rapidly changing situation. Older people in many cases get admitted following an acute event (e.g. a stroke, collapse, fracture, etc.). This alters the needs of these people dramatically and, as a result, their living situation prior to the admission may not reflect their current accommodation needs if the assessment is done very soon after the admission. However, the CANE may identify current and future needs for assessment in particular domains.

When applying the CANE to patients who for various reasons have been on the ward or have been on different wards for some time (a few months or longer), certain items on the CANE can also be applied to the person's needs on the ward. Items such as daytime activities, company and intimate relationships remain highly relevant, even in the confines of the ward, and have to be considered when the assessment is carried out. Conversely, other needs like accommodation, looking after the home, food and self-care tend to be met in an in-patient setting. For longer-stay patients, particular attention has to be given to the details of these needs.

By using the framework provided by the CANE, a comprehensive assessment of needs can be undertaken, perhaps highlighting needs that are commonly overlooked in certain settings. Items such as memory, psychotic symptoms, psychological distress (e.g. depression and anxiety) or risk of deliberate self-harm might be particularly relevant in the setting of a medical ward. Similarly, items on eyesight/hearing/communication, mobility, continence, physical health and drugs are useful within a ward setting.

Some specific need areas

These are some specific areas of the CANE for which these additional assessment prompts and comments have been modified for the population.

Food

In a hospital setting, generally this area is rated a no need or a met need. However, particular patients will have specific dietary requirements (e.g. those with celiac disease), and these have to be addressed. This will be a met need if the individual can supplement/complement the diet requirement by some means (e.g. food from home, canteen, etc.).

Daytime activities

Traditionally, by assuming the sick role, one is expected to lose social and leisure activities. This is particularly the case when an individual is in a general hospital and reduction of the level of daytime activities from the usual activities is expected and indeed desirable. This might be noted as a met need or no need, depending on the circumstances.

Mobility

Some very frail individuals on the wards will be bed-bound, and care plans will be formulated around this. This area would be a met need if the current level of mobility is acceptable and appropriate interventions are being conducted, such as the need to keep joints mobile to prevent contractors (e.g. need for physiotherapy) or the need for turning to prevent pressure sores.

Company

On acute medical wards, issues such as whether patients have adequate social company may not be a high priority, but in longer-stay patients this can be an important issue and may be easily missed. Therefore, this need should be carefully considered, as visits from friends, relatives or local organisations (e.g. church, community groups) can play a vital role in maintaining quality of life.

Vignette 4 – Margaret

Margaret is a 73-year-old patient, who was admitted to hospital after a fall at home. She was referred from the medical rehabilitation ward for a psychiatric assessment as the medical team had noticed that she was depressed.

The staff on the rehabilitation ward reported that she had been in the ward for over 2 months and the physiotherapist and occupational therapist were currently working with her. Over the past 3 weeks, however, staff reported that she was not motivated with her physiotherapy and was seen to be mobilising poorly. The medical team could not point to any physical cause to explain this. She was also noted to be isolating herself and not taking part in any activities, and was needing more help with her personal care. She was also noted to be more forgetful, misplacing her things about the ward and forgetting her appointments.

Her daughter, who used to visit her regularly about twice a week prior to her current admission, reported that her mother used to be very independent, needed no help in her personal care and had no problems with her memory prior to admission. Her mobility was good, and she used to enjoy the company of people and was very keen to attend various social clubs up to three times a week. After assessment of the patient, it was clear that she was moderately depressed and had decreased confidence as a result. She scored 22/30 on the MMSE, indicating mild impairment in cognition with the main problem in her level of concentration.

Scoring vignette 4

Some of the categories that the CANE highlighted as needs for this patient were: *self-care, daytime activities, memory, mobility, psychological distress* and *company*. The need for *self-care* was being met as the ward staff helped her on a daily basis. A reassessment in this area would be advisable much closer to the time of discharge, as she might have become more independent as her mood improved. The *psychological distress* area would be scored as unmet, as she was not currently receiving any appropriate intervention (e.g. antidepressants or psychotherapy) to address her depressed mood. The areas of need for *daytime activities* and *company* needed to be examined more closely. Margaret had been very socially active and currently on the ward she was isolated and did not take part in daytime activities. However, these needs were scored as met needs because appropriate interventions had been put in place by the ward staff but because of Margaret's depression she was unwilling to participate in these activities. This example demonstrates how one area of need can affect the scoring of other needs. Likewise *mobility* was also scored as a met need, as plans were in place to address the area of

CANE Assessment Summary Sheet

User name Margaret _____ Date of assessment _____ / _____ / _____

Ratings: 0 = no need 1 = met need 2 = unmet need 9 = unknown

Sections 2–4a show raters' overall ratings

	U	C	S	R	Section 2 Informal help	Section 3a Formal help	Section 3b Help needed	Section 4a Type of help	Section 4b User satisfaction
1 Accommodation	0	0	0	0					
2 Looking after the home	0	0	9	9					
3 Food	0	0	1	1	1	3	3	1	
4 Self-care	1	0	1	1	0	2	2	1	
5 Caring for someone else	0	0	0	0					
6 Daytime activities	0	2	1	2	1	1	2	1	
7 Memory	0	0	0	0					
8 Eyesight/hearing/communication	0	0	0	0					
9 Mobility/falls	2	2	1	1	1	3	3	1	
10 Continence	0	0	0	0					
11 Physical health	1	1	1	1	0	3	3	1	
12 Drugs	0	0	1	1	0	3	3	1	
13 Psychotic symptoms	0	0	0	0					
14 Psychological distress	0	2	2	2	1	0	2	0	
15 Information	0	0	0	0					
16 Deliberate self-harm	0	0	0	0					
17 Inadvertent self-harm	0	0	0	0					
18 Abuse/neglect	0	0	0	0					
19 Behaviour	0	0	0	0					
20 Alcohol	0	0	0	0					
21 Company	0	1	1	1	3	1	1	1	
22 Intimate relationships	0	0	0	0					
23 Money/budgeting	0	0	9	0					
24 Benefits	0	0	0	0					
A Carer's need for information									
B Carer's psychological distress									
Met needs (Count the number of 1s in the column)	2	2	7	6					
Unmet needs (Count the number of 2s in the column)	1	3	1	2					
Total needs (Add number of met and unmet needs)	3	5	8	8					
Total level of help given, needed and level of satisfaction (add scores, rate 9 as 1)					7	16	19	7	

mobility (i.e. installing a ramp at Margaret's home), but owing to her depression these had yet to be implemented. Margaret's problem with *memory* would be marked as an unmet need because there seemed to be a clear problem that had not been adequately assessed, even though it could be argued that her memory difficulties were related to her depression. Margaret was not on any treatment for depression and it is likely that her memory would improve with treatment of her depression. This is an example of two different needs that could be met by a common intervention and hence they both have to be scored as being presently unmet.

Vignette 5 – Joan

Joan is an 80-year-old patient referred from a medical ward for a psychiatric opinion, mainly to assess her capacity to consent as she was refusing to accept services when discharged home. Needs were identified by assessment with social services and the occupational therapist. The information from the staff and the carer indicated that she was admitted following a chest infection and worsening of confusion, and she stayed in the hospital for more than 2 months. She had been noted by staff to be forgetful and confused, and scored 20/30 on the MMSE. She also needed significant help with her personal care and a home visit revealed that she was not capable of cooking safely or doing much of the housework. Joan herself complained of loneliness and of having nothing much to do during the day. Talking to her, it was evident that she had moderate impairment in her cognitive functions. She was aware of the different areas of need and the interventions suggested, and it was felt that she was capable of deciding what help she would accept despite her cognitive difficulties. Joan said she was willing to accept meals on wheels. She was not willing to accept home help or referral to a day centre, as she felt she could not afford this. In the social worker report, Joan was documented as receiving appropriate benefits and had no major money concerns. There were no other clinical symptoms of depression present.

Scoring Vignette 5

The need for *accommodation* would be a no need as Joan had a flat that was in a satisfactory state (although untidy) and she wanted to return to it. The area *food* was scored as met, as she had accepted meals on wheels. On the other hand, Joan was clearly not capable of *looking after her home* and she had refused to accept home help, hence this area was scored as an unmet need. Likewise, the need for *daytime activities* and *company* were also scored as unmet needs. Joan herself identified these areas as unmet needs, yet refused referral to a day centre to address them. Other avenues should be explored with her to satisfactorily assist her to meet these unmet needs and see whether other interventions (e.g. a befriender) may be acceptable to her. This is an example where the needs are scored as unmet as a result of refusal by the patient/client to accept the intervention suggested.

Application of CANE in community/home visit assessment

A community or home visit is usually carried out by a member of the multidisciplinary team. Assessment of an individual within the community has become an important and pivotal part of elderly multidisciplinary team work. This shift has occurred because a greater number of individuals who require assessment are being cared for in their own home. In the past, these individuals would have been relocated to an acute assessment ward, or would be residing in a long-term hospital or another care facility. This move to providing care in the community means that individuals do not have to be disruptively moved, at risk to themselves and their supportive community networks, and also means that the assessor can make a more complete assessment of the person in their own environment. The

CANE Assessment Summary Sheet

User name Joan _____ Date of assessment _____ /____ /_____

Ratings: 0 = no need 1 = met need 2 = unmet need 9 = unknown

Sections 2–4a show raters' overall ratings

	U	C	S	R	Section 2 Informal help	Section 3a Formal help	Section 3b Help needed	Section 4a Type of help	Section 4b User satisfaction
1 Accommodation	0		0	0					
2 Looking after the home	0		2	2	0	0	2	1	
3 Food	1		2	1	0	2	2	1	1
4 Self-care	0		9	2	0	0	2	1	
5 Caring for someone else	0		0	0					
6 Daytime activities	2		2	2	0	0	1	1	0
7 Memory	0		2	2	0	0	2	1	
8 Eyesight/hearing/communication	0		0	0					
9 Mobility/falls	0		1	0					
10 Continence	0		0	0					
11 Physical health	0		1	1	0	1	1	1	
12 Drugs	0		1	1	0	2	2	1	
13 Psychotic symptoms	0		0	0					
14 Psychological distress	0		0	0					
15 Information	0		1	1	0	2	2	1	
16 Deliberate self-harm	0		0	0					
17 Inadvertent self-harm	0		1	0					
18 Abuse/neglect	0		0	0					
19 Behaviour	0		0	0					
20 Alcohol	0		0	0					
21 Company	2		2	2	0	0	1	1	0
22 Intimate relationships	0		0	0					
23 Money/budgeting	2		9	0					
24 Benefits	9		1	1	0	2	2	1	
A Carer's need for information									
B Carer's psychological distress									
Met needs (Count the number of 1s in the column)	1		6	5					
Unmet needs (Count the number of 2s in the column)	3		5	5					
Total needs (Add number of met and unmet needs)	4		11	10					
Total level of help given, needed and level of satisfaction (add scores, rate 9 as 1)					0	9	17	10	1

individual and their family also do not have to cope with sometimes costly periods of assessment in an acute assessment ward environment, where their behaviour and functioning may be different than if they were seen in their natural home environment.

While there are many advantages of having an assessment of current problems conducted in the individual's own home, the professional conducting the assessment must be confident and competent to undertake an assessment in this setting. This professional must be able to collect information about a number of health and social areas, and be prepared to report this information back to the team or coordinate with other disciplines to ensure the completion of a comprehensive assessment. The CANE is an ideal tool for use in this type of assessment situation. The broad range of environmental, social, physical, and psychological needs covered by the CANE means that the health or social care professional can complete a comprehensive assessment of the individual's needs and feed this information back to the multidisciplinary team for further consideration and establishment of care planning. The CANE also triggers a wide range of possible support for the individual, meaning that the person's own local network is acknowledged and is used to support the person in their own home.

Specific areas of need must be assessed during a home visit. The assessment of immediate and potential risk may be monitored via structured and prolonged observation in a hospital ward environment, but such assessment may not be available in the individual's home. Therefore the need for a comprehensive assessment of risk in the community is paramount. The CANE provides assessment of the person's risk of harming themselves and of being harmed by others. In addition, the CANE can highlight risks for the individual in multiple settings (e.g. mobility, physical health, access to appropriate food and so forth).

Vignette 6 – Anna

Anna, an 83-year-old married woman with a history of multiple sclerosis, chair-bound and dependant on her husband, was referred to the psychiatric services on account of low mood. She had a past history of depression.

Interview with Anna

Anna was interviewed by her bedside, where she had been for the past week. She felt that her inability to do things for herself and total dependence on her husband made life not worth living. She had contemplated suicide several times and said that she had not been motivated to continue with her usual activities of helping out with small jobs about the home or talking with her family.

Interview with Anna's husband – Mark

In meeting all of Anna's needs in respect of her personal care, assistance with mobility, meals, looking after the home and having to be with her all the time, Mark had begun to find it increasingly difficult, despite support from his children. Mark said that he frequently became upset at Anna and occasionally wanted to strike her or leave the house for long periods of time in order to have a break from caring for her.

Scoring of Vignette 6

Anna was assessed as suffering from a recurrent depressive disorder, complicated by her physical disabilities, and inadequate social support leading to distress in her husband. A few days after her first visit, Anna took an overdose of her own tablets, and further revealed an unhappy married life and

CANE Assessment Summary Sheet

User name Anna   Date of assessment _____/_____/_____

Ratings: 0 = no need 1 = met need 2 = unmet need 9 = unknown

Sections 2–4a show raters' overall ratings

	U	C	S	R	Section 2 Informal help	Section 3a Formal help	Section 3b Help needed	Section 4a Type of help	Section 4b User satisfaction
1 Accommodation	0	0		0					
2 Looking after the home	1	1		1	3	0	1	1	1
3 Food	1	1		1	3	0	1	1	1
4 Self-care	1	1		1					
5 Caring for someone else	0	0		0	2	0	1	0	0
6 Daytime activities	2	0		2					
7 Memory	0	0		0					
8 Eyesight/hearing/communication	0	0		0					
9 Mobility/falls	1	1		1	2	0	0	1	1
10 Continence	0	0		0					
11 Physical health	1	1		1	1	1	1	1	1
12 Drugs	0	0		2	0	0	3	0	
13 Psychotic symptoms	0	0		0					
14 Psychological distress	2	2		2	1	0	3	0	0
15 Information	0	0		0					
16 Deliberate self-harm	2	0		2	1	0	3	0	0
17 Inadvertent self-harm	0	0		0					
18 Abuse/neglect	0	2		2	0	0	2	0	
19 Behaviour	0	0		0					
20 Alcohol	0	0		0					
21 Company	0	0		2	1	0	2	0	
22 Intimate relationships	2	0		2	1	0	3	0	0
23 Money/budgeting	1	1		1	3	0	0	1	1
24 Benefits	1	1		1					
A Carer's need for information	0	0		2					
B Carer's psychological distress	0	2		2					
Met needs (Count the number of 1s in the column)	7	7		7					
Unmet needs (Count the number of 2s in the column)	4	2		7					
Total needs (Add number of met and unmet needs)	11	9		14					
Total level of help given, needed and level of satisfaction (add scores, rate 9 as 1)					18	1	20	5	5

feelings of isolation. Treatment offered included hospitalisation, antidepressant therapy and cognitive therapy, with the possibility of marital therapy and homecare to be explored.

Vignette 7 – Arnold

Arnold was an 85-year-old widower, a retired scientist who suffered from progressive memory loss, self-neglect and wandering. He had moved to live with his daughter owing to increased concerns over his safety when living alone. He received thrice daily home care, but carers expressed increased concerns over his personal hygiene.

Interview with Arnold

Arnold reported that he had no concerns over his present living situation, his personal hygiene, care or his mental health. He was oblivious to any other concerns about his health and well-being.

Interview with Arnold's daughter Julie

Julie said that she was unhappy with some aspects of the home care offered such as the time-keeping of carers, who would call around to the house at irregular intervals during the day. Otherwise, Julie felt that all her father's needs were met by her when she had time to tend to him or by Arnold himself.

Interview with the homecare staff

Staff were concerned about Arnold's personal hygiene, in that he was doubly incontinent and his daughter refused to let him use incontinence pads. They had noted that there were traces of faeces smeared on the floor, clothing and walls. The homecare staff also thought that Arnold was at risk of becoming physically unwell because of lack of attention to his hygiene difficulties. In addition, the staff reported that they often arrived at the home to find Arnold wandering around looking for his daughter, who was not in the house.

Scoring of Vignette 7

Arnold was assessed as suffering from severe dementia. Julie appeared to have a poor understanding of his illness and his needs. Her expectations of her father and the home carers were at times unrealistic, in that she believed he was not incontinent and just needed some bowel retraining. Though not recognised by her, there was clearly some strain in her family life by taking on the responsibility of her father's care at the expense of her marital relationship and caring for her own children. The assessment identified the need for carer information, respite care to alleviate distress in the family and appropriate management of incontinence.

Application of the CANE in younger people with dementia

The CANE has been used to investigate the needs of people under 65 years old where their needs have been deemed to be similar to those of older people, particularly those with early-onset dementia (Hammond et al, Chapter 10). The fact that younger people, in this case under the age of 65, are being assessed using a tool designed for older people, may seem inappropriate. However, dementia remains a rare condition in younger people and is more typically found in older people. Hence the

CANE Assessment Summary Sheet

User name <u>Arnold</u>   Date of assessment ____/ ____/ ____

Ratings: 0 = no need 1 = met need 2 = unmet need 9 = unknown

Sections 2–4a show raters' overall ratings

	U	C	S	R	Section 2 Informal help	Section 3a Formal help	Section 3b Help needed	Section 4a Type of help	Section 4b User satisfaction
1 Accommodation	0	1	1	1	1	0	0	1	
2 Looking after the home	0	1	1	1	2	0	0	1	
3 Food	0	1	1	1	3	0	0	1	
4 Self-care	0	1	2	2	1	3	3	9	
5 Caring for someone else	0	0	0	0					
6 Daytime activities	0	0	0	0					
7 Memory	0	1	2	2	0	1	2	0	
8 Eyesight/hearing/communication	0	0	0	0					
9 Mobility/falls	0	0	0	0					
10 Continence	0	0	2	2	1	1	3	0	
11 Physical health	0	0	0	0					
12 Drugs	0	0	0	0					
13 Psychotic symptoms	0	0	0	0					
14 Psychological distress	0	0	0	0					
15 Information	0	0	0	0					
16 Deliberate self-harm	0	0	0	0					
17 Inadvertent self-harm	0	1	2	2	0	1	2	0	
18 Abuse/neglect	0	0	2	2	0	1	2	0	
19 Behaviour	0	0	2	2	1	1	2	0	
20 Alcohol	0	0	0	0					
21 Company	0	0	0	0					
22 Intimate relationships	0	0	0	0					
23 Money/budgeting	0	1	1	1	3	0	0	1	
24 Benefits	0	1	1	1	2	1	1	1	
A Carer's need for information	0	0	2	2	0	0	2	0	
B Carer's psychological distress	0	0	0	2	0	0	1	0	
Met needs (Count the number of 1s in the column)	0	8	5	5					
Unmet needs (Count the number of 2s in the column)	0	0	6	6					
Total needs (Add number of met and unmet needs)	0	8	11	11					
Total level of help given, needed and level of satisfaction (add scores, rate 9 as 1)					14	9	15	6	

use of the CANE is appropriate, as the typical areas of need are similar between the younger and older populations. There are a number of factors, however, that make the needs of the younger person with dementia different to the needs of older people. A major and obvious factor is that of age, with the comparison of the typically frail and elderly group with people who are potentially in their 30s, 40s and 50s, and often quite physically active. To demonstrate the use of the CANE with the younger client group, an example of the full CANE follows, and after each section there is an explanation of common issues that may arise when assessing needs within this specialist population.

Vignette 8 – Jack

Jack was a 54-year-old man who lived with his wife, Hilda. Jack was unable to participate in the CANE interview due to severe dementia. Therefore, the CANE was completed by two separate interviews, one with Hilda as his main carer and one with his community psychiatric nurse, who was his keyworker.

1. Accommodation

Hilda expressed concerns about the layout of the house. Jack was presently getting around the house adequately, but difficulties were anticipated in the future when she foresaw that he would become more confused and less mobile. Both the carer and professional recognised that this was a serious problem area and scored 2.

Both the carer and the professional recognised that Jack received a lot of help with his accommodation from friends and relatives. The carer needed to do a great deal of work around the house to maintain a safe environment, and both scored this as 3. Both the carer and the professional recognised that there was no support coming in from local services, and this was scored as 1, and while the carer accepted this was adequate, the professional identified the need for more support from local services such as minor work and scored this as 0. Both felt that Jack was receiving the right type of help with accommodation, with both scoring this as 1, and the carer was satisfied that the right amount of help was being received.

Some people with young onset dementia have difficulties with their present accommodation. Some are unable to manage stairs and this often restricts them to half of the house as they have to stay on one level. Residential or nursing accommodation can also present problems for people, as this is not always suitable and people often live with others considerably older than themselves.

2. Looking after the home

Prior to his illness, Jack would help with tasks around the home, but this had stopped owing to his condition worsening, with the additional burden going to Hilda. Both the carer and the professional identified that because of the extra input from the carer, this was a moderate problem and both scored 1 to the first question. Both indicated that there was a high amount of help given by the carer, and scored 3 with the help received from friends and relatives. Both indicated no help was received from local services, with the professional indicating no further help was needed. Hilda, however, felt she could do with more help, not withstanding that she worked full-time. Therefore the carer felt the right type of support was not being received, while the professional felt that it was. Overall, there was satisfaction with the help being received to look after the home.

Generally, this type of problem with looking after the home is typical in young-onset dementia. Issues can arise regarding the loss of skills that are important to maintain as much as possible.

CANE Assessment Summary Sheet

User name Jack _____   Date of assessment _____/_____/_____

Ratings: 0 = no need 1 = met need 2 = unmet need 9 = unknown

Sections 2–4a show raters' overall ratings

	U	C	S	R	Section 2 Informal help	Section 3a Formal help	Section 3b Help needed	Section 4a Type of help	Section 4b User satisfaction
1 Accommodation		2	2	2	3	0	1	1	
2 Looking after the home		1	1	1	3	0	1	1	
3 Food		1	1	1	3	1	2	0	
4 Self-care		1	2	1	2	0	1	1	
5 Caring for someone else		0	0	0					
6 Daytime activities		2	2	2	1	1	2	0	
7 Memory		2	2	2	3	1	2	1	
8 Eyesight/hearing/communication		0	0	0					
9 Mobility/falls		0	0	0					
10 Continence		0	0	0					
11 Physical health		0	0	0					
12 Drugs		1	1	1	2	1	1	1	
13 Psychotic symptoms		1	0	1	1	0	0	1	
14 Psychological distress		0	2	1	2	1	1	1	
15 Information		0	0	0					
16 Deliberate self-harm		0	0	0					
17 Inadvertent self-harm		1	1	1	2	0	1	1	
18 Abuse/neglect		0	1	1	1	1	1	1	
19 Behaviour		0	0	0					
20 Alcohol		0	0	0					
21 Company		2	2	2	2	1	2	1	
22 Intimate relationships		0	0	0					
23 Money/budgeting		1	1	1	3	0	0	1	
24 Benefits		2	1	1	2	1	1	1	
A Carer's need for information		1	1	1	1	2	2	1	
B Carer's psychological distress		2	2	2	1	0	1	0	
Met needs (Count the number of 1s in the column)		7	7	10					
Unmet needs (Count the number of 2s in the column)		5	6	4					
Total needs (Add number of met and unmet needs)		12	13	14					
Total level of help given, needed and level of satisfaction (add scores, rate 9 as 1)					30	8	16	12	

3. Food

Food was identified by both Hilda and the keyworker as a moderate problem area, because of the unpredictability of meals during the day when Hilda was working. Jack was unable to prepare any food for himself. Both Hilda and the keyworker identified Hilda as providing a lot of help to resolve this by preparing all meals, and scored 3 for help from family and friends. There was some help from local services, a lunch club that provided meals twice a week. However, with Hilda needing to work 5 days a week, this left the meals for the rest of the time unpredictable, and as such did not meet all Jack's and Hilda's needs.

The issue of individuals with dementia being alone for long periods, leading to doubts about whether they are eating properly, is potentially a major concern within the younger client group.

4. Self-care

Both Hilda and the keyworker identified difficulties with Jack's personal hygiene, although Hilda thought this was a moderate problem and the keyworker considered it to be a serious problem. Both acknowledged that Hilda helped Jack a lot with his self-care. Hilda did not identify any help from elsewhere, and felt the help received was adequate and of the right type. The keyworker recognised help from elsewhere, but did not consider that Jack had the right amount of help.

Younger people identify the need for services that help with self-care to be more flexible and tie in with carer employment (e.g. running later at night and earlier in the morning).

5. Caring for someone else

Jack does not care for anyone else and this did not present a problem for any of the other people. Therefore, this was scored as 0 by both Hilda and the keyworker.

6. Daytime activities

This area was described by both the keyworker and Hilda as a serious problem area, with limited support from family and friends and local services, and generally not enough or of the right type. Therefore, both were not satisfied with the amount of help they were receiving and this was scored as an unmet need.

Daytime activities has been shown to be one of the most frequent unmet needs and most of the people have identified that there are no appropriate day activities for active younger people with dementia (Hammond et al, Chapter 10). Carers have identified the need for activities to be more akin to the person's hobbies, with an element of individualism being required, rather than a formal day care approach. Flexibility of services is also needed, as there is often a need to cover times when a carer is working.

7. Memory

Both Hilda and the keyworker identified a moderate problem with memory, with significant help being given by friends, relatives and local services. However, this help was identified as being insufficient to meet the need for more stimulating activities, to assist with cognitive difficulties.

Memory is frequently a problem highlighted by many younger people, although another concern is related to the prescribing of anti-dementia drugs, suggesting that if this had happened earlier, the person with dementia could have gained more benefit.

8. Eyesight/hearing/communication

Both Jack's keyworker and Hilda identified no problems with his eyesight or hearing.

This area has not been identified to any great extent within the younger population apart from some people with perceptual problems and losing glasses.

9. Mobility/falls

Jack had no problems with his mobility and this was identified by both interviewees as not a problem area.

Many of the problems with mobility with this group are that they are either not very active and prone to falls and accidents, or are too active and liable to wander. As with Jack, there are problems in organising their own transport or using public transport effectively.

10. Continence

Jack is presently not incontinent, and both interviewees described this as not an area of need.

There may be variation in the services available to meet peoples' needs for continence. There is some general acceptance of incontinence problems in people with dementia and, as a result, investigations into the cause of the problem may not be carried out thoroughly.

11. Physical health

Jack had few physical health problems, and both interviewees described this area as one of no need.

Unlike people over 65, those under 65 have a mixture of minor physical health problems, but the frequency of this need is lower.

12. Drugs

Jack was on an acetylcholinesterase-inhibitor drug, which required administration by Hilda. He did not experience any adverse side-effects. Therefore, both interviewees regarded this as a met need, due to help given. There was identification of the community psychiatric nurse's role in monitoring this, and agreement that Jack was receiving the right type of help.

Compliance when self-administering medication can be an issue for people with dementia. Some need is identified when a person is considered to have benefited from an earlier prescription of the acetylcholinesterase-inhibitor drugs, while others experience side-effects and identify the need for more professional involvement in prescribing and explaining the medication.

13. Psychotic symptoms

Jack's carer identified that he had some moderate problems with hallucinations, but these had been resolved by her being involved in coping strategies. The keyworker did not identify any psychotic symptoms.

There are frequently issues identified with hallucinating and episodes of paranoia, but these are not always taken seriously; the issue is also raised that psychotic symptoms need to be monitored more frequently.

14. Psychological distress

Both Hilda and the keyworker identified that Jack had times when he felt quite low in mood, potentially because he was left alone for long periods. The keyworker identified that he was receiving the right type of help, but needed more of it, while the carer did not feel that he was receiving any help from local services.

Carers frequently identify a number of problems that could make the younger person with dementia sad or low in mood, often as a result of having some insight into their problems and identifying that they are unoccupied or under-stimulated. There are issues that depression is not taken seriously in people with dementia, and carers identify the need for monitoring of the person's mental state.

15. Information (on condition and treatment)

Jack knew that he had Alzheimer's disease and watched out for information on this. Both the carer and the professional did not regard this as an area of need.

16. Deliberate self-harm

Hilda and the keyworker felt that Jack would not harm himself, and both scored this as a no need area. However, there were some concerns regarding the perception that he was, at times, low in mood, and that he might harm himself then.

It has been noted that people who are bored and frustrated with being alone for long periods pose a risk for self-harm.

17. Inadvertent self-harm

Both Hilda and the keyworker identified this as a met area of need area due to help given, with both having some concerns because of the long periods that Jack was left alone. There was identification that friends and family offered periodic supervision, and both Hilda and the keyworker identified little or no help from local services, while a moderate amount was needed. Hilda also identified that this issue could get worse in the future.

The main problem identified is the long periods of time that a younger person with dementia could spend alone, which would heighten the potential for inadvertent self-harm with everyday household items, such as the cooker, for which carers would have to make decisions about how to make them safe.

18. Abuse/neglect

While Hilda did not recognise this as a problem area, the keyworker identified some potential for abuse, although they identified that the support they received from their carer and local services would meet these needs.

Some younger people with dementia could be at risk of abuse. This could be sexual or financial in nature and for many the presence of a carer can lessen the risk of abuse, as, for example, they could take a stronger hand in a person's finances. Again, the issue of being left at home for long periods of time should heighten peoples' concerns about the person they are caring for being abused by another person.

19. Behaviour

Both interviewees identified Jack's behaviour as an area of no need.

Some aggressive and inappropriate sexual behaviour have been areas of need for younger people with dementia, but for most people these needs are met.

20. Alcohol

Again this was an area where neither interviewee had concerns about Jack.

This area is not frequently identified as a major problem for people with dementia. Some individuals with Korsakoff's syndrome require supervision by a carer.

21. Company

Both interviewees identified that Jack had an unmet need for help with social contact and company. Much of this related to the long periods of time that he would spend at home alone, while his wife worked. Both regarded the main source of support as his relatives and friends, and although he was getting support from local services, they identified a need for more assistance.

This is frequently a common problem for young people with dementia and their carers. The other area of concern is with people in long-term care, who have a need for more one-to-one and social input.

22. Intimate relationships

This was considered to be an area of no need for Jack as he still had a good relationship with Hilda.

For most people with young-onset dementia this area is not considered an area of need, with people being content with their present arrangements. However, for a few users this area is unmet and evidenced by the person seeking out inappropriate contact with others, making it an unmet need for the person.

23. Money

Hilda and the keyworker both identified this as a met need, as Hilda was managing all of Jack's finances. Hilda was satisfied that this was the right type of help, and did not identify that support was needed from local services.

Typically, most people feel that the complete management of the person with dementia's finances is a met need. There can be some major issues about people having to obtain Enduring Power of Attorney to access finances in the name of the person with dementia, and issues of access joint accounts, when someone has dementia. There was often some uncertainty about the legal position, regarding finances.

24. Benefits

Jack's carer was not sure whether she was getting the correct benefits and their social worker was advising her on this. The keyworker was sure they were getting their full entitlement.

This area is one in which carers frequently request more information. People largely identify that they are getting what they are entitled to, but feel they do not get it easily, and they often have difficulty seeking assistance when needed.

A. Carer's need for information

Both Hilda and the keyworker identified that Hilda was well informed about Jack's illness and regarded this as an area of no need. Hilda said that she had struggled with information when Jack was first diagnosed, but was now in contact with appropriate associations.

Other carers often report that information is not always easy to access, and that sometimes there is too much information, often in a format that is difficult for them to access.

B. Carer's psychological distress

Both Hilda and the keyworker identified a serious unmet need for help with Hilda's own psychological distress. She identified that there were other problems present, which potentially she would have normally handled well. However, with the additional stresses of caring, this was an added factor on top of other concerns. The keyworker was able to identify that Hilda had issues that left her stressed, but felt that support was available to her on request.

Most carers acknowledge that they feel stressed from the pressures of caring. Some report the use of anti-depressants or are receiving counselling. Others can feel guilty about the use of what they consider to be inappropriate facilities.

12 References

Age Concern (1998) *Older People in the United Kingdom: Some basic facts*. London: Age Concern.

Altman, D. G. (1991) *Practical Statistics for Medical Research*. London: Chapman & Hall.

Alzheimer's Disease Society (1993) *The Younger People with Dementia*. London: Alzheimer's Disease Society.

Alzheimer's Society (2000) *National Database of Services for Younger People with Dementia*. London: Alzheimer's Society.

American Psychiatric Association (1994) *Diagnostic and Statistical Manual of Mental Disorders*, 4th edn (DSM–IV). Washington, DC: American Psychiatric Association.

Anderson, D. N. & Philpott, R. M. (1991) The changing pattern of referrals for psychogeriatric consultation in the general hospital: an eight year study. *International Journal of Geriatric Psychiatry*, **6**, 801–807.

Andrews, G. & Henderson, S. (eds) (1999) *Unmet Needs in Psychiatry: Problems, Resources, Responses*. Cambridge: Cambridge University Press.

Arie, T. (1974) Day care in geriatric psychiatry. *Gerontologia Clinica*, **17**, 31–39.

Arie, T. & Jolley, D. (1982) Making services work: organisation and style of psychogeriatric services. In *The Psychiatry of Later Life* (eds R. Levy & F. Post), pp. 222–251. Oxford: Blackwell.

Aronson, M. K., Cox, D., Guastadisegni, P., *et al* (1992) Dementia and the nursing home: association with care needs. *Journal of the American Geriatrics Society*, **40**, 27–33.

Ashaye, O. A., Livingston, G. & Orrell, M. W. (2003) Does standardised needs assessment improve the outcome of psychiatric day hospital care for older people? A randomised controlled trial. *Aging and Mental Health*, **7**, 195–199.

Audini, B., Lelliott, P., Banerjee, S., *et al* (2001) *Old Age Psychiatric Day Hospital Survey*. London: Royal College of Psychiatrists' Faculty for the Psychiatry of Old Age & College Research Unit. http://www.rcpsych.ac.uk/college/faculty/oap/dayhospitals/oapdayhospsurvey.pdf

Audit Commission (1997) *The Coming of Age: Improving Care Services for Older People*. London: Audit Commission.

Audit Commission (1999a) *Audit Guide: Mental Health Services for Older People*. London: Audit Commission.

Audit Commission (1999b) *Best Value and the Audit Commission in England*. London: Audit Commission.

Audit Commission (2000) *Forget-me-not: Mental Health Services for Older People*. London: Audit Commission.

Bach, M., Hofmann, W. & Nikolaus, T. (1995) *Geriatrisches Basisassessment. Handlungsanleitungen für die Praxis*. Munich: MMV Medizin Verlag.

Badger, T. A. (1998) Depression, physical health impairment and service use among older adults. *Public Health Nursing*, **15**, 136–145.

Baker, A. A. & Byrne, R. J. F. (1977) Another style of psychogeriatric service. *British Journal of Psychiatry*, **130**, 123–126.

Ball, C. (1993) The rise and fall of day hospitals. *International Journal of Geriatric Psychiatry*, **8**, 783–784.

Barker, J. C., Mitteness, L. S. & Wood, S. J. (1988) Gate-keeping: residential managers and elderly tenants. *The Gerontologist*, **28**, 610–619.

Beats, B., Trinkle, D. & Levy, R. (1993) Day hospital provision for the elderly mentally ill within the SE Thames Regional Health Authority. *International Journal of Geriatric Psychiatry*, **8**, 442–443.

Bebbington, P. E., Marsden, L. & Brewin, C. R. (1997) The need for psychiatric treatment in the general population: the Camberwell Needs for Care Survey. *Psychological Medicine*, **27**, 821–834.

Bedford, S., Melzer, D., Dening, T., *et al* (1996) What becomes of people with dementia referred to community psychogeriatric teams? *International Journal of Geriatric Psychiatry*, **11**, 1051–1056.

Beecham, J. & Knapp, M. (1992) Costing psychiatric interventions. In *Measuring Mental Health Needs* (eds G. Thornicroft, C. Brewin & J. K. Wing), pp. 200–224. London: Gaskell.

Bell, J. S. & Gilleard, C. J. (1986) Psychometric prediction of psychogeriatric day care outcome. *British Journal of Clinical Psychology*, **25**, 195–200.

Bergmann, K., Foster, E. M., Justice, A. W., et al (1978) Management of the demented elderly patient in the community. *British Journal of Psychiatry*, **132**, 441–449.

Blessed, G., Tomlinson, B. E. & Roth, M. (1968) The association between quantitative measures of dementia and of senile change in the cerebral grey matter of elderly subjects. *British Journal of Psychiatry*, **114**, 798–811.

BMFSFJ (Bundesministerium für Familie, Senioren, Frauen und Jugend (Hrsg.)) (2001) *Vierter Altenbericht. Risiken, Lebensqualität und Versorgung Hochaltriger – unter besonderer Berücksichtigung demenzieller Erkrankungen.* Bonn: BMFSFJ.

Boardman, A. P, Hodgson, R. E, Lewis, M., et al (1999) North Staffordshire community beds study: longitudinal evaluation of psychiatric in-patient units attached to community mental health centres. I: Methods, outcome and patient satisfaction. *British Journal of Psychiatry*, **175**, 70–78.

Bollini, P., Muscettola, G. & Piazza, A. (1986) Mental health care in southern Italy: application of care-control methodology for the evaluation of the impact of the 1978 psychiatric reform. *Psychological Medicine*, **16**, 701–707.

Bowling, A., Formby, J., Grant, K., et al (1991) A randomized controlled trial of nursing home and long-stay geriatric ward care for elderly people. *Age and Ageing*, **20**, 316–324.

Bramesfeld, A., Adler, G., Brassen, S., et al (2001) Day-clinic treatment of late-life depression. *International Journal of Geriatric Psychiatry*, **16**, 82–87.

Brewin, C. R. & Wing, J. K. (1993) The MRC Needs for Care Assessment: progress and controversies. *Psychological Medicine*, **23**, 837–841.

Brewin, C. R., Wing, J. K., Mangen, S. P., et al (1987) Principles and practice of measuring needs in the long-term mentally ill: The MRC needs for care assessment. *Psychological Medicine*, **17**, 971–981.

Brewin, C. R., Wing, J. K., Mangen, S. P., et al (1988) Needs for care among the long-term mentally ill: a report from the Camberwell high contact survey. *Psychological Medicine*, **18**, 457–468.

British Geriatrics Society & the Health Visitors' Association (1986) *Health visiting for the health of the aged: a joint policy statement.* London: BGS/HVA.

Brown, K. & Groom, L. (1995) General practice health checks of elderly people: a countywide survey. *Health Trends*, **27**, 89–91.

Brown, K., Boot, D., Groom, L., et al (1997). Problems found in the over-75s by the annual health check. *British Journal of General Practitioners*, **47**, 31–35.

Bula, C. J., Berod, A. C., Stuck, A. E., et al (1999) Effectiveness of preventative in-home geriatric assessment in well functioning, community dwelling older people: secondary analysis of a randomised trial. *Journal of the American Geriatric Society*, **47**, 389–395.

Bullinger, M., Kirchberger I. (1998) *SF-36 Fragebogen zum Gesundheitszustand.* Handanweisung. Göttingen: Hogrefe.

Burch, S., Longbottom, J., McKay, M., et al (1999) A randomized controlled trial of day hospital and day centre therapy. *Clinical Rehabilitation*, **13**, 105–112.

Burch, S., Longbottom, J., McKay, M., et al (2000) The Huntingdon Day Hospital Trial: secondary outcome measures. *Clinical Rehabilitation*, **14**, 447–453.

Butler, A., Oldman, C. & Greve, J. (1983) *Sheltered Housing for the Elderly: Policy Practice and the Consumer.* London: Allen & Unwin.

Butler, M. M. (1987) *Health visitors' use of risk criteria in an experimental screening project.* In *Preventive Care of the Elderly: A Review of Current Developments* (eds R. C. Taylor & E. G. Buckley). Occasional Paper 35. London: Royal College of General Practitioners.

Butterworth, M. (1993) *Pre-senile dementia: Results of the questionnaire.* London: Alzheimer's Disease Society.

Campbell, A. J., McCosh, L. M., Reinken, J., et al (1983) Dementia in old age and the need for services. *Age and Ageing*, **12**, 11–16.

Carter, M. F., Crosby, C., Geertshuis, S., et al (1996) Developing reliability in client-centred mental health needs assessment. *Journal of Mental Health*, **5**, 233–243.

Caslyn, R. J., Roades, L. A. & Caslyn, D. S. (1992) Acquiescence in needs assessment studies of the elderly. *The Gerontologist*, **32**, 246–252.

Cassel, C. K. (1994) Researching the health needs of elderly people (Editorial). *BMJ*, **308**, 1655–1656.

Chester, R. & Bender, M. (1999) *Reconstructing Dementia: The man with the worried eyes.* London: Sage.

Cole, M. G., Fenton, F. R., Engelsmann, F., et al (1991) Effectiveness of geriatric consultations in an acute care hospital: A randomized clinical trial. *Journal of American Geriatric Society*, **39**, 183–188.

Cooper, B. (1993) Principles of service provision in old age psychiatry. In *Psychiatry in the Elderly* (eds R. Jacoby & C. Oppenheimer), pp. 274–300. London: Oxford University Press.

Cooper, B. (1997) Principles of service provision in old age psychiatry. In *Psychiatry in the Elderly,* 2nd edn (eds R. Jacoby & C. Oppenheimer), pp. 357–375. Oxford: Oxford University Press.

Cooper, B. & Bickel, H. (1989) Prävalenz und Inzidenz von Demenzerkrankungen in der Altenbevölkerung. *Nervenarzt*, **60**, 472–482.

Copeland, J. R. M., Dewey, M. E., Wood, N., *et al* (1987) Range of mental illness among the elderly in the community. Prevalence in Liverpool using the GMS–AGECAT package. *British Journal of Psychiatry*, **150**, 815–823.

Corcoran, E., Guerandel, A. & Wringley, M. (1994) The day hospital in psychiatry of old age – what difference does it make. *Irish Journal of Psychological Medicine*, **11**, 110–115.

Crome, P. & Phillipson, C. (2000) Assessment of need (Editorial). *Age and Ageing*, **29**, 479–480.

Currie, A., McAllister-Willams, R. H. & Jacques, A. (1995) A comparison study of day hospital and day centre attenders. *Health Bulletin*, **53**, 365–372.

Dech, H. (2001) Die versteckten Opfer der Demenz – Zur Situation pflegender Angehöriger. In Hessisches Sozialministerium (Hrsg): *Altenhilfe in Europa*. Wiesbaden: HSM.

Dech, H., Ndetei, D. M. & Machleidt, W. (2003) Social change, globalization and transcultural psychiatry. *Psychiatrica Neurologica Japonica*, **105**, 17–27.

Department of Health (1995) *Building Bridges. A Guide to Arrangements for Interagency Working for the Care and Protection of Severely Mentally Ill People*. London: Department of Health.

Department of Health (1995) *NHS Responsibilities for Meeting Continuing Health Care Needs*. London: HMSO

Department of Health (1998) *A First Class Service: Quality in the New NHS*. London: HMSO.

Department of Health (1999) *Modernising the Care Programme Approach*. London: Department of Health.

Department of Health (2000) *Effective Care Co-ordination in Mental Health Services: A Policy Booklet. National Service Framework Project: Care Programme Approach*. http://www.info-exchange.org.uk/nsf/cpa/

Department of Health (2001) *National Service Framework for Older People: Modern Standards and Service Models*. London: HMSO.

Department of Health (2002) *The Single Assessment Process: Assessment Tools and Scales*. London: HMSO.

Department of Health Social Services Inspectorate (1990) *The Care Programme Approach for People with a Mental Illness Referred to the Specialist Psychiatrist Service*. London: HMSO.

Deutscher Bundestag (Hrsg) (2002) *Enquête-Kommission Demographischer Wandel. Herausforderungenunserer älter werdenden Gesellschaft an den Einzelnen und die Politik*. Berlln Deutscher Bundestag.

Dowd, S. & Davidhizar, R. (1999) Opening up to the Katz Index. *Elderly Care*, **11**, 9–12.

Drennan, V. (1987) Working with groups of elderly people. In *Health Visiting and Older People* (ed. L. Day). London: Health Education Authority.

Drennan, V., Iliffe, S., Haworth, D., *et al* (2003) A picture of health. *Health Services Journal*, **113**, 22–24.

Ebrahim, S., Hedley, R. & Sheldon, M. (1984) Low levels of ill health among elderly non-consulters in general practice. *BMJ*, **289**, 1273–1275.

Fasey, C. (1994) The day hospital in old age psychiatry: The case against. *International Journal of Geriatric Psychiatry*, **9**, 519–523.

Feldman, E., Mayou, R., Hawton, K., *et al* (1987) Psychiatric disorder in medical inpatients. *Quarterly Journal of Medicine*, **241**, 405–412.

Field, E., Walker, M. & Orrell, M. (2002) Social networks and health of older people living in sheltered housing. *Aging & Mental Health*, **6**, 376–390.

Finch, J. & Orrell, M. (1999) *Standards for Mental Health Services for Older People*. London: Health Advisory Service & Pavilion Publishing.

Folstein, M. F., Folstein, S. E. & McHugh, P. R. (1975) Mini-mental state: A practical method for grading the cognitive state of patients for the clinician. *Journal of Psychiatric Research*, **12**, 189–198.

Forster, A., Young, J. & Langhorne, P. (1999) Systematic review of day hospital care for elderly people. *BMJ*, **318**, 837–841.

Forster, A., Young, J. & Langhorne, P. (2001) Medical day hospital care for the elderly versus alternative forms of care. Cochrane Review. In *The Cochrane Library*, Issue 2 Oxford: Update Software.

Freer, C. (1987) Detecting hidden needs in the elderly: screening or case finding. In *Preventive Care of the Elderly: A Review of Current Developments* (eds R. C. Taylor & E. G. Buckley). Occasional Paper 35. London: Royal College of General Practitioners.

Freyne, A., Kidd, N., Coen, R., *et al* (1999) Burden in carers of dementia patients: higher levels in carers of younger sufferers, *International Journal of Geriatric Psychiatry*, **14**, 784–788.

Furness, L., Simpson, R., Chakrabarti, S., *et al* (2000) A comparison of elderly day care and day hospital attenders in Leicestershire: client profile, carer stress and unmet need. *Aging & Mental Health*, **4**, 326–331.

Furst, M. & Sperlinger, D. (1992) *Hour to Hour, Day to Day: A Survey of the Service Experiences of Carers of People with Pre-senile Dementia in the London Borough of Sutton*. Sutton: Department of Psychology, St Helier NHS Trust.

Garms-Homolova, V., Gilgen, R. & Weiss, U. (1996) *Resident Assessment Instrument (RAI) System zur Klientenbeurteilung und Dokumentation*. Koeln: Kuratorium Deutsche Altershilfe.

Gilleard, C. J. (1987) Influence of emotional distress among supporters on the outcome of psychogeriatric day care. *British Journal of Psychiatry*, **150**, 219–223.

Gilleard, C. & Pattie, A. (1979) *Clifton Assessment Procedures for the Elderly*. Windsor: NFER/Nelson.

Gilleard, C. J., Gilleard, E. & Whittick, J. E. (1984) Impact of psychogeriatric day hospital care on the patient's family. *British Journal of Psychiatry*, **145**, 487–492.

Goldberg, D. P. (1978) *Manual of the General Health Questionnaire*. Windsor: NFER.

Goldberg, D. P. (1985) Identifying psychiatric illness among general medical patients. *BMJ*, **291**, 161–162.

Goldberg, D. P., Bridges, K., Duncan-Jones, P., et al (1988) Detecting anxiety and depression in general medical settings. *BMJ*, **97**, 897–899.

Gordon, D. S., Carter, H. & Scott, S. (1997) Profiling the care needs of the population with dementia: A survey in central Scotland. *International Journal of Geriatric Psychiatry*, **12**, 753–759.

Grant, G. & Wenger, G. C. (1993) Dynamics of support networks: Differences and similarities between vulnerable groups. *Irish Journal of Psychology* (Special issue: Psychological aspects of ageing: Well-being and vulnerability), **14**, 79–98.

Greene, J. G. & Timbury, G. C. (1979) A geriatric day hospital service: a five-year review. *Age and Ageing*, **8**, 49–53.

Gurland, B., Golden, R. R., Teresi, J. A., et al (1984) The Short–CARE: an efficient instrument for the assessment of depression, dementia, and disability. *Journal of Gerontology*, **39**, 166–169.

Gustafson, Y., Berggren, D., Brannstrom, B., et al (1988) Acute confusional states in elderly patients treated for femoral neck fracture. *Journal of the American Geriatrics Society*, **36**, 525–530.

Hamid, W. A. (1997) The elderly homeless men in Bloomsbury hostels: their needs for services. *International Journal of Geriatric Psychiatry*, **12**, 724–727.

Hamid, W. A., Howard, R. & Silverman, M. (1995) Needs assessment in old age psychiatry: a need for standardization. *International Journal of Geriatric Psychiatry*, **10**, 533–540.

Hancock, G. A., Reynolds, T., Woods, B., et al (2003) The needs of older people with mental health problems according to the user, the carer, and the staff. *International Journal of Geriatric Psychiatry*, **18**, 803–811.

Harrison, R., Savla, N. & Kafetz, K. (1990) Dementia, depression, and physical disability in a London borough: a survey of elderly people in and out of residential care and implications for future developments. *Age and Ageing*, **19**, 97–103.

Harvey, R. J. (1998) *Young Onset Dementia: Epidemiology, clinical symptoms, family burden, support and outcome*. London: North Thames NHS Executive.

Herrman, H., Schofield, H., Murphy, B., et al (1994) The experiences and quality of life of informal caregivers. In *Quality of Life Assessment: International Perspectives. WHO and IPSEN Foundation Joint Meeting Proceedings*. (Paris, 2–3 July 1993) (eds J. Orley & W. Kuyken), pp. 131–150. Heidelberg: Springer-Verlag.

Hirsch, R. D., Holler, G., Reichwaldt, W., et al (1999) *Leitfaden für die ambulante und teilstationäre gerontopsychiatrische Versorgung*. Baden-Baden: Nomos Verlagsgesellschaft.

Hogg, L. I. & Marshall, M. (1992) Can we measure needs in the homeless mentally ill? Using the MRC Needs for Care Assessment in hostels for the homeless. *Psychological Medicine*, **22**, 1027–1034.

Holshouser, W. L (1988) *Ageing in Place: The demographics and service needs of elders in urban public housing*. Boston, MA: Citizens Housing and Planning Association.

House of Commons (1990) *The National Health Service and Community Care Act*. London: HMSO.

House of Commons (1995) *The Carer Recognition and Services Act*. London: HMSO.

Howard, R. (1994) Day hospitals: The case in favour. *International Journal of Geriatric Psychiatry*, **9**, 525–529.

Huckle, P. L. (1994) Review: Families and dementia. *International Journal of Geriatric Psychiatry*, **9**, 735–741.

Hughes, J., Stewart, K., Challis, D., et al (2001) Care management and the care programme approach: towards integration in old age mental health services. *International Journal of Geriatric Psychiatry*, **16**, 266–272.

Hurrelmann, K. (Hrsg) (1999) *Gesundheitswissenschaften*. Berlln Springer-Verlag.

Husband, H. J. & Shah M. N. (1999) Information and advice received by carers of younger people with dementia. *Psychiatric Bulletin*, **23**, 94–96.

Ihl, R. & Frölich, L. (1991) *Die Reisberg-Skalen*. Weinheim: Beltz.

Iliffe, S., Haines, A., Gallivan, S., et al (1991a) Assessment of elderly people in general practice.1. Social circumstances and mental state. *British Journal of General Practice*, **41**, 9–12.

Iliffe, S., Haines, A., Gallivan, S., et al (1991b) Assessment of elderly people in general practice. 2. Functional abilities and medical problems. *British Journal of General Practice*, **41**, 13–15.

Iliffe, S., Gould, M. M. & Wallace, P. (1999) Assessment of older people in the community: lessons from Britain's '75 and over checks. *Reviews in Clinical Gerontology*, **9**, 305–316.

Impallomeni, M. & Starr, J. (1995) The changing face of community and institutional care for the elderly. *Journal of Public Health Medicine*, **17**, 171–178.

Jackson, S. & Mittelmark, M. B. (1997) Unmet needs for formal home and community services among African-American and white older adults: The Forsyth County ageing study. *Journal of Applied Gerontology*, **16**, 298–316.

Janzon, K., Law, S., Watts, C., et al (2000) Lost and confused. *Health Service Journal*, **9**, 26–29.

Jewell, M., Wurr, S. & Zadik, T. (1997) Kindred spirits. *PSIGE Newsletter*, issue 59.

Jiménez, J. F., Moreno, B., Rodríguez, E., et al (1995) *CAN Cuestionario de Evaluación de Necesidades de Camberwell*. Granada: Grupo de Investigación de Salud Mental Granada Sur. Publicación patrocinada por Laboratorios Upjhon/Duphar.

Johnston, M., Wakeling, A., Graham, N., *et al* (1987) Cognitive impairment, emotional disorder and length of stay of elderly patients in a district general hospital. *British Journal of Medical Psychology*, **60**, 133–139.

Jolley, D. (1994) The development of day hospitals and day hospital care. In *Principles and Practice of Geriatric Psychiatry* (eds J. R. M. Copeland, M. Abou-Saleh & D. Blazer), pp. 905–910. Chichester: John Wiley.

Jolley, D. & Arie, T. (1992) Developments in psychogeriatric services. In *Recent Advances in Psychogeriatric Services* (ed. T. Arie), pp. 117–135. Edinburgh: Churchill Livingstone.

Jones, J. & Hunter, D. (1996) Consensus methods for medical and health services research. In *Qualitative Research in Health Care* (eds N. Mays & C. Pope), pp. 46–58. London: BMJ Publishing Group.

Jorm, A. F. & Jacomb, P. A. (1989) The Informant Questionnaire on Cognitive Decline in the Elderly (IQCODE): socio-demographic correlates, reliability, validity and some norms. *Psychological Medicine*, **19**, 1015–1022.

Jorm, A. F., Korten, A. E. & Henderson, A. S. (1987) The prevalence of dementia: a quantitative integration of the literature. *Acta Psychiatrica Scandinavica*, **76**, 465–479.

Kamis-Gould, E. & Minsky, S. (1995) Needs assessment in mental health service planning. *Administration and Policy in Mental Health*, **23**, 43–58.

Kay, D. W. K. (1989) Ageing of the population: measuring the need for care. *Age and Ageing*, **18**, 73–76.

Kaye, L. & Monk, A. (1991) Social relations in enriched housing for the aged: a case study. *Journal of Housing for the Elderly*, **9**, 111–126.

Kewley, J. (1984) Self-help for the elderly. *Community View*, April.

Kitchen, G., Reynolds, T., Ashaye, O., *et al* (2002) A comparison of methods for the evaluation of mental health day hospitals for older people. *Journal of Mental Health*, **11**, 667–675.

Kitzinger, J. (1996) Introducing focus groups. In *Qualitative Research in Health Care* (eds N. Mays & C. Pope), pp. 36–45. London: BMJ Publishing Group.

Lam, D., Sewell, M., Bell, G., *et al* (1989) Who needs psychogeriatric continuing care? *International Journal of Geriatric Psychiatry*, **4**, 109–114.

Lawton, M. P. & Brody, E. M. (1969) Assessment of older people: self-maintaining and instrumental activities of daily living. *Gerontologist*, **9**, 179–186.

Leese, M., Johnson, S., Slade, M, *et al* (1998) User perspectives on needs and satisfaction with mental health services. PRiSM Psychosis Study. 8. *British Journal of Psychiatry*, **173**, 409–415.

Levin, E. (1997) Carers – problems, strains and services. In *Psychiatry In The Elderly*, 2nd edn (eds R. Jacoby & C. Oppenheimer), pp. 392–402. Oxford: Oxford University Press.

Light, E., Niederehe, G. & Lebowitz, B. (1994) *Stress Effects on Family Caregivers of Alzheimer's Patients. Research and Interventions*. New York: Springer.

Little, A. & Doherty, B. (1996) Going beyond cognitive assessment: assessment of adjustment, behaviour and the environment. In *Handbook of Clinical Psychology of Ageing* (ed. R. T. Woods), pp. 475–508. Chichester: John Wiley & Sons.

Lloyd, M. P. (1993) *Early Onset Dementia in the Maidstone Area: Identifying needs of sufferers and carers*. Maidstone Health Authority/ Mid Kent Area Social Services.

Lobo, A., Pérez-Echeverría, M. J. & Artal, J. (1986) Validity of the scaled version of the General Health Questionnaire (GHQ–28) in a Spanish population. *Psychological Medicine*, **16**, 135–140.

Lobo, A., Montón, C., Campos, R., *et al* (1994) *Detección de morbilidad psíquica en la práctica médica. El Nuevo Instrumento EADG*. Zaragoza: Editorial Luzán.

Luscombe, G., Brodaty, H. & Freeth, S. (1998) Younger people with dementia: diagnostic issues, effects on carers and use of services, *International Journal of Geriatric Psychiatry*, **13**, 323–330.

Macdonald, A. J. D., Mann, A. H., Jenkins, R., *et al* (1982) An attempt to determine the impact of four types of care upon the elderly in London by the study of matched groups. *Psychological Medicine*, **12**, 93–200.

Macleod, E. & Mein, P. (1987) The nursing care team: a task force approach. In *Preventive Care of the Elderly: A Review of Current Developments* (eds R. C. Taylor & E. G. Buckley). Occasional Paper 35. London: Royal College of General Practitioners.

Mahoney, F. I. & Barthel, D. W. (1965) Functional evaluation. The Barthel Index. *Maryland State Medical Journal*, **14**, 61–65.

Marshall, M., Hogg, L. I., Gath, D. H., *et al* (1995) The Cardinal Needs Schedule – a modified version of the MRC Needs for Care Assessment Schedule. *Psychological Medicine*, **25**, 605–617.

Martin, M., Pehrson, J. & Orrell, M. (1999) A survey of social services needs assessments for elderly mentally ill people in England and Wales. *Age and Ageing*, **28**, 575–577.

Martin, M. D., Hancock, G. A., Richardson, D., *et al* (2002) An evaluation of needs in elderly continuing care settings. *International Psychogeriatrics*, **14**, 379–404.

Maslow, A. H. (1954) *Motivation and Personality*. New York: Harper and Row.

Mateos, R. & Rodríguez, A. (1989) *Estudio de Epidemiología Psiquiátrica en la Comunidad Gallega*. Santiago de Compostela: Xunta de Galicia.

Mateos, R., Camba, M. T., Gómez, R., *et al* (1994) La Unidad de Psicogeriatría del Area de Salud. Un dispositivo asistencial novedoso en la red de Salud Mental de Galicia. Saúde Mental e Sociedade. *Proceedings of the*

2nd Congress of the Asociación Galega de Saúde Mental (28–29 May 1993, Santiago de Compostela, Spain), pp. 259–275. Vigo: Asociación Galega de Saúde Mental.

Mateos, R., González, F., Páramo, M., et al (2000) The Galicia Study of Mental Health of the Elderly I: general description of methodology. *International Journal of Methods in Psychiatry Research*, **9**, 165–173.

McCabe, R., Bavin, D., Lenihan, P., et al (2000) Primary care for older people: investigating the needs of older people in the community. *Community Practitioner*, **73**, 832–834.

McEwan, E. (1992) The consumer's perception of need. In *Long-Term Care for Elderly People* (eds D. Seely & J. Kitc). London: Department of Health/HMSO.

McWalter, G., Toner, H., McWalter, A., et al (1998) A community needs assessment: The Care Needs Assessment Pack for Dementia (CARENAPD) – its development, reliability and validity. *International Journal of Geriatric Psychiatry*, **13**, 16–22.

Medical Research Council (1994) *Topic review on care of the elderly*. London: MRC.

Ministry of Housing and Local Government (1969) *Housing Standards and Costs: Accommodation Specially Designed for Old People*. Circular 82/69. London: HMSO.

Moos, R. H. & Lemke, S. (1992) *Multiphasic Environmental Assessment Procedure*. Palo Alto, CA: Centre for Health Care Evaluation, Stanford University Medical Center.

Montorio, I. & Izal, M. (1996) The geriatric depression scale: a review of its development and utility. *International Psychogeriatrics*, **8**, 103–112.

Morris, J. N., Hawes, C., Fries, B. E., et al (1990) Designing the National Resident Assessment Instrument for nursing homes. *Gerontologist*, **30**, 293–307.

Murphy, E. (1991) Community mental health services: a vision for the future. *BMJ*, **302**, 1064–1065.

Murphy, E. (1992) A more ambitious vision for residential long-term care (Editorial). *International Journal of Geriatric Psychiatry*, **7**, 851–852.

Murphy, E. (1994) The day hospital debate. *International Journal of Geriatric Psychiatry*, **9**, 517–518.

Neville, P., Boyle, A. & Baillon, S. (1999) A descriptive survey of acute bed usage for dementia care in old age psychiatry. *International Journal of Geriatric Psychiatry*, **14**, 348–354.

Nikolaus, T. (2001) Geriatrisches Assessment. *Zeitschrift für Gerontologie und Geriatrie*, **34** (suppl.) 1, 36–42.

Nikolaus, T. & Specht-Leible, N. (1992) *Das geriatrische Assesssment*. Munich: MMV.

Nikolaus, T., Specht-Leible, N., Bach, M., et al (1999) A randomised trial of comprehensive geriatric assessment and home intervention in the care of hospitalised patients. *Age and Ageing*, **28**, 543–550.

Nolan, M. & Grant, G. (1992) *Regular Respite: An Evaluation of a Hospital Rota Bed Scheme for Elderly People*. Age Concern Institute of Gerontology. London: Ace Books.

Nolan, M., Grant, G., Caldock, K., et al (1994) *A Framework for Assessing the Needs of Family Carers: A Multi-Disciplinary Guide*. Stoke-on-Trent: BASE Publications.

Nolan, M. R., Keady, J. & Grant, G. (1995) CAMI: a basis for assessment and support with family carers. *British Journal of Adult/Elderly Care Nursing*, **1**, 822–826.

O'Brien, J., Ames, D. & Burns, A. (2000) *Dementia*. London: Arnold.

O'Donovan, S. (1999) The service needs of younger people with dementia. *Signpost*, **4**(3), 3–6.

O'Driscoll, C. (1993) The TAPS Project 7: Mental hospital closure – a literature review of outcome studies and evaluative techniques. *British Journal of Psychiatry*, **162** (suppl. 19), 7–17.

O'Driscoll, C. & Leff, J. (1993) The TAPS Project 8: Design of the research study on long-stay patients. *British Journal of Psychiatry*, **162** (suppl. 19), 18–24.

Pampalon, R., Saucier, A., Berthiaume, N., et al (1996) The selection of needs indicators for regional resource allocation in the fields of health and social services in Québec. *Social Scicence and Medicine*, **42**, 909–922.

Pattie, A. H. & Gilleard, C. J. (1975) A brief psychogeriatric assessment schedule: validation against psychiatric diagnosis and discharge from hospital. *British Journal of Psychiatry*, **127**, 489–493.

Pattie, A. H. & Gilleard, C. J. (1979) *Manual of the Clifton Assessment Procedures for the Elderly (CAPE)*. Sevenoaks: Hodder & Stoughton Educational.

Pearce, S. M. (1982) Review of day-hospital provision in psychogeriatrics. *Health Trends*, **14**, 92–95.

Penfold, M. (1998) *The Forgotten Age: a report on the circumstances and service needs of young people with dementia and their carers*. London: Metropolitan Housing Trust and Hexagon Housing Association.

Phelan, M., Slade, M., Thornicroft, G., et al (1995). The Camberwell Assessment of Need: the validity and reliability of an instrument to assess the needs of people with severe mental illness. *British Journal of Psychiatry*, **167**, 589–595.

Philp, I. (1997) *Outcomes Assessment for Healthcare in Elderly People*. London: Farrand Press.

Philp, I., McKee, K. J., Meldrum, P., et al (1995) Community care for demented and non-demented elderly people: a comparison study of financial burden, service use, and unmet needs in family supporters. *BMJ*, **310**, 1503–1506.

Pitt, B. (1991a) The mentally disordered old person in the general hospital ward. In *Handbook of Studies on General Hospital Psychiatry* (eds. F. K. Judd, G. D. Burrows & D. R. Lipsett), pp. 225–230. New York: Amsterdam: Elsevier.

Pitt, B. (1991*b*) Depression in the general hospital setting. *International Journal of Geriatric Psychiatry*, **6**, 363–370.

Pryce, I. G., Griffiths, R. D., Gentry, R. M., *et al* (1993) How important is the assessment of social skills in current long-stay in-patients? An evaluation of clinical response to needs for assessment, treatment, and care in a long-stay psychiatric in-patient population. *British Journal of Psychiatry*, **162**, 498–502.

Querido J. (1959) An investigation into the clinical, social and mental factors determining the results of hospital treatment. *British Journal of Preventive Social Medicine*, **13**, 33–49.

Ramsay, M., Winget, C. &. Higginson, I. (1995) Review: measures to determine the outcome of community service for people with dementia. *Age and Ageing*, **24**, 73–83.

Regier, D. A., Kaelber, C. T., Rae, D. S., *et al* (1998) Limitations of diagnostic criteria and assessment instruments for mental disorders. Implications for research and policy. *Archives of General Psychiatry*, **55**, 109–115.

Reich, J. W. & Zautra, A. J. (1991) Experimental measurement approaches to internal control in at-risk older adults. *Journal of Social Issues*, **47**, 143–158.

Reisberg, B., Ferris, S. H., deLeon, M. J., *et al* (1982) The Global Deterioration Scale (GDS): an instrument for the assessment of primary degenerative dementia. *American Journal of Psychiatry*, **139**, 1136–1139.

Reuben, D. B., Frank, J. C., Hirsch, S. H., *et al* (1999) A randomised clinical trial of outpatient comprehensive geriatric assessment coupled with an intervention to increase adherence to recommendations. *Journal of American Geriatric Society*, **47**, 269–276.

Reynolds, T. & Orrell, M. (2001) Needs assessment in mental health care for older people. In *Measuring Mental Health Needs* (ed. G Thornicroft), pp. 393–406. London: Gaskell.

Reynolds, T., Thornicroft, G., Abas, M., *et al* (2000) Camberwell Assessment of Need for the Elderly (CANE): development, validity and reliability. *British Journal of Psychiatry*, **176**, 444–452.

Richter, D., Lowens, S. & Liekenbrock, A. (2000) Need for psychosocial nursing care in a psychogeriatric nursing home. *Zeitschrift für Gerontologie und Geriatrie*, **33**, 17–23.

Robinson, S. (1961) Problems of drug trials in elderly people. *Gerontologia Clinica*, **3**, 247–257.

Rockwood, K. (1989) Acute confusion in elderly medical patients. *Journal of the American Geriatrics Society*, **37**, 150–154.

Rodriguez-Ferrera, S. & Vassilas, C. A. (1998) Older people with schizophrenia: providing services for a neglected group (Editorial). *BMJ*, **317**, 293–294.

Rook, K. S. (1998) Investigating the positive and negative sides of personal relationships: through a lens darkly? In *The Dark Side of Close Relationships* (eds B. H. Spitzberg & W. R. Cupach), pp. 369–393. Mahwah, NJ: Lawrence Erlbaum Associates.

Rosenvinge. H. P. (1994) The role of the psychogeriatric day hospital. A consensus document. *Psychiatric Bulletin*, **18**, 733–736.

Sartorius, N. (1999) Assessing needs for psychiatric services. In *Unmet Needs in Psychiatry: Problems, Resources, Responses* (eds G. Andrews & S. Henderson), pp. 3–7. Cambridge: Cambridge University Press.

Sidell, M. (1995) *Health in Old Age: Myth, Mystery and Management*. Milton Keynes: Open University Press.

Simmons, P. & Orrell, M. (2001) State funded continuing care for the elderly mentally ill: a legal and ethical solution? *International Journal of Geriatric Psychiatry*, **16**, 1–4.

Slade, M. & Thornicroft, G. (1995) Health and social needs of the long-term mentally ill. *Current Opinion in Psychiatry*, **8**, 126–129.

Slade, M., Phelan, M., Thornicroft, G., *et al* (1996) The Camberwell Assessment of Need (CAN): comparison of assessments by staff and patients of the needs of the severely mentally ill. *Social Psychiatry and Psychiatric Epidemiology*, **31**, 109–113.

Slade, M., Leese, M., Taylor, R., *et al* (1999) The association between needs and quality of life in an epidemiologically representative sample of people with psychosis. *Acta Psychiatrica Scandinavica*, **100**, 149–157.

Slade, M., Phelan, M. & Thornicroft, G. (1998) A comparison of needs assessed by staff and by an epidemiologically representative sample of patients with psychosis. *Psychological Medicine*, **28**, 543–550.

Slaets, J. P., Kauffmann, R. H., Duivenvoodrden, H. J., *et al* (1997) A randomized trial of geriatric liason intervention in elderly medical inpatients. *Psychosomatic medicine*, **59**, 585–591.

SPSS (1993) *SPSS for Windows, Version 6*. Chicago, IL: SPSS Inc.

Stevens, A. & Gabbay, J. (1991) Needs assessment, needs assessment. *Health Trends*, **23**, 20–23.

Strauss, A. & Corbin, J. (1998) *Basics of Qualitative Research: Techniques and procedures for developing grounded theory*, 2nd edn. Thousand Oaks, CA: Sage Publications.

Stuck, A. E. (1997) Multidimensionales Geriatrisches Assessment. In *Checkliste Geriatrie* (ed. A. Wettstein), pp. 101–104. Stuttgart: Thieme.

Stuck, A. E., Siu, L. A., Wieland, A. G., *et al* (1993) Comprehensive geriatric assessment: a meta-analysis of controlled trials. *Lancet*, **342**, 1032–1036.

Stuck, A. E., Aronow, H. U., Steiner, A., *et al* (1995) A trial of annual in-home comprehensive geriatric assessments for elderly people living in the community. *New England Journal of Medicine*, **333**, 1184–1189.

Stuck, A. E., Egger, M., Hammer, A., *et al* (2002) Home visits to prevent nursing home admission and functional decline in elderly people: systematic review and meta-regression analysis. *Journal of the American Medical Association*, **287**, 1022–1028.

Taylor, R. C. & Buckley, E. G. (eds) (1987) *Preventive Care of the Elderly: A Review of Current Developments.* Occasional paper 35. London: Royal College of General Practitioners.

Thornicroft, G., Brewin, C. R. & Wing, J. (1992) *Measuring Mental Health Needs.* London: Gaskell.

Tracy, L. (1986) Towards an improved need theory: in response to legitimate criticism. *Behavioural Science*, **31**, 205–218.

Tulloch, A. J. & Moore, V. L. (1979) A randomised controlled trial of geriatric screening and surveillance in general practice. *BMJ*, **29**, 733–742.

UK700 Group (1999) Predictors of quality of life in people with severe mental illness. Study methodology with baseline analysis in the UK700 trial. *British Journal of Psychiatry*, **175**, 426–432.

Van den Akker, M., Buntinx, F., Metsemakers, J. F. M., *et al* (1998) Multimorbidity in general practice: Prevalence, incidence, and determinants of co-occurring chronic and recurrent disease. *Journal of Clinical Epidemiology*, **51**, 367–375.

Vaughan, P. J. (1985) Developments in psychiatric day care. *British Journal of Psychiatry*, **147**, 1–4.

Victor, C. R. (1991) *Health and Health Care in Later Life.* Milton Keynes: Open University Press.

Wade, D. T. & Collin, C. (1988) The Barthel ADL Index: a standardised measure of physical disability? *International Disabilities Studies*, **10**, 64–67.

Walker, M., Orrell, M., Manela, M., *et al* (1998) Do health and use of services differ in residents of sheltered accommodation? A pilot study. *International Journal of Geriatric Psychiatry*, **13**, 617–624.

Walters, K., Iliffe, S., See Tai, S., *et al* (2000) Assessing need from patient, carer and professional perspectives: a feasibility study of the Camberwell Assessment of Need for the Elderly in primary care. *Age & Ageing*, **29**, 505–510.

Walters, K., Iliffe, S. & Orrell, M. (2001) An exploration of help-seeking behaviour in older people with unmet needs. *Family Practice*, **18**, 277–282.

Ware, J. E., Gandek, B. (1998) Overview of the SF–36 Health Survey and the International Quality of Life Assessment (IQOLA) Project. *Journal of Clinical Epidemiology*, **51**, 903–912.

Warrington, J. & Eagles, J. M. (1996) A comparison of cognitively impaired attenders and their coresident carers at day hospitals and day centres in Aberdeen. *International Journal of Geriatric Psychiatry*, **11**, 251–256.

Wattis, P. J., Hobson, J. & Barker, G. (1992) Needs for continuing care of demented people: a model for estimating needs. *Psychiatric Bulletin*, **16**, 465–467.

Wattis, J., Wattis, L. & Arie, T. (1981) Psychogeriatrics: a national survey of a new branch of psychiatry. *BMJ*, **282**, 1529–1533.

Wenger, C. G. (1988) *Old Peoples' Health and Experience of the Caring Services: Accounts from Rural Communities in North Wales.* Liverpool: Liverpool University Press.

Wenger, G. C. (1994) *Support Networks of Older People: A Guide for Practioners.* Bangor: University of Wales Centre for Social Policy Research & Development.

Wenger, G. C. (1997) Social networks and the prediction of elderly people at risk. *Ageing and Mental Health*, **1**, 311–320.

Wenger, C. G. & Shahtahmasebi, S. (1991) Survivors: Support network variation and sources of help in rural communities. *Journal of Cross Cultural Gerontology*, **6**, 41–82.

Weyerer, S., Mann, A. H. & Ames, D. (1995) Praevalenz von Depression und Demenz bei Altenheimbewohnern. *Zeitschrift für Gerontologie und Geriatrie*, **28**, 169–178.

Wilcox, J., Jones, B. & Alldrick, D. (1995) Identifying the support needs of people with dementia and older people with mental illness on a joint community team. A preliminary report. *Journal of Mental Health* (special section: Dementia care), **4**, 157–163.

Wild, C. & Gibis, B. (2003) Evaluations of health interventions in social insurance-based countries: Germany, the Netherlands, and Austria. *Health Policy*, **63**, 187–196.

Williams, E. I. (1987) Scope for intervention following case identification. In *Preventive Care of the Elderly: A Review of Current Developments* (eds R. C. Taylor & E. G. Buckley). Occasional Paper 35. London: Royal College of General Practitioners.

Williams, G. (1986) *Meeting the Housing Needs of the Elderly: Private Initiative or Public Responsibility?* Department of Town & Country Planning Occasional Paper No. 17. Manchester: University of Manchester.

Williams, I. (1974) A follow-up of geriatric patients after socio-medical assessment. *Journal of the Royal College of General Practitioners*, **24**, 341–346.

Williams, I. (1975) A case for screening the elderly. *Update*, **2**, 1275–1285.

Williamson, J., Stokoe, I. H., Gray, S., *et al* (1964) Old people at home; their unreported needs. *Lancet*, **13**, 1117–1120.

Wing, J. K. (1990) Meeting the needs of people with psychiatric disorders. *Social Psychiatry and Psychiatric Epidemiology*, **25**, 2–8.

Wing, J. K., Brewin, C. R. & Thornicroft, G. (1992) Defining mental health needs. In *Measuring Mental Health Needs* (eds G. T. Thornicroft, C. R. Brewin & J. K. Wing), pp. 1–17. London: Gaskell.

Woods, R. T. (2001) Discovering the person with Alzheimer's disease: cognitive, emotional, and behavioural aspects. *Ageing and Mental Health*, **5** (suppl. 1), S7–S16.

Wing, J. K. & Roth, R. (1996) Effectiveness of psychological interventions with older people. In *What Works for Whom? A Critical Review of Psychotherapy Research* (eds A. Fonagy & P. Roth), pp. 321–340. New York: Guilford Press.

Woolrych, R. (1998) *Springboard Housing Association Report on Sheltered Housing Schemes*. London: Springboard Housing Association.

Xenitidis, K., Thornicroft, G., Leese, M., *et al* (2000) Reliability and validity of the CANDID – a needs assessment instrument for adults with learning disabilities and mental health problems. *British Journal of Psychiatry*, **176**, 473–478.

Ybarzábal, M., Mateos, R., García-Álvarez, M. J., *et al* (2002) Validación de la versión española del CANE. Escala de Evaluación de Necesidades para Ancianos de Camberwell. *Revista Psicogeriatría*, **2**, 38–44.

Yesavage, J. A., Brink, T. L., Rose, T. L., *et al* (1983) Development and validation of a geriatric depression scale: a preliminary report. *Journal of Psychiatric Research*, **22**, 37–49.

Young, S. (1993) *Private Tenanted Sheltered Accommodation and the Elderly: A Study into Independence, Security and Social Relationships*. BSc thesis. Guildford: University of Surrey.

Index

Appendix 1

Camberwell Assessment of Need for the Elderly (CANE)

How to use the CANE

The CANE is a comprehensive, person-centred needs assessment tool that has been designed for use with the elderly. It is suitable for use in a variety of clinical and research settings. The CANE has a person-centred approach which allows views of the professional, user and carer to be recorded and compared. The instrument uses the principle that identifying a need means identifying a problem plus an appropriate intervention which will help or alleviate the need. Therefore the CANE models clinical practice and relies on professional expertise for ratings to be completed accurately. Professionals using the CANE need to have had training and experience working with older people and an adequate knowledge of clinical interviewing and decision-making. They should also have good working knowledge of the concepts of need, met need and unmet need. This knowledge can be gained with experience of full CANE assessments and reference to the manual.

There are 24 topics relating to the user and two (A & B) relating to the carer. There are four columns to document ratings so that one or more of the user (U), staff member (S), carer (C) or rater (clinician/researcher) (R) can each express their view.

Section 1

This section aims to assess whether there is currently a need in the specific area. A need is defined as a problem with a potential remedy or intervention. Use the prompts below each area in *italics* on the record form to establish the user's current status with regard to the need area. If there has been a need, then assess whether it was met appropriately. Score each interviewee independently, even though their perceptions of need in each area may differ from one another. The administrator should ask additional questions, probing into the area until he/she can establish whether the person has a significant need that requires assistance and whether they are getting enough of the right type of help. Once this information has been gathered a rating of need can be made. Judgement of rating in this section should be based on normal clinical practice. The CANE is intended to be a framework for assessment grounded in good professional practise and expertise. Although Section 1 in each problem area is the main section of interest to CANE administrators, it often cannot be rated until adequate information has been collected about the area. Indeed, some administrators have found it easier to rate Section 1 once information has been collected from the other Sections 2 to 5. When adequate information has been gathered the rater should clearly be able to make a clinical judgement as to whether the area is a met need, an unmet need or is not a need for the person. Confusion with ratings can be avoided by not directly asking a closed question about whether there is a problem in a certain area (e.g. "Do you have any problems with the food here?") because the person can answer "No". This response may then be mistaken as a 'No need' where in fact it is a 'Met need' because the person is assisted by someone else.

© *The Royal College of Psychiatrists, 2004. This page may be photocopied freely.*

0 = no need If there is no need in the area then, go on to the next page. In this situation the user is coping well independently and does not need any further assistance. For example, the user has reported that they are successfully administering their own medication and do not have any problematic side-effects. Or the staff member reports that the user appeared to be comfortable in his/her home environment and that no alterations to the building are needed or planned.

1 = met need A need is met when there is a mild, moderate or serious problem which is receiving an intervention or assessment which is appropriate and potentially of benefit. This category is also used for problems which would normally not be of clinical significance and would not require a specific intervention. For example, the user is receiving an assessment for poor eyesight or a district nurse is overseeing the administration of medications each day.

2 = unmet need If the need is currently unmet, there is a serious problem requiring intervention or assessment, which is currently receiving no assistance or the *wrong* type or level of help. For example, if a staff member reported that the user was incontinent of large amounts of urine every night despite toileting twice during the night and the use of pads. Or a carer reported that the user had become very hard of hearing and had not received an assessment or suitable hearing aid.

9 = unknown If the person does not know about the nature of the problem or about the assistance he/she receives, go on to the next page. Such a score may mean that further information is needed to make a rating.

For any topic, if Section 1 is rated as 1 or 2, complete Sections 2–4. If Section 1 for the topic is rated as 0 or 9, do not complete Sections 2–4 but go to the next topic area.

Section 2

This section asks about assistance from informal sources during the past month. Informal sources include family, friends or neighbours. Use the examples on the assessment form to prompt the interviewee. Score 1 when assistance is given very occasionally or infrequently. Score 2 when assistance is given more frequently or involves more time/effort. Score 3 when assistance is given daily or is intensive (e.g. long periods of respite). Score 4 when assistance is very intensive and/or daily (e.g. family lives with the user and gives them full assistance with most tasks). Score 9 if the interviewee is unsure of the level of assistance provided.

Section 3

Part 1

This section asks whether the user receives any assistance from local services to help with the problem. These formal supports are defined above to include paid carers, residential care, long-term wards, formal respite, day care centres, hospitals, community psychiatric nurses or other staff. Use the examples on the assessment form to prompt the interviewee. Score 1 for minimal support, occasional support, or light support. Score 2 for more regular assistance, maybe once a week or more significant support occasionally. Score 3 for specialist assistance, currently under assessment or more frequent assistance. Score 9 if the interviewee is unsure of the level of assistance provided.

© *The Royal College of Psychiatrists, 2004. This page may be photocopied freely.*

Part 2

The second part to Section 3 asks what formal supports the interviewer feels the user *requires*, using the same scale as in (i) of Section 3. This second part indicates under-met need, where the person is getting (Part 1) less than they require (Part 2) or over-provision of need, where the person is getting (Part 1) a higher level of service than they require (Part 2).

Section 4

Part 1

This section asks whether the person feels that the user is receiving the right type of help with the problem. The answer to this question may have been obvious from the responses to the previous sections, especially Section 1. However, if in doubt, ask more specifically. As well as highlighting unmet needs, this section can point out over-provision of needs, where the person reported that the user was receiving a higher level of assistance than they required.

Part 2

The second question in Section 4 asks about the user's satisfaction with the assistance they are receiving. Again this may be obvious from prior responses, but please ask specifically.

Section 5

This section is for noting the individual details of the assessment and the details of the help the user receives and requires (particularly the nature of the unmet needs identified) in order to formulate an action plan. Problems with current interventions or care plans and indicating plans in progress should also be documented in this section. Use codes to document which informant has provided the information (i.e. U = user, S= staff, C = carer, R = rater/professional). User perspectives on their expectations, personal strengths and resources should be noted here. Individual spiritual and cultural information should also be noted in this section. This information is vital for establishing an effective individualised care plan.

Scoring

It is to be noted that scoring is a secondary aspect of the CANE, as its primary purpose is to identify and assess individual unmet needs. The total CANE score is based on the rating of Section 1 of each of the 24 problem areas. The two areas (A and B) relating to carer's needs are not added into this total score. Count total number of met needs (rated as a 1 in Section 1), out of a maximum 24. Count total number of unmet needs identified (rated as a 2 in Section 1), out of a maximum score 24. Count total number of needs identified (rated as a 1 or 2 in Section 1), out of a maximum 24. The rater's (clinician's or researcher's) ratings are made based on all the information gathered through the assessment. Raters ratings of Section 1 are used as the basis for total CANE scores.

© The Royal College of Psychiatrists, 2004. *This page may be photocopied freely.*

Contents

© *The Royal College of Psychiatrists, 2004.* *This page may be photocopied freely.*

Background details (Please fill in blanks or circle where applicable)

Code number   _____

Date of birth   Age _____ (years)

Gender   Male / Female

Ethnicity   Asian / African / African–American / Black Caribbean / White / Other _____

Religion   Christian / Muslim / Hindu / Jewish / Other _____

First language   English / Other _____

Marital status   Single / married / divorced / separated / widowed

Living situation   Alone / with partner / with other relatives / with others

Living environment   Flat / house / sheltered / residential / nursing / other

Previous occupation
(or partner's)   _____

Education   _____ (years)

Current status   In-patient / day patient / community patient / (psychiatric / geriatric / other)

Main diagnoses
(DSM–IV/ICD–10)   _____
                       _____
                       _____

Current medication   _____
                       _____
                       _____

Disease prevention   (e.g. blood pressure/smoking/sleep pattern/exercise/screening/vaccination)
                       _____
                       _____

Does the person have   Yes / No
a carer?

Is the person a carer? Yes / no

© The Royal College of Psychiatrists, 2004.   This page may be photocopied freely.

1 Accommodation

Does the person have an appropriate place to live?

What kind of home do you live in?
Do you have any problems with accommodation?

Rating	Meaning	Example
0	No need	Has an adequate and appropriate home (even if currently in hospital). No need for assistance
1	Met need	Home undergoing adaptation/redecoration. Needs and is getting help with accommodation, e.g. in residential care, sheltered housing
2	Unmet need	Homeless, inappropriately housed or home lacks basic facilities such as water, electricity, heating or essential alterations
9	Not known	

If rated 0 or 9 go to Question 2

How much help with accommodation does/will the person receive from friends or relatives?

Rating	Meaning	Example
0	None	
1	Low help	Occasionally does odd jobs concerning accommodation, e.g. minor redecorations
2	Moderate help	Substantial help with improving accommodation such as organising redecoration or specific adaptations
3	High help	Living with a relative because own accommodation is unsatisfactory
9	Not known	

How much help with accommodation does the person receive from local services?

How much help with accommodation does the person need from local services?

Rating	Meaning	Example
0	None	
1	Low help	Minor redecoration, referral to housing agency/assisted housing
2	Moderate help	Major improvements, actively pursuing change in accommodation
3	High help	Being rehoused, living in supported accommodation, residential care, nursing home or continuing care hospital ward
9	Not known	

Overall, does the person receive the right type of help with their accommodation?
(0=No; 1=Yes; 9=Not known)

Overall, is the person satisfied with the amount of help they are receiving with accommodation?
(0=Not satisfied; 1=Satisfied; 9=Not known)

Comments:

© The Royal College of Psychiatrists, 2004. This page may be photocopied freely.

2 Looking after the home

Does the person have difficulty looking after their home?

Are you able to look after your home?
Does anyone help you?

Rating	Meaning	Example
0	No need	Independent in looking after the home, home may be untidy but kept basically clean
1	Met need	Limited in looking after home and has appropriate level of domestic help
2	Unmet need	Not receiving appropriate level of domestic assistance. Home is a potential health/fire/escape hazard
9	Not known	

If rated 0 or 9 go to Question 3

How much help does the person receive from relatives or friends with looking after the home?

Rating	Meaning	Example
0	None	
1	Low help	Prompts or helps tidy up or clean occasionally
2	Moderate help	Prompts or helps clean at least once a week
3	High help	Does most or all of the household tasks
9	Not known	

How much help does the person receive from local services with looking after the home?

How much help does the person need from local services with looking after the home?

Rating	Meaning	Example
0	None	
1	Low help	Prompting/supervision by staff
2	Moderate help	Some assistance with houselhold tasks
3	High help	Majority of household tasks done by staff
9	Not known	

Overall, does the person receive the right type of help with looking after the home?

(0=No; 1=Yes; 9=Not known)

Overall, is the person satisfied with the amount of help they are receiving with looking after the home?

(0=Not satisfied; 1=Satisfied; 9=Not known)

Comments:

© The Royal College of Psychiatrists, 2004.   This page may be photocopied freely.

3 Food

Does the person have difficulty in getting enough to eat?

Are you able to prepare your own meals and do your own shopping?
Are you getting the right sort of food?

Rating	Meaning	Example
0	No need	Able to buy and/or prepare adequate meals independently
1	Met need	Unable to prepare food and has meals provided to meet need
2	Unmet need	Very restricted diet, culturally inappropriate food, unable to obtain adequate food, difficulty swallowing normal food
9	Not known	

If rated 0 or 9 go to Question 4

How much help does the person receive from relatives or friends with getting enough to eat?

Rating	Meaning	Example
0	None	
1	Low help	Occasional meal provided and/or occasional help with shopping
2	Moderate help	Help with weekly shopping and/or meals provided more than weekly, but not daily
3	High help	Assistance with food provided daily
9	Not known	

How much help does the person receive from local services with getting enough to eat?

How much help does the person need from local services with getting enough to eat?

Rating	Meaning	Example
0	None	
1	Low help	1–4 meals a week provided or assisted for one meal a week
2	Moderate help	More than 4 meals a week provided or assisted for all meals. Weekly shopping
3	High help	All meals provided
9	Not known	

Overall, does the person receive the right type of help with getting enough to eat?
(0=No; 1=Yes; 9=Not known)

Overall, is the person satisfied with the amount of help they are receiving with getting enough to eat?
(0=Not satisfied; 1=Satisfied; 9=Not known)

Comments:

© The Royal College of Psychiatrists, 2004. This page may be photocopied freely.

4 Self-care

Assessments
User Carer Staff Rater

Does the person have difficulty with self-care?

Do you have any difficulty with personal care like washing, cutting your nails or dressing?
Do you ever need help?

Rating	Meaning	Example
0	No need	Appropriately dressed and groomed independently
1	Met need	Needs and gets appropriate help with self-care
2	Unmet need	Poor personal hygiene, unable to wash or dress, not receiving appropriate help
9	Not known	

If rated 0 or 9 go to Question 5

How much help does the person receive from relatives or friends with self-care?

Rating	Meaning	Example
0	None	
1	Low help	Prompts (e.g. to change clothes) or help occasionally
2	Moderate help	Regular assistance, e.g. weekly or more often
3	High help	Daily assistance with care, e.g. dressing, bathing, weekly laundry
9	Not known	

How much help does the person receive from local services with self-care?

How much help does the person need from local services with self-care?

Rating	Meaning	Example
0	None	
1	Low help	Occasional prompting by staff
2	Moderate help	Supervise weekly washing and some other aspects of self-care
3	High help	Supervise most aspects of self-care, assist most days
9	Not known	

Overall, does the person receive the right type of help with self-care?

(0=No; 1=Yes; 9=Not known)

Overall, is the person satisfied with the amount of help they are receiving with self-care?

(0=Not satisfied; 1=Satisfied; 9=Not known)

Comments:

© *The Royal College of Psychiatrists, 2004. This page may be photocopied freely.*

5 Caring for someone else

Does the person have difficulty caring for someone else?

Is there anyone that you are caring for?
Do you have any difficulty in looking after them?

Rating	Meaning	Example
0	No need	No one to care for or no problem in caring
1	Met need	Difficulties with caring and receiving help
2	Unmet need	Serious difficulty in looking after or caring for another person
9	Not known	

If rated 0 or 9 go to Question 6

How much help does the person receive from relatives or friends with looking after someone else?

Rating	Meaning	Example
0	None	
1	Low help	Occasional help, less than once a week
2	Moderate help	Help most days
3	High help	Cared for person goes to stay with friends or relatives, assistance required every day
9	Not known	

How much help does the person receive from local services with caring?

How much help does the person need from local services with caring?

Rating	Meaning	Example
0	None	
1	Low help	Person goes to day care, weekly assistance at home
2	Moderate help	Nearly daily assistance at home, ongoing carer support/training for user
3	High help	Respite care, 24-hour package or plans for alternative care for the cared for person
9	Not known	

Overall, does the person receive the right type of help with caring?
(0=No; 1=Yes; 9=Not known)

Overall, is the person satisfied with the amount of help they are receiving with caring?
(0=Not satisfied; 1=Satisfied; 9=Not known)

Comments:

© The Royal College of Psychiatrists, 2004. This page may be photocopied freely.

6 Daytime activities

Does the person have difficulty with regular, appropriate daytime activities?

How do you spend your day?
Do you have enough to do?

Rating	Meaning	Example
0	No need	Adequate social, work, leisure or learning activities, can arrange own activities
1	Met need	Some limitation in occupying self, has appropriate activities organised by others
2	Unmet need	No adequate social, work or leisure activities
9	Not known	

If rated 0 or 9 go to Question 7

How much help does the person receive from relatives or friends with daytime activities?

Rating	Meaning	Example
0	None	
1	Low help	Occasional help in arranging activities
2	Moderate help	Help at least weekly
3	High help	Daily help with arranging or providing activities
9	Not known	

How much help does the person receive from local services with daytime activities?

How much help does the person need from local services with daytime activities?

Rating	Meaning	Example
0	None	
1	Low help	Adult education, weekly day activity
2	Moderate help	Day centre 2–4 days a week. Day hospital attendance. Adequate activities 2–4 days a week
3	High help	Provision of suitable activity 5 or more days a week, e.g. day hospital or day centre
9	Not known	

Overall, does the person receive the right type of help with daytime activities?

(0=No; 1=Yes; 9=Not known)

Overall, is the person satisfied with the amount of help they are receiving with daytime activities?

(0=Not satisfied; 1=Satisfied; 9=Not known)

Comments:

© The Royal College of Psychiatrists, 2004.   This page may be photocopied freely.

7 Memory

Does the person have a problem with memory?

Do you often have a problem remembering things that happened recently?
Do you often forget where you've put things?

Rating	Meaning	Example
0	No need	Occasionally forgets, but remembers later. No problem
1	Met need	Some problems, but having investigations/assistance
2	Unmet need	Clear deficit in recalling new information: loses things, becomes disorientated in time and/or place, not receiving appropriate assistance
9	Not known	

If rated 0 or 9 go to Question 8

How much help does the person receive from relatives or friends for memory loss?

Rating	Meaning	Example
0	None	
1	Low help	Prompting, occasional notes, reminders
2	Moderate help	Assistance/supervision most days
3	High help	Living with a relative, constant supervision
9	Not known	

How much help does the person receive from local services for memory loss?

How much help does the person need from local services for memory loss?

Rating	Meaning	Example
0	None	
1	Low help	Some advice/assistance with memory, GP clinic reviews
2	Moderate help	Undergoing investigations. Regularly sees health care professional, e.g. memory clinic, day hospital, specialist day facility. Modified environment
3	High help	Specially modified care because of memory needs. Intensive assistance
9	Not known	

Overall, does the person receive the right type of help for memory loss?

(0=No; 1=Yes; 9=Not known)

Overall, is the person satisfied with the amount of help they are receiving for memory loss?

(0=Not satisfied; 1=Satisfied; 9=Not known)

Comments:

© The Royal College of Psychiatrists, 2004. This page may be photocopied freely.

8 Eyesight/hearing/communication

Does the person have a problem with sight or hearing?

Do you have any difficulty hearing what someone says to you in a quiet room?
Do you have any difficulty in seeing newsprint or watching television?
Are you able to express yourself clearly?

Rating	Meaning	Example
0	No need	No difficulties (wears appropriate corrective lenses or hearing aid, is independent)
1	Met need	Some difficulty, but aids help to some extent, receiving appropriate investigations or assistance to care for aids
2	Unmet need	A lot of difficulty seeing or hearing, does not receive appropriate assistance
9	Not known	

If rated 0 or 9 go to Question 9

How much help does the person receive from relatives or friends with sight or hearing?

Rating	Meaning	Example
0	None	
1	Low help	Help making appointments for sight/hearing problems. Occasional assistance
2	Moderate help	Regular help with difficult tasks such as reading correspondence
3	High help	Help with most tasks that are difficult because of a hearing/vision problem
9	Not known	

How much help does the person receive from local services with sight/hearing?

How much help does the person need from local services with sight/hearing?

Rating	Meaning	Example
0	None	
1	Low help	Advice about impairment, aids provided or monitored
2	Moderate help	Investigations/treatment. Aids regularly reviewed. Regular assistance with tasks
3	High help	Assistance several days a week. Hospital appointments, specialist services or specialist day facilities
9	Not known	

Overall, does the person receive the right type of help with sight/hearing?

(0=No; 1=Yes; 9=Not known)

Overall, is the person satisfied with the amount of help they are receiving with sight/hearing?

(0=Not satisfied; 1=Satisfied; 9=Not known)

Comments:

© The Royal College of Psychiatrists, 2004.   This page may be photocopied freely.

9 Mobility/falls

Does the person have restricted mobility, falls or any problems using public transport?

Do you have trouble moving about your home? Do you have falls?
Do you have trouble with transport?

Rating	Meaning	Example
0	No need	Physically able and mobile
1	Met need	Some difficulty walking, climbing stairs or using public transport, but able with assistance (walking aids, wheelchair). Occasional fall. Safety plan in place
2	Unmet need	Very restricted mobility, even with walking aid. Frequent falls. Lack of appropriate help
9	Not known	

If rated 0 or 9 go to Question 10

How much help does the person receive from relatives or friends for mobility problems?

Rating	Meaning	Example
0	None	
1	Low help	Occasional help, e.g. with transport, support
2	Moderate help	Regular help with mobility/public transport. Help organising home access alterations
3	High help	Daily help and supervision with mobility/transport
9	Not known	

How much help does the person receive from local services for mobility problems?

How much help does the person need from local services for mobility problems?

Rating	Meaning	Example
0	None	
1	Low help	Advice, one or more aids
2	Moderate help	Currently undergoing investigation and/or OT/physiotherapy assessments. Regular transport, e.g. to day centre, light mobility assistance given
3	High help	Fully appropriate home alterations and aids. Substantial assistance most days. Care home because of mobility needs
9	Not known	

Overall, does the person receive the right type of help for mobility problems?

(0=No; 1=Yes; 9=Not known)

Overall, is the person satisfied with the amount of help they are receiving for mobility problems?

(0=Not satisfied; 1=Satisfied; 9=Not known)

Comments:

© The Royal College of Psychiatrists, 2004.   This page may be photocopied freely.

10 Continence

Does the person have incontinence?

Do you ever have accidents/find yourself wet if you can't get to the toilet quickly?
How much of a problem? Ever any soiling? Are you getting any help?

Rating	Meaning	Example
0	No need	No incontinence/independent in managing incontinence
1	Met need	Some incontinence. Receiving appropriate help/ investigations
2	Unmet need	Regularly wet or soiled. Deteriorating incontinence needing assessment
9	Not known	

If rated 0 or 9 go to Question 11

How much help does the person receive from relatives or friends for incontinence?

Rating	Meaning	Example
0	None	
1	Low help	Prompts to maintain continence
2	Moderate help	Regular help with laundry, hygiene and use of aids
3	High help	Full assistance with continence (laundry, hygiene, aids)
9	Not known	

How much help does the person receive from local services for incontinence?

How much help does the person need from local services for incontinence?

Rating	Meaning	Example
0	None	
1	Low help	Prompts to maintain continence and provision of aids
2	Moderate help.	Investigations/treatment. Regular help with laundry, hygiene and use of aids
3	High help	Planned medical intervention (e.g. surgery). Constant care and assistance because of incontinence (e.g. in care home). Substantial continence programme in place
9	Not known	

Overall, does the person receive the right type of help for incontinence?
(0=No; 1=Yes; 9=Not known)

Overall, is the person satisfied with the amount of help they are receiving for incontinence?
(0=Not satisfied; 1=Satisfied; 9=Not known)

Comments:

© The Royal College of Psychiatrists, 2004.   This page may be photocopied freely.

11 Physical health

Does the person have any physical illness?

How well do you feel physically?
Are you getting any treatment from your doctor for physical problems?

Rating	Meaning	Example
0	No need	Physically well. Receiving no medical interventions
1	Met need	Physical ailment such as high blood pressure under control, receiving appropriate treatment/investigation. Reviews of physical conditions
2	Unmet need	Untreated serious physical ailment. Significant pain. Awaiting major surgery
9	Not known	

If rated 0 or 9 go to Question 12

How much help does the person receive from relatives or friends for physical health problems?

Rating	Meaning	Example
0	None	
1	Low help	Arranging appointments to see doctor
2	Moderate help	Accompanied regularly to doctor/clinics
3	High help	Daily help with condition arising out of physical health problems
9	Not known	

How much help does the person receive from local services for physical health problems?

How much help does the person need from local services for physical health problems?

Rating	Meaning	Example
0	None	
1	Low help	Given dietary or health advice. Occasional visit to GP
2	Moderate help	Prescribed significant medications. Regularly seen by health care professional
3	High help	In-patient admissions, 24-hour nursing care. Very regular or intensive treatment
9	Not known	

Overall, does the person receive the right type of help for physical health problems?

(0=No; 1=Yes; 9=Not known)

Overall, is the person satisfied with the amount of help they are receiving for physical health problems?

(0=Not satisfied; 1=Satisfied; 9=Not known)

Comments:
(Consider oral health, skin care and foot care, particularly in those people who are very frail or who have chronic medical conditions)

© The Royal College of Psychiatrists, 2004. This page may be photocopied freely.

12 Drugs

Does the person have problems with medication or drugs?

Do you have any problems (e.g. side-effects) with medication? How many different tablets are you on? Has your medication been recently reviewed by your doctor? Do you take drugs that are not prescribed?

Rating	Meaning	Example
0	No need	No problems with compliance, side-effects, drug misuse or dependency
1	Met need	Regular reviews, advice, district nurse/CPN administers medication, dosette boxes/aids
2	Unmet need	Poor compliance, dependency or misuse of prescribed or non-prescribed drugs, inappropriate medication given
9	Not known	

If rated 0 or 9 go to Question 13

How much help does the person receive from relatives or friends with their medication?

Rating	Meaning	Example
0	None	
1	Low help	Occasional prompt. Advice about drug misuse
2	Moderate help	Collection, regular reminding and checking of medication. Advice about agencies
3	High help	Administers and holds medication. Support during drug withdrawal programme
9	Not known	

How much help does the person receive from local services with their medication?

How much help does the person need from local services with their medication?

Rating	Meaning	Example
0	None	
1	Low help	Advice from GP, prompts to take medication
2	Moderate help	Supervision by district nurse/CPN/day hospital/care facility administers drugs
3	High help	Intensive programme regarding drug administration, complience, misuse or dependency (e.g. supervised withdrawal programme for drug dependency)
9	Not known	

Overall, does the person receive the right type of help with medication?

(0=No; 1=Yes; 9=Not known)

Overall, is the person satisfied with the amount of help they are receiving with medication?

(0=Not satisfied; 1=Satisfied; 9=Not known)

Comments:

© The Royal College of Psychiatrists, 2004.   This page may be photocopied freely.

13 Psychotic symptoms

Does the person have symptoms such as delusional beliefs, hallucinations, formal thought disorder or passivity?

Do you ever hear voices, see strange things or have problems with your thoughts?
Are you on medication for this?

Rating	Meaning	Example
0	No need	No definite symptoms. Not at risk or in distress from symptoms and not on medication for psychotic symptoms
1	Met need	Symptoms helped by medication or other help, e.g. coping strategies, safety plan
2	Unmet need	Currently has symptoms or is at risk
9	Not known	

If rated 0 or 9 go to Question 14

How much help does the person receive from relatives or friends for these psychotic symptoms?

Rating	Meaning	Example
0	None	
1	Low help	Some support
2	Moderate help	Carers involved in helping with coping strategies or medication compliance
3	High help	Constant supervision of medication and helping with coping strategies
9	Not known	

How much help does the person receive from local services with these psychotic symptoms?

How much help does the person need from local services with these psychotic symptoms?

Rating	Meaning	Example
0	None	
1	Low help	Mental state and medication reviewed 3-monthly or less often, support group
2	Moderate help	Mental state and medication reviewed more frequently than 3-monthly. Frequent specific therapy, e.g. day hospital, high CPN input
3	High help	Active treatment/24-hour hospital care, daily day care or crisis care at home
9	Not known	

Overall, does the person receive the right type of help with these symptoms?

(0=No; 1=Yes; 9=Not known)

Overall, is the person satisfied with the amount of help they are receiving with these symptoms?

(0=Not satisfied; 1=Satisfied; 9=Not known)

Comments:

© *The Royal College of Psychiatrists, 2004. This page may be photocopied freely.*

14 Psychological distress

Does the person suffer from current psychological distress?

Have you recently felt very sad or fed up?
Have you felt very anxious, frightened or worried?

Rating	Meaning	Example
0	No need	Occasional or mild distress. Copes independently
1	Met need	Needs and gets ongoing support
2	Unmet need	Distress affects life significantly, e.g. prevents person from going out
9	Not known	

If rated 0 or 9 go to Question 15

How much help does the person receive from relatives or friends for this distress?

Rating	Meaning	Example
0	None	
1	Low help	Some sympathy and support
2	Moderate help	Has opportunity at least once a week to talk about distress and get help with coping strategies
3	High help	Constant support and supervision
9	Not known	

How much help does the person receive from local services for this distress?

How much help does the person need from local services for this distress?

Rating	Meaning	Example
0	None	
1	Low help	Assessment of mental state or occasional support
2	Moderate help	Specific psychological or social intervention for distress. Counselled by staff at least once a week, e.g. at day hospital
3	High help	24-hour hospital care, or crisis care at home, daily assistance for distress
9	Not known	

Overall, does the person receive the right type of help for this distress?
(0=No; 1=Yes; 9=Not known)

Overall, is the person satisfied with the amount of help they are receiving for this distress?
(0=Not satisfied; 1=Satisfied; 9=Not known)

Comments:

© The Royal College of Psychiatrists, 2004.   This page may be photocopied freely.

15 Information

Has the person had clear verbal or written information about their condition and treatment?

Have you been given clear information about your condition, medication or other treatment?
Do you want such information? How helpful has the information been?

Rating	Meaning	Example
0	No need	Has received and understood adequate information. Has not received but does not want information
1	Met need	Receives assistance to understand information. Information given that is appropriate for the person's level of communication/understanding
2	Unmet need	Has received inadequate or no information
9	Not known	

If rated 0 or 9 go to Question 16

How much help does the person receive from relatives or friends in obtaining such information?

Rating	Meaning	Example
0	None	
1	Low help	Some advice
2	Moderate help	Given leaflets/fact sheets or in touch with self-help groups
3	High help	Regular liaison with mental health staff or voluntary groups (e.g. Alzheimer's Society) by friends and relatives
9	Not known	

How much help does the person receive from local services in obtaining such information?

How much help does the person need from local services in obtaining such information?

Rating	Meaning	Example
0	None	
1	Low help	Brief verbal or written information on illness/problem/treatment
2	Moderate help	Given details of self-help groups. Long verbal information sessions, e.g. day hospital attendance
3	High help	Has been given specific personal education with or without detailed written information
9	Not known	

Overall, does the person receive the right type of help in obtaining information?

(0=No; 1=Yes; 9=Not known)

Overall, is the person satisfied with the amount of help they are receiving in obtaining information?

(0=Not satisfied; 1=Satisfied; 9=Not known)

Comments:

© The Royal College of Psychiatrists, 2004. This page may be photocopied freely.

16 Deliberate self-harm

Is the person a danger to themselves?

Do you ever think of harming yourself or actually harm yourself?

Rating	Meaning	Example
0	No need	No thoughts of self-harm or suicide
1	Met need	Suicide risk monitored by staff, receiving counselling, adequate safety plan in place
2	Unmet need	Has expressed suicidal intent, deliberately neglected self or exposed self to serious danger in the past month
9	Not known	

If rated 0 or 9 go to Question 17

How much help does the person receive from relatives or friends to reduce the risk of deliberate self-harm?

Rating	Meaning	Example
0	None	
1	Low help	Able to contact friends or relatives if feeling unsafe
2	Moderate help	Friends or relatives are usually in contact and are likely to know if feeling unsafe
3	High help	Friends or relatives in regular contact and are very likely to know and provide help if feeling unsafe
9	Not known	

How much help does the person receive from local services to reduce the risk of deliberate self-harm?

How much help does the person need from local services to reduce the risk of deliberate self-harm?

Rating	Meaning	Example
0	None	
1	Low help	Someone to contact if feeling unsafe
2	Moderate help	Staff check at least once a week: regular supportive counselling
3	High help	Daily supervision: in-patient care because of risk
9	Not known	

Overall, does the person receive the right type of help to reduce the risk of deliberate self-harm?

(0=No; 1=Yes; 9=Not known)

Overall, is the person satisfied with the amount of help they are receiving to reduce this risk?

(0=Not satisfied; 1=Satisfied; 9=Not known)

Comments:

© The Royal College of Psychiatrists, 2004.   This page may be photocopied freely.

17 Inadvertent self-harm

Is the person at inadvertent risk to themselves?

Do you ever do anything that accidentally puts you in danger, such as leaving gas taps on, leaving the fire unattended or getting lost?

Rating	Meaning	Example
0	No need	No accidental self-harm
1	Met need	Specific supervision or help to prevent harm, e.g. memory notes, prompts, secure environment, observation
2	Unmet need	Dangerous behaviour, e.g. getting lost, gas/fire hazard, no safety plan in place
9	Not known	

If rated 0 or 9 go to Question 18

How much help does the person receive from relatives or friends to reduce the risk of inadvertent self-harm?

Rating	Meaning	Example
0	None	
1	Low help	Periodic supervision, weekly or less
2	Moderate help	Supervision on 3–5 days a week
3	High help	Almost constant supervision/24-hour care because of risk
9	Not known	

How much help does the person receive from local services to reduce the risk of inadvertent self-harm?

How much help does the person need from local services to reduce the risk of inadvertent self-harm?

Rating	Meaning	Example
0	None	
1	Low help	Check on behaviour weekly or less, risk assessment completed
2	Moderate help	Daily supervision, specific plan to prevent harm
3	High help	Constant supervision, e.g. residential care because of risk of inadvertent self-harm
9	Not known	

Overall, does the person receive the right type of help to reduce the risk of inadvertent self-harm?

(0=No; 1=Yes; 9=Not known)

Overall, is the person satisfied with the amount of help they are receiving to reduce this risk?

(0=Not satisfied; 1=Satisfied; 9=Not known)

Comments:

© The Royal College of Psychiatrists, 2004.   This page may be photocopied freely.

18 Abuse/neglect

Is the person at risk from others?

Has anyone done anything to frighten or harm you, or taken advantage of you?

Rating	Meaning	Example
0	No need	No abuse/neglect issues in the past month
1	Met need	Needs and gets ongoing support or protection. Safety plan in place
2	Unmet need	Regular shouting, pushing or neglect, financial misappropriation, physical assault
9	Not known	

If rated 0 or 9 go to Question 19

How much help does the person receive from relatives or friends to reduce the risk of abuse?

Rating	Meaning	Example
0	None	
1	Low help	Occasional advice
2	Moderate help	Regular support and protection
3	High help	Constant support, very regular protection, negotiation
9	Not known	

How much help does the person receive from local services to reduce the risk of abuse?

How much help does the person need from local services to reduce the risk of abuse?

Rating	Meaning	Example
0	None	
1	Low help	Someone to contact when feeling threatened
2	Moderate help	Regular support, occasional respite
3	High help	Constant supervision, legal involvement via services, separation from abuser
9	Not known	

Overall, does the person receive the right type of help to reduce the risk of abuse?

(0=No; 1=Yes; 9=Not known)

Overall, is the person satisfied with the amount of help they are receiving to reduce the risk of abuse?

(0=Not satisfied; 1=Satisfied; 9=Not known)

Comments:

© The Royal College of Psychiatrists, 2004.   This page may be photocopied freely.

19 Behaviour

Is the person's behaviour dangerous, threatening, interfering or annoying to others?

Do you come into conflict with others, e.g. by interfering with their affairs, frequently annoying, threatening or disturbing them? What happens?

Rating	Meaning	Example
0	No need	No disturbance to others
1	Met need	Under supervision/treatment because of potential risk
2	Unmet need	Recent violence, threats or seriously interfering behaviour
9	Not known	

If rated 0 or 9 go to Question 20

How much help does the person receive from relatives or friends to reduce annoying or disturbing behaviour?

Rating	Meaning	Example
0	None	
1	Low help	Help/supervision weekly or less
2	Moderate help	Help/supervision more often than weekly
3	High help	Almost constant help/supervision due to persistently disturbing behaviour
9	Not known	

How much help does the person receive from local services to reduce annoying or disturbing behaviour?

How much help does the person need from local services to reduce annoying or disturbing behaviour?

Rating	Meaning	Example
0	None	
1	Low help	Check on behaviour weekly or less
2	Moderate help	Daily supervision or night-sitting service, active care plan in place
3	High help	Constant supervision, intensive behaviour management programme
9	Not known	

Overall, does the person receive the right type of help to reduce annoying or disturbing behaviour?

(0=No; 1=Yes; 9=Not known)

Overall, is the person satisfied with the amount of help they are receiving to reduce these behaviours?

(0=Not satisfied; 1=Satisfied; 9=Not known)

Comments:

© The Royal College of Psychiatrists, 2004.   This page may be photocopied freely.

20 Alcohol

Does the person drink excessively or have a problem controlling their drinking?

Do you drink alcohol? How much? Does drinking cause you any problems?
Do you ever feel guilty about it? Do you ever wish you could cut down on your drinking?

Rating	Meaning	Example
0	No need	Does not drink or drinks sensibly
1	Met need	At risk from alcohol misuse and receiving assistance
2	Unmet need	Current drinking harmful or uncontrollable, not receiving appropriate assistance
9	Not known	

If rated 0 or 9 go to Question 21

How much help does the person receive from relatives or friends for their drinking?

Rating	Meaning	Example
0	None	
1	Low help	Advised to cut down
2	Moderate help	Advised about helping agencies, e.g. Alcoholics Anonymous
3	High help	Constant support and/or monitoring of alcohol intake
9	Not known	

How much help does the person receive from local services for their drinking?

How much help does the person need from local services for their drinking?

Rating	Meaning	Example
0	None	
1	Low help	Given information and told about risks
2	Moderate help	Given support and details of helping agencies, access to drink is supervised
3	High help	Attends alcohol clinic, supervised withdrawal programme
9	Not known	

Overall, does the person receive the right type of help for their drinking?

(0=No; 1=Yes; 9=Not known)

Overall, is the person satisfied with the amount of help they are receiving for their drinking?

(0=Not satisfied; 1=Satisfied; 9=Not known)

Comments:

© The Royal College of Psychiatrists, 2004. This page may be photocopied freely.

21 Company

Does the person need help with social contact?

Are you happy with your social life? Do you wish you had more social contact with others?

Rating	Meaning	Example
0	No need	Able to organise enough social contact with friends
1	Met need	Lack of company identified as a problem. Has specific intervention for company needs, e.g. lonely at night but attends a drop-in or day centre. Social work involvement
2	Unmet need	Frequently feels lonely and isolated. Very few social contacts
9	Not known	

If rated 0 or 9 go to Question 22

How much help does the person receive from relatives or friends with social contact?

Rating	Meaning	Example
0	None	
1	Low help	Friends help with social contact or visit less than weekly to provide company
2	Moderate help	Friends help with social contact weekly or more often
3	High help	Friends help with social contact at least four times a week
9	Not known	

How much help does the person receive from local services in organising social contact?
How much help does the person need from local services in organising social contact?

Rating	Meaning	Example
0	None	
1	Low help	Occasional visits from befriender or voluntary worker. Referral to centre
2	Moderate help	Regular attendance at day centre, regular lunch club, organised social activity
3	High help	Day centre or social home visits 3 or more times a week, social skills training, social worker involvement
9	Not known	

Overall, does the person receive the right type of help with social contact?
(0=No; 1=Yes; 9=Not known)

Overall, is the person satisfied with the amount of help they are receiving with social contact?
(0=Not satisfied; 1=Satisfied; 9=Not known)

Comments:

© The Royal College of Psychiatrists, 2004. This page may be photocopied freely.

22 Intimate relationships

Does the person have a partner, relative or friend with whom they have a close emotional/physical relationship?

Do you have a partner, relative or friend you feel close to? Do you get on well?
Can you talk about your worries or problems? Do you lack physical contact/intimacy?

Rating	Meaning	Example
0	No need	Happy with current relationships or does not want an intimate relationship
1	Met need	Has problems concerning intimate relationships, specific plan/counselling/support that is helpful
2	Unmet need	Desperately lonely. Lack of confidant
9	Not known	

If rated 0 or 9 go to Question 23

How much help does the person receive from relatives or friends with intimate relationships or loneliness?

Rating	Meaning	Example
0	None	
1	Low help	Occasional emotional support
2	Moderate help	Regular support
3	High help	Help contacting counselling services (e.g. bereavement/ marriage counselling) and possibly accompanying the person there
9	Not known	

How much help does the person receive from local services with intimate relationships or loneliness?

How much help does the person need from local services with intimate relationships or loneliness?

Rating	Meaning	Example
0	None	
1	Low help	Some support/advice
2	Moderate help	Regular support/advice/contact
3	High help	Intensive support. Specific therapy, e.g. marital or bereavement counselling
9	Not known	

Overall, does the person receive the right type of help with relationships?

(0=No; 1=Yes; 9=Not known)

Overall, is the person satisfied with the amount of help they are receiving with relationships?

(0=Not satisfied; 1=Satisfied; 9=Not known)

Comments:

© The Royal College of Psychiatrists, 2004. This page may be photocopied freely.

23 Money/budgeting

Does the person have problems managing or budgeting their money?

Do you have any difficulty managing your money? Are you able to pay your bills?

Rating	Meaning	Example
0	No need	Able to buy essential items and pay bills independently
1	Met need	Benefits from help with managing affairs and budgeting
2	Unmet need	Often has no money for essential items or bills. Unable to manage finances
9	Not known	

If rated 0 or 9 go to Question 24

How much help does the person receive from relatives or friends with managing their money?

Rating	Meaning	Example
0	None	
1	Low help	Occasional help sorting out household bills
2	Moderate help	Frequent assistance, calculating weekly budget, collecting pension
3	High help	Complete management of finances. Power of attorney
9	Not known	

How much help does the person receive from local services with managing their money?

How much help does the person need from local services with managing their money?

Rating	Meaning	Example
0	None	
1	Low help	Occasional help with budgeting
2	Moderate help	Supervised in paying rent, given weekly spending money
3	High help	Virtual or complete management of finances, Court of Protection, enduring Power of Attorney
9	Not known	

Overall, does the person receive the right type of help with managing their money?

(0=No; 1=Yes; 9=Not known)

Overall, is the person satisfied with the amount of help they are receiving with managing their money?

(0=Not satisfied; 1=Satisfied; 9=Not known)

Comments:

© The Royal College of Psychiatrists, 2004. *This page may be photocopied freely.*

24 Benefits

Is the person definitely receiving all the benefits that they are entitled to?

Are you sure that you are getting all the money that you are entitled to?

Rating	Meaning	Example
0	No need	Has no need of benefits or receiving full entitlement
1	Met need	Receives appropriate help in claiming benefits, social worker involvement over past month
2	Unmet need	Not sure/not receiving full entitlement of benefits
9	Not known	

If rated 0 or 9 go to carer's section A

How much help does the person receive from relatives or friends in obtaining their full benefit entitlement?

Rating	Meaning	Example
0	None	
1	Low help	Occasionally asks whether person is getting any money
2	Moderate help	Makes enquiries about entitlements and helps fill in forms
3	High help	Has ensured full benefits are being received
9	Not known	

How much help does the person receive from local services with obtaining their full benefit entitlement?

How much help does the person need from local services with obtaining their full benefit entitlement?

Rating	Meaning	Example
0	None	
1	Low help	Occasional advice about entitlements
2	Moderate help	Help with applying for extra entitlements
3	High help	Comprehensive evaluation of current entitlement in the past month
9	Not known	

Overall, does the person receive the right type of help in obtaining their full benefit entitlement?

(0=No; 1=Yes; 9=Not known)

Overall, is the person satisfied with the amount of help they are receiving in obtaining their full benefit entitlement?

(0=Not satisfied; 1=Satisfied; 9=Not known)

Comments:

© The Royal College of Psychiatrists, 2004.   This page may be photocopied freely.

A Carer's need for information

Has the carer been given clear information about the person's condition and all the treatments available?

Have you been given clear information about their condition and all the treatments and services available? How helpful has this information been?

Rating	Meaning	Example
0	No need	Received and understood
1	Met need	Has not received or understood all information, receives help with information
2	Unmet need	Has received little or no information, has not understood information given
9	Not known	

If rated 0 or 9 go to carer's section B

How much help does the carer receive from relatives or friends in obtaining such information?

Rating	Meaning	Example
0	None	
1	Low help	Has had some advice
2	Moderate help	Given leaflets/fact sheets or put in touch with self-help groups
3	High help	Regular liaison with doctors, other professionals, self-help or support groups by friends or relatives
9	Not known	

How much help does the carer receive from local services in obtaining such information?
How much help does the carer need from local services in obtaining such information?

Rating	Meaning	Example
0	None	
1	Low help	Brief verbal or written information on condition/problem/treatment
2	Moderate help	Given details of self-help groups. Personal explanations of drugs, alternative treatments and services and the likely course of the condition
3	High help	Has been given detailed written information or has had specific personal education, e.g. from keyworker
9	Not known	

Overall, does the carer receive the right type of help in obtaining such information?

(0=No; 1=Yes; 9=Not known)

Overall, is the carer satisfied with the amount of help they are receiving in obtaining such information?

(0=Not satisfied; 1=Satisfied; 9=Not known)

Comments:

© The Royal College of Psychiatrists, 2004.   This page may be photocopied freely.

B Carer's psychological distress

Is the carer currently psychologically distressed?

Do you find it difficult or stressful caring for this person?
Do you feel that you need a break or much more support for yourself?

Rating	Meaning	Example
0	No need	Coping well
1	Met need	Some stress, but receiving help/contact/support that is beneficial
2	Unmet need	Very stressed or depressed. Wants relief from caring
9	Not known	

If rated 0 or 9 finish

How much help does the carer receive from relatives or friends for this distress?

Rating	Meaning	Example
0	None	
1	Low help	Occasional advice/support
2	Moderate help	Weekly practical and/or emotional support and/or relief from caring
3	High help	Regular respite and assistance with tasks (3–4 times a week)
9	Not known	

How much help does the carer receive from local services for this distress?

How much help does the carer need from local services for this distress?

Rating	Meaning	Example
0	None	
1	Low help	Advice, e.g. about their other options such as residential care
2	Moderate help	Weekly day care, occasional respite, CPN visits, carers' support groups
3	High help	Regular respite admissions. Treatment and/or counselling for stress/depression
9	Not known	

Overall, does the carer receive the right type of help for this distress?

(0=No; 1=Yes; 9=Not known)

Overall, is the carer satisfied with the amount of help they are receiving for this distress?

(0=Not satisfied; 1=Satisfied; 9=Not known)

Comments:

© The Royal College of Psychiatrists, 2004.   This page may be photocopied freely.

CANE Assessment Summary Sheet

User name _____ Date of assessment _____/_____/_____

Ratings: 0 = no need 1 = met need 2 = unmet need 9 = unknown

	U	C	S	R	Section 2 Informal help	Section 3a Formal help	Section 3b help needed	Section 4a Right type of help	4b User satisfaction
					Section 2–4a rater's overall ratings				
1 Accommodation									
2 Looking after the home									
3 Food									
4 Self-care									
5 Caring for someone else									
6 Daytime activities									
7 Memory									
8 Eyesight/hearing									
9 Mobility/falls									
10 Continence									
11 Physical health									
12 Drugs									
13 Psychotic symptoms									
14 Psychological distress									
15 Information									
16 Safety to self									
17 Inadvertant self-harm									
18 Abuse/neglect									
19 Behaviour									
20 Alcohol									
21 Company									
22 Intimate relationships									
23 Money/budgeting									
24 Benefits									
A Carer's need for information									
B Carer's psychological distress									
Met needs (Count the number of 1s in the column)									
Unmet needs (Count the number of 2s in the column)									
Total needs (Add number of met and unmet needs)									
Total level of help given, needed and level of satisfaction (add scores, rate 9 as 1)									

© The Royal College of Psychiatrists, 2004.   This page may be photocopied freely.

Appendix 2

Camberwell Assessment of Need
for the Elderly – Short Version (CANE–S)

How to use the CANE–S

The CANE–S is a comprehensive, person-centred needs assessment tool that has been designed for use with the elderly. It is suitable for use in a variety of clinical and research settings. The CANE has a person-centred approach which allows views of the professional, user and carer to be recorded and compared. The instrument uses the principle that identifying a need means identifying a problem plus an appropriate intervention which will help or alleviate the need. Therefore the CANE models clinical practice and relies on professional expertise for ratings to be completed accurately. Administrators need to have an adequate knowledge of clinical interviewing and decision-making. Administrators should also have good working knowledge of the concepts of need, met need and unmet need. This knowledge can be gained with experience of full CANE assessments and reference to the manual.

There are 24 topics relating to the user and two (A & B) relating to the carer. There are four columns to document ratings so that one or more of the user (U), staff member (S), carer (C) or rater (clinician/researcher) (R) can each express their view.

The CANE–S aims to assess whether there is currently a need in the specific area. A need is defined as a problem with a potential remedy or intervention. Use the prompts below each area on the record form to establish the user's current status with regard to the need area. If there has been a need, then assess whether it was met appropriately. Score each interviewee independently, even though their perceptions of need in each area may differ from one another. The administrator should ask additional questions probing into the area until he/she can establish whether the person has a significant need that requires assistance and whether they are getting enough of the right type of help. Once this information has been gathered a rating of need can be made. Judgement of rating in this section should be based on normal clinical practice. The CANE is intended to be a framework for assessment grounded in good professional practise and expertise. Although Section 1 in each problem area is the main section of interest to CANE administrators, it often cannot be rated until adequate information has been collected about the area. When adequate information has been gathered the rater should clearly be able to make a clinical judgement as to whether the area is a met need, an unmet need or is not a need for the person. Confusion with ratings can be avoided by not directly asking a closed question about whether there is a problem in a certain area (e.g. "Do you have any problems with the food here?") because the person can answer "No". This response may then be mistaken as a 'No Need' where in fact it is a 'Met Need' because the person is assisted by someone else.

© The Royal College of Psychiatrists, 2004.   This page may be photocopied freely.

0 = no need   If there is no need in the area, then go on to the next question. In this situation the user is coping well independently and does not need any further assistance.

1 = met need   A need is met when there is a mild, moderate or serious problem which is receiving an intervention or assessment which is appropriate and potentially of benefit. This category is also used for problems which would normally not be of clinical significance and would not require a specific intervention.

2 = unmet need   If the need is currently unmet, there is a serious problem requiring intervention or assessment, which is currently receiving no assistance or the *wrong* type or level of help.

9 = unknown   If the person does not know about the nature of the problem or about the assistance he/she receives, go on to the next question. Such a score may mean that further information is needed to make a rating.

Scoring

It is to be noted that scoring is a secondary aspect of the CANE, as its primary purpose is to identify and assess individual unmet needs. The total CANE score is based on the rating of Section 1 of each of the 24 problem areas. The two areas (A and B) relating to carer's needs are not added into this total score. Count total number of met needs (rated as a 1 in Section 1), out of a maximum 24. Count total number of unmet needs identified (rated as a 2 in Section 1), out of a maximum score 24. Count total number of needs identified (rated as a 1 or 2 in Section 1), out of a maximum 24. The rater's (clinician's or researcher's) ratings are made based on all the information gathered through the assessment. Raters ratings of Section 1 are used as the basis for total CANE scores.

© *The Royal College of Psychiatrists, 2004. This page may be photocopied freely.*

Camberwell Assessment of Need for the Elderly
Short Version (CANE–S)

User name	0 = No need 1= Met need
Date of assessment __/__/__ Initials of assessor _____	9 = Not known 2 = Unmet need

		User	Carer	Staff	Rater
1.	**Accommodation** *Does the person have an appropriate place to live?*				
2.	**Looking after the home** *Does the person look after their home?*				
3.	**Food** *Does the person get enough of the right type of food to eat?*				
4.	**Self-care** *How does the person look after their self-care?*				
5.	**Caring for someone else** *Does the person care for another? Can they manage this caring?*				
6.	**Daytime activities** *How does the person occupy their day?*				
7.	**Memory** *Does the person have a problem with memory?*				
8.	**Eyesight/hearing/communication** *How is the person's eyesight and hearing?*				
9.	**Mobility/falls** *How does the person get around inside and outside their home?*				
10.	**Continence** *Does the person have incontinence?*				
11.	**Physical health** *How is the person's physical health?*				
12.	**Drugs** *Does the person have problems with medication or drugs?*				
13.	**Psychotic symptoms** *Does the person ever see or hear things others don't?*				
14.	**Psychological distress** *Does the person have problems with mood or anxiety?*				
15.	**Information (on condition and treatment)** *Has the person had clear information about their condition?*				
16.	**Deliberate self-harm** *Is the person a danger to themselves?*				
17.	**Inadvertent self-harm** *Does the person have accidents?*				
18.	**Abuse/neglect** *Is the person at risk from others?*				
19.	**Behaviour** *Is the person's behaviour problematic for others?*				
20.	**Alcohol** *Does the person have a drinking problem?*				
21.	**Company** *Does the person have an adequate social life?*				
22.	**Intimate relationships** *Does the person have a close emotional/physical relationship?*				
23.	**Money/budgeting** *How does the person manage their money?*				
24.	**Benefits** *Is the person receiving the benefits he/she is entitled to?*				
A	**Carer's need for information** *Has the carer been given all the information they need about the person's condition and treatment?*				
B	**Carer's psychological distress** *Is the carer currently psychologically distressed?*				

	User	Carer	Staff	Rater
Met needs: count the number of 1s in the column (1–24 only)				
Unmet needs: count the number of 2s in the column (1–24 only)				
Total number of needs: add number of met needs and unmet needs (1–24 only)				

© *The Royal College of Psychiatrists, 2004.   This page may be photocopied freely.*

Appendix 3

Training overheads

1 The CANE and Individual Needs Assessment

- User-based approaches to care

- Person-centred assessment and treatment

© The Royal College of Psychiatrists, 2004.   *This page may be photocopied freely.*

2 Definition of need

- Hierarchies of need

- Lower and higher needs – fundamental and complex

- Needs and the relationship with well-being and ill health

- Needs as wants

- Needs as personally defined personal perceptions

- Needs and the relationship to appropriate interventions

© *The Royal College of Psychiatrists, 2004. This page may be photocopied freely.*

3 Development

- **Background**

- **Reliability:**
  Test–retest reliability
  Inter-rater reliability

- **Validity:**
  Face validity
  Content validity
  Concurrent validity
  Construct validity

© *The Royal College of Psychiatrists, 2004.* *This page may be photocopied freely.*

4 Areas of the CANE

1	Accommodation
2	Looking after the home
3	Food
4	Self-care
5	Caring for someone else
6	Daytime activities
7	Memory
8	Eyesight/hearing/communication
9	Mobility/falls
10	Continence
11	Physical health
12	Drugs
13	Psychotic symptoms
14	Psychological distress
15	Information
16	Deliberate self-harm
17	Inadvertent self-harm
18	Abuse/neglect
19	Behaviour
20	Alcohol
21	Company
22	Intimate relationships
23	Money/budgeting
24	Benefits
A	Carer's need for information
B	Carer's psychological distress

© *The Royal College of Psychiatrists, 2004.*   *This page may be photocopied freely.*

5 Classification of need

No need
Individual has no problem in the area, or has a problem but manages independently

Met need
Individual has a problem in the area for which they require assistance, which they receive and it is appropriate to meet that need

Unmet need
Individual has a significant problem in the area for which they are not receiving appropriate assistance or assessment

Overmet need
Individual is receiving more assistance than their problem requires

© *The Royal College of Psychiatrists, 2004.   This page may be photocopied freely.*

6 Instructions

Section 1
Asks whether there is currently a need in the specific area. A need is defined as a significant problem with a potential remedy or intervention.

Section 2
Assistance from informal sources?

Section 3
Assistance from local services?

Section 4
(i)   Right type of help with the problem?
(ii) User's satisfaction?

Section 5
Notes individual details of the assessment, user perspectives, expectations, cultural/religious issues, personal strengths and resources in order to establish an effective, individualised care plan.

© *The Royal College of Psychiatrists, 2004.   This page may be photocopied freely.*

7 CANE example

7. Memory

Does the person have a problem with memory?

"Do you often have a problem remembering things that happened recently?"
"Do you often forget where you've put things?"

0 = no need
e.g. occasionally forgets, but remembers later

1 = met need
e.g. some problems, but having investigations/ assistance

2 = unmet need
e.g. clear deficit in recalling new information, loses things, becomes disorientated in time and/or place, and is not receiving appropriate assistance

9 = not known

© *The Royal College of Psychiatrists, 2004.   This page may be photocopied freely.*

8 Application of CANE in special populations

- Primary care

- Community

- Residential/nursing care

- Sheltered accommodation

- Day hospitals

- Specialist mental health units

- Younger-onset dementia

© *The Royal College of Psychiatrists, 2004.   This page may be photocopied freely.*

9 Issues when assessing the needs of older people

- Privacy and confidentiality

- External parties, family, carers, others

- Specialist services involved

- Dementia and communication problems

- Refusal of services

© *The Royal College of Psychiatrists, 2004.   This page may be photocopied freely.*

10 Scoring

- For research, outcome measurement, population surveys, efficacy of intervention package

- Count number of met needs (1s)

- Count number of unmet needs (2s)

- Count number of met and unmet needs for number of needs identified (1s and 2s)

© *The Royal College of Psychiatrists, 2004.   This page may be photocopied freely.*

WA 305 AM ORR X

WA 305 AM ORR X